Branding, like retail, is in a constant evolution—Kevin Perlmutter gives us 21st-century coaching.
Paco Underhill, global bestselling author of *Why We Buy*

Kevin is a thought leader you can trust. Recognizing our industry's need for experts who do more than identify strategic gaps, he offers the practical guidance to fix them by openly detailing his entire approach to more effective branding. I'm among his biggest supporters because he's honest and willing—qualities I look for in the people who I listen to and learn from.
Flavia Barbat, Editor-in-Chief at *Brandingmag*

This book shines a light on one of the most powerful (and most overlooked) principles in marketing: Only if you truly understand what moves people and their behavior can you be a builder of great brands and businesses. *Brand Desire* reveals precisely how to act on this simple and timeless human truth.
Dominik Prinz-Barley, Head of Brand at Google

Perlmutter's *Brand Desire* insightfully catapults brand strategy into a new era—one that evolves from persuasion-based approaches to creating meaningful connections rooted in the emotional drivers of customer decisions.
Stephan Gans, SVP, Chief Consumer Insights and Analytics Officer at PepsiCo

The smart, new way to spark brand desire. Perlmutter reveals exactly how any brand, big or small, B2B or B2C, can identify and implement emotional insights to refine their strategy for attracting customers. *Brand Desire* is an indispensable compass for marketers, as well as brand and business leaders.
Nancy Harhut, Co-Founder and Chief Creative Officer at HBT Marketing, and author of *Using Behavioral Science in Marketing*

This book is a masterclass in unlocking the emotional drivers of consumer behavior—offering insight and inspiration far beyond any textbook. Perlmutter blends human understanding and real-world application with clarity and heart. He outlines an intuitive and practical guide for creating emotionally intelligent brand strategies. *Brand Desire* is now on my consumer behavior class reading list because it captures what students need to understand most.
Barry Martin, branding consultant and Adjunct Professor of Consumer Behavior at New York University

Perlmutter's Limbic Sparks approach is unique, and helped my company evolve our branding to better connect with the underlying emotions of our most important stakeholders. Whether you're a branding veteran steeped in marketing and behavioral science, or an executive looking to strengthen brand credibility and relevance to your customers, *Brand Desire* simplifies the process with real world examples that translate to practical application in organizations.
Craig Albright, Chief Executive Officer at Valera Health

In an age of influencers and exponential messaging, brand clarity and emotional resonance is ever more important. Great brands have always captured our hearts and Perlmutter's approach forces us to seek deep customer insights, while embracing the science of emotion, to accelerate sparks of connection.
Dr. Jez Frampton, Adjunct Professor at University of Westminster London Business School and former Global Chief Executive Officer at Interbrand

Brand Desire shares clear direction that will enable any CEO to uncover blind spots in their brand strategy. These are not just conjectures or ideas—rather, actionable pillars of brand management that I've found to be indispensable in steering organizations internally, so that the brand delivers the best possible experience for customers externally.
Rajiv Pancholy, Global Chief Executive Officer and Brand Practitioner

Perlmutter's focus on aligning the emotional motivations of customers and brands is a great reminder of what really drives successful branding. His Focus-Connect-Evolve model adds structure to emotion-centric branding, echoing key principles in behavioral science. Reading it was a joy and even made me reflect on how emotion shows up in my own work.
Michelle Niedziela PhD, Neuroscientist and Behavioral Science Consultant at Nerdoscientist

As a creative lead, I know that there's nothing more frustrating than being challenged to create effective marketing with a less than helpful brief. Kevin's Limbic Sparks approach to understanding the "who" reminds us that emotional impact is often why people respond and remain loyal to a brand. It's those nuggets of customer understanding that feel like a secret cheat code to elevate the work with emotional storytelling that connects.

Della Mathew, Executive Creative Director at 22Squared, formerly with Ogilvy NY, Arnold Worldwide NY, and Publicis NY

Brand Desire

Spark Customer Interest
Using Emotional Insights

Kevin Perlmutter

KoganPage

First published in Great Britain in 2025 by Kogan Page Limited

Kogan Page

Kogan Page Ltd, 2nd Floor, 45 Gee Street, London EC1V 3RS, United Kingdom
Kogan Page Inc, 8 W 38th Street, Suite 902, New York, NY 10018, USA
www.koganpage.com

EU Representative (GPSR)

Authorised Rep Compliance Ltd, Ground Floor, 71 Baggot Street Lower, Dublin D02 P593, Ireland
www.arccompliance.com

Kogan Page books are printed on paper from sustainable forests.

© Kevin Perlmutter 2025

Trademarks

Limbic Sparks® and Limbic Brand Evolution® are registered trademarks of Limbic Brand Evolution, LLC. All other trademarks, service marks, and company names are the property of their respective owners.

ISBNs

Hardback	978 1 3986 2109 1
Paperback	978 1 3986 2104 6
Ebook	978 1 3986 2108 4

British Library Cataloguing-in-Publication Data

A CIP record for this book is available from the British Library.

Library of Congress Control Number

2025939073

Typeset by Integra Software Services, Pondicherry
Print production managed by Jellyfish
Printed and bound by CPI Group (UK) Ltd, Croydon, CR0 4YY

This book is dedicated to
Sarah, Emily, and Rebecca
My loves and my greatest inspiration

CONTENTS

PART FOUR

Evolve

PART FIVE

Lead

ONLINE RESOURCES

Additional information, supporting materials, and ways to learn more from Kevin can be found at www.LimbicBrandEvolution.com.

Kevin also invites you to connect with him on LinkedIn at www.linkedin.com/in/kevinperlmutter/

ABOUT THE AUTHOR

Kevin Perlmutter is a brand strategy trailblazer. He is chief strategist and founder of Limbic Brand Evolution and creator of Limbic Sparks Brand Strategy, which puts emotional insight at the center of how brands spark desire. Based in the New York City area, he works with business and brand leaders to create stronger connections between their brand and the people they want to reach. Prior, he served as chief strategist and chief innovation officer at a sonic branding music studio. There, he collaborated with a pioneering behavioral science research company to create an award-winning, neuroscience-based research capability, fueling his understanding of the overwhelming influence of our emotional instincts. Earlier he was senior director of brand strategy at global brand consultancy Interbrand, where he led the creation of their first global customer experience practice. Kevin is a frequent writer and speaker on the intersection of brand strategy, emotion, and customer engagement, including being a podcast host and contributing writer for *Brandingmag*.

Throughout Kevin's 30+ year career he's worked with dozens of top global brands in various roles and has consistently guided the development of more effective methods for brand evolution and customer engagement. This book is both a culmination of everything he's learned and created. It's also the start of a new conversation among brand leaders who are eager to overcome the limitations of traditional brand strategy, so they can increase the ROI of their marketing efforts and spark meaningful, business-driving, emotional connections with their customers.

FOREWORD

by Ruth Gaviria, Chief Marketing Officer & CMO Advisor

I've had the pleasure of collaborating with Kevin for over a decade on brand and rebranding initiatives for Fortune 500 companies, nonprofits, and digital-first brands across a diverse range of industries.

Through our work together, I've learned that traditional brand strategy frequently misses the mark. It often prioritizes the brand's identity over the customer experience, leading to ineffective recommendations. Data, frameworks, analysis, and buzzwords are often used, but they fail to connect with the core truth, the subconscious value, or the unmet desires of customers. This is where Kevin's revolutionary approach, outlined in this book, truly shines.

This body of work is a disciplined approach to being curious about humanity, and humanizing marketing and branding. As a long-time chief marketing officer, I know that not everything is about performance marketing; as a matter of fact, that is a misguided concept geared to reduce cost, and in my mind is extractive, not additive. At the heart of this book lies a simple yet powerful premise: Brand leaders who understand and address the emotional motivations of their customers lead the brands that thrive. By tapping into the way people want to feel, and activating "Limbic Sparks," those instinctive, emotionally driven responses that originate in the subconscious mind, brands can forge deep and lasting connections with their audiences.

I am reminded of Brené Brown's *Atlas of the Heart* and how she talks about how choosing to be curious lets us be vulnerable and surrender to uncertainty. Yet, marketers falsely believe that we can predict everything and will it into success without becoming emotionally involved. The work we do in branding must be emotional. It requires us to be vulnerable and to get into a real conversation with our customers. We don't know if our brand is going to be successful solely because it is innovative, high-quality, or affordable. When we launch or re-launch a brand, we enter the unknown, regardless of the data we have accumulated. What we do know is that people's decision-making is informed by their emotional state, their desires, and their intention to have their needs met. This information resides in the limbic system part of the brain that regulates emotion, behavior, and memory. Gaining access to these motivations requires us to go deeper into the subconscious mind or unarticulated thoughts of our customers. Kevin is brilliant at mining for those juicy morsels of information—emotional insights that will enable our brands to be more successful.

I've witnessed the transformative power of Limbic Sparks Brand Strategy firsthand. In a crowded market where every brand is vying for attention, understanding the emotional drivers of customer decisions is no longer a luxury—it's a necessity.

Kevin's methodology tackles the challenges of traditional brand strategy head-on. He encourages us to move beyond surface-level information and embrace a more human-centric approach. He emphasizes the importance of deep customer understanding, not just accumulating data. It includes figuring out what Kevin calls the "Shared Emotional Motivation"—the intersection of what truly motivates both the brand and the customer—which is key to creating a compelling and sustainable brand strategy and is missing from traditional approaches.

This method benefits business leaders across a wide spectrum of industries. Whether you're a tech startup, a healthcare provider, an entertainment company, a professional services firm, or a consumer goods company, understanding the emotional context of your target audience is critical to success.

What sets Kevin's approach apart from brand strategy practices of the past is the singular focus on emotional intelligence to deliver on a business strategy. It's not about manipulating emotions through clever marketing tactics. It's about genuinely understanding and addressing the deep-seated needs and desires of your customers—and once understood, then creating or evolving products and services, marketing, and brand experiences that are rooted in reasons why customers will want to bring your offering into their life.

This book is a call to action for all brand builders and marketers. It's a must-read for emerging and experienced leaders, consultants, and students. It's a guide to a new era of branding—one that prioritizes emotional insight so that your brand can reign supreme in people's minds. It offers a practical, actionable framework for creating brands that resonate and earn loyalty.

Step into the world of "Limbic Sparks." Embrace the power of emotional insights. Discover how to build a brand that truly connects with your customers on a human level. The future of branding is emotional. Are you ready to lead the way?

PREFACE

You're curious, aren't you? Curious about how to get more people interested in the brand you're responsible for. You know it has a fantastic offering and very happy customers, but something isn't right. You wish you could more effectively convey the brand's benefits, so that more people feel compelled to bring it into their life.

Often, the difference between great results and discouraging results comes from a shift in perspective and approach.

I started out as a traditional brand strategist at a top global brand consultancy, after many years in advertising. I became a student of how the world's most valuable brands stay strong, and I guided the evolution of some of the most well-known brands. I also led the creation of this consultancy's first ever global customer experience practice—my first entry into understanding the impact that emotion has on brand loyalty.

A few years later, I joined a sonic branding music studio to be their chief strategist and chief innovation officer. There, I led the creation of a proprietary research capability in collaboration with a pioneering behavioral science research company. Working with my newfound behavioral science mentors, I experienced a massive shift in perspective. I was suddenly immersed in neuroscientific understanding and details about the limbic system part of our brain. Our research studies proved an incredibly high correlation between how something makes us feel subconsciously and our conscious desire to have the experience again, or not. I was fascinated, learning more and more about the overwhelming influence that our instinctive emotional reactions have on our conscious behavior, and just how much activity happens subconsciously that we are never made aware of.

I contrast this behavioral science perspective with what I had been experiencing and observing in my own industry and with so many brands. Brand strategy frameworks that are all about what company insiders want people to know, with shallow details about what matters to customers. Supposed best practices that don't reflect the science of how people make decisions. Creative briefs that are loaded with persuasion-era proof points and reasons to believe, but light on customer insights and reasons to care. Ad agency creative teams who place more value on winning creative awards with funny or sentimental ads, than on insightfully addressing business objectives and customer motivations. I saw brand leaders struggle to have influence in their organizations because of pressure to move the needle for their brand without robust customer insights to guide the way. I became even more skeptical when I thought about how so many brand leaders are fixated on articulating their brand's "Why," without nearly as much regard for understanding their "Who."

I came to the realization that this inextricable link between emotion and desire, that is fundamental in human behavior, is largely absent from traditional brand strategy. It's certainly not insight that most brand leaders understand or apply to their work, and it's a big source of underperforming marketing and sales efforts. It was clear to me that traditional brand strategy was broken, and in need of a behavioral science-rooted evolution.

In 2019, I created Limbic Sparks Brand Strategy and launched Limbic Brand Evolution to address this gap in my own industry. Limbic Sparks Brand Strategy puts emotional insight at the center of how brands spark desire. It prioritizes discovery of the emotional motivations that drive customer behavior, as a critical input to developing brand strategy and marketing. It's about finding the relevant intersection of "why" and "who" to create what I call Limbic Sparks, which are what you feel when your emotional motivation meets brand desire. Think about a brand that you'd prefer not to live without, and how it makes you feel. What you're feeling are Limbic Sparks.

This book is neither theoretical nor overly scientific, though it draws on behavioral science understanding that barely makes its way into most brand leadership initiatives. It reveals a detailed playbook for how you can put emotional insight at the center of how the brand you're responsible for sparks desire. It shares examples of how this approach has been put into practice through the eyes of brand leaders who have benefited from using it. This book is for you if you are a small business owner, a brand leader in any size organization, a consultant, or a student. It's for you if you are eager to become fluent in an approach that is more efficient and effective at igniting customer enthusiasm for what your brand has to offer.

Each chapter will inspire you and teach you how to move beyond the limitations of traditional brand strategy. You'll learn about the three steps to sparking brand desire—Focus, Connect, and Evolve—and you will become a believer and practitioner of the idea that understanding and addressing how people want to feel will be what sets your brand apart. Whether you're doing the work yourself or guiding your team, you'll be able to put this emotion-centric mindset into practice every day, even when a big brand evolution is not underway.

Admittedly, this approach is not something I learned overnight. Like anything worth doing well, it took practice and ongoing refinement. I'll never forget one of my first client presentations back in 2019. It was to my long-time friend and first Limbic client, Michelle Holmes, who was VP and chief marketing officer at the AT&T Performing Arts Center. A few weeks into the project, after a significant amount of insights discovery, I was sharing initial brand strategy ideas. It was a first-round presentation, my first ever as an independent consultant, and it did not go as well as I'd hoped. Michelle, never afraid to tell me what's on her mind, said: "I don't know, Kevin. I'm just not feeling the Limbic Sparks." The video call got quiet as those words hung in the air. Everyone was waiting for my response. Then I smiled, a big smile. Michelle said to me, "What's that look on your face?" I said, "Michelle, you're the first person ever to use my words and new trademark, Limbic Sparks, in a sentence, and it's making me so happy." Michelle was right. She helped me see beyond what I could see myself, and it led to improvements in the Limbic Sparks approach.

Several years and many brand evolutions later, the results are consistent and clear. Limbic Sparks is not traditional brand strategy. Limbic Sparks is an approach that puts emotional insight at the center of how brands spark desire, and increasingly what it takes to be a desirable brand going forward.

If you're still curious, keep reading. I'll reveal how.

ACKNOWLEDGMENTS

I'm grateful for the love, support, inspiration, and motivation that I have, thanks to so many people—those who ignite Limbic Sparks for me.

My wife Sarah Anderson, and my daughters Emily Perlmutter and Rebecca Perlmutter—who are the loves of my life.

My dad Norman Perlmutter, who has inspired me from day one, my mom Sandra Wachs, who I miss so much and who would be so proud, my incredibly loving and supportive stepmom Jane Perlmutter, stepdad Howard Wachs, and mother-in-law Nancy Anderson, my grandparents who I miss always, and the rest of my amazing family of brothers, sisters, in-laws, nieces, and nephews—Ali, Brian, and Zachary Glaser; Melissa, Scott, Andrew, Lindsay, and Matthew Makower; Jonathan, Gabrielle, and Gavin Punko and Keri Willis; Paige, Nora, and Ian Menchini; Martha, Megan, Caitlin, and John Sanborn; Robin, Shawn, Erika, and Kaitlyn Burst; Brian, Katie, Juliana, and Jacob Wachs; Henry Mitchell and Poutine.

My close friends, informal advisers, and collaborators who motivate and inspire me in so many ways on my Limbic journey—Rebeca Arbona, Katherine Ardizone, Catherine Avery, Megan Baker, Flavia Barbat, Paul Barnett, Ilan Beesen, Anne Bentley, Peter Carrabba, Maxine Cunningham, Melissa Curtis, Penelope Davis, David Edwards, Vincent Fatato, Darcy Flanders, Eric Fernandez, Susana Fonticoba, Jez Frampton, Ruth Gaviria, Rob Guissanie, Ed Han, Nancy Harhut, Sarah Harper, Gregg Heard, Maria Hernandez, Michelle Holmes, Ashley Julig, Steve Keller, Rahul Khosla, Agnes Konopka, Leslie Koppel, Amanda Lee, Samantha Liss, Frank Liu, Nicole Loughrey, Barry Martin, Cyrus McCandless, Jody McKinley, Nathanael Meyers, Jasmine Moradi, Krista Oraa, Rajiv Pancholy, Tim Peterson, Michael Pincus, Elaine Pofeldt, Lisa Richner, Diana Rojas, Jonathan Rosen, Jordan Ruden, Diana Sabloff, George Sanchez, Joe Sauer, Diamond Michael Scott, Ellen Smolko, Remo Strada, Esther-Mireya Tejeda, Danielle Venne, Katrina Villani, Nancy Walker-Laudenberger, Will Weisser, Betsy Wise, Sivapriya Yallapragada.

My clients who generously allowed me to share the details of our work together in this book. Thank you to Debbie Storey, Chis Heinbaugh, Lin Sang, Xiran Liu, Kyle Pexton, Rob Principe, Kish Melwani.

My friends, collaborators, clients, advocates, and book contributors, who, while not mentioned by name, are all people to whom I am so grateful for your friendship and trust in me. Also, my past colleagues and mentors, who helped me set the foundation for what I'm doing today.

My *Let's Talk Limbic Sparks* podcasts guests, interviewees for my *Brandingmag* articles, and anyone whose insights I have shared in this book.

My wonderful friends who are part of Collaberex—the peer advisory community that has been a constant source of inspiration.

My fellow board members, the incredible staff, and volunteers who are part of Rise—the awe-inspiring social services nonprofit where I proudly serve as a board member.

My subscribers at LimbicSparks.Substack.com.

My fantastic Kogan Page team members who believed in me and guided me through the creation of this book, especially George Boutros Sleiman, Donna Goddard-Skinner, Theresa Persona, Jeylan Ramis, Nancy Wallace, Natalie Weaver, and Bobbi-Lee Wright.

There are so many wonderful people in my life that it would be impossible to name you all. For anyone I may have missed, please accept my sincerest apology, and my gratitude.

PART ONE

Feel

01

Evolving Brand Strategy

People won't forget how you made them feel. This idea, popularized by a quote credited to Maya Angelou, suggests that what you say or do is far less memorable than how people feel as a result.

If you are responsible for running a business or brand, I believe it suggests a fundamental question that you should always have in the forefront of your mind: "How do people want to feel?"

Behavioral scientists will tell you that we gravitate toward the things that make us feel good, and away from the things that make us feel bad. This idea is rooted in Approach Avoidance Motivation Theory, which suggests that we are constantly weighing the potential positives and negatives associated with things we encounter during our day-to-day activities. When something feels positive, we are open to bringing it into our life, and when something feels negative, our instinct is to avoid it (Feltman and Elliot, 2012).

Brands That Spark Desire

Consider a brand that you've made a consistent part of your life. How does it make you feel? At some point, it caught your attention, then it sparked your desire, and you started using it. Now, you not only like it, but you would rather not live without it. As a result of these feelings, it's most likely a brand that you go out of your way for, one that you tell other people about, and one that you forgive for any rare frustrating experience.

For me, this includes brands like Ben & Jerry's—not just because of the great ice cream and brand aesthetic, but also because of their commitment to social justice and environmental causes. It includes Bose—not just because of the great sound quality, but also because on two occasions they replaced items I bought for free with no fuss or questions (one was my fault and one was normal wear and tear past the warranty). It includes Marriott Bonvoy—because there's always a hotel brand property to fit the occasion wherever I travel, their app makes booking and communicating with the property easy, and by aggregating my purchase on Bonvoy American Express cards I earn wonderful travel rewards. It even includes the relationships I have with my long-time financial advisor and my accountant, both of whom are super-attentive and always make me feel like a valued client whenever I ask for their support, and often when I don't.

When a brand makes you feel this way, you're experiencing what I call Limbic Sparks.

Limbic Sparks

What you feel when your emotional motivation meets brand desire.

Thanks to how the brand communicates, the experiences it delivers and, most importantly, the way it makes you feel, this brand has earned your interest, engagement, desire, and repeated business. You've connected with the brand on an emotional level, and you've made it a part of your life.

FIGURE 1.1 Limbic Sparks

Brand Motivations

Customer Motivations

Limbic Sparks are what you feel when your emotional motivation meets brand desire

NOTE This is what it's all about—creating Limbic Sparks at the intersection of brand and customer emotional motivations.

Now think about a brand that you've had bad experiences with, or one that you simply ignore. In this case, Limbic Sparks aren't igniting. Your interactions with many brands are just fleeting transactions. Perhaps you use them out of habit, out of convenience, or begrudgingly only when you need to. Regardless, you're just not that into it. Maybe you go out of your way to avoid some brands altogether, and you're probably not shy about telling people why.

For me, this includes brands where I don't feel valued, where my time does not feel respected, or where I dread interactions because I anticipate they will not be pleasant—my internet provider, online stores where I make one purchase and they send me daily promotional emails afterwards, the many solutions providers who spam me with irrelevant emails to sell me services for my business, some businesses where leaders have acted in ways that are not in sync with my values, and some brand experiences that made me feel more like a burden than a valued customer or showed no appreciation for my business.

Brand

A unique combination of elements representing an organization, product, or service that evokes an overall impression people have based on all their associations and experiences.

It's important to recognize that your brand will mean different things to different people, based on their individual associations and experiences. You're creating Limbic Sparks when someone interacts with your brand, and they decide to bring it into their life.

If you are someone who the leaders of a brand want to attract, and you were made to feel indifferent or, even worse, bad, after a brand experience, it's highly likely that they did not prioritize and act on questions like "How do people want to feel?" Perhaps they are relying on traditional brand strategy that often suffers from a lack of emotional insight, or no thoughtful strategy at all for attracting and retaining customers. As a result, they either do not understand or do not address what matters most to you, and they're not doing what it takes to become and remain a meaningful part of your life.

Emotional Insights

A deep understanding of the underlying emotions that drive our decisions and behavior.

"Great brand experiences are largely emotional and don't happen by accident—they are actively designed." This was shared with me by brand leader Gregg Heard, whose specialty is brand design and experience leadership at large global companies (Limbic Brand Evolution, 2021).

He's right. Our interest in brands happens when brand leaders do what it takes to uncover insights around what matters most to the people who their brand is for, and then use that insight to improve the product and service offering, the marketing, and the brand experience. When we feel an emotional connection to a brand, it happens because they have found that Limbic Sparks intersection of what the brand does for people and what people truly care about. It happens because they convey brand messaging and/or deliver brand experiences in ways that stand apart from other similar brands, and it makes us feel something that sparks our interest and desire.

What's more, we most often find that the reasons people choose and stick with specific brands, products, and services are rooted in emotional benefits that brand leaders had not considered. Most brand leaders tend to focus brand messaging on the product features and benefits that they believe are most important. However, when talking with a brand's customers, other reasons emerge, and they are most often less tangible emotional benefits. Time and again I'm reminded of just how powerful a role emotion plays in our judgments and behaviors, and once brand leaders understand how to unlock these emotional insights, there are significant competitive advantages that can be gained.

Your Greatest Competitive Advantage

For much of my life I was a competitive long-distance runner. Early on I learned how to have a competitive edge without a lot of extra effort. Here are a few things core to my approach: I'd lengthen my stride, enabling every step to take me further using the same energy. I'd run along the inside of turns to make my run less distance than it is for those who inefficiently run in the middle of the road. I'd power up hills and pass people who were struggling both physically and mentally, and then power down the other side with an extra-long stride while recovering. All these little tricks helped me extend my lead from those who weren't as strategic in their efforts.

If you're like most business and brand leaders, your job is consumed with finding ways to be more successful in attracting and retaining customers. You want the results of your ongoing efforts to have an even greater impact on customer acquisition and retention. We're all looking for ways to improve performance and have a competitive advantage. Oftentimes, the difference between great results and disappointing results comes from a twist in perspective or approach.

What if you had an opportunity to improve the results of your efforts, and gain a competitive advantage, by applying a strategy that is both efficient and effective, rooted in behavioral science?

We all know that there are many aspects to gaining competitive advantage. Some relate to functional aspects of your offering—such as product or service quality, pricing strategy, and availability—which are no doubt essential to get right. Other ways to gain a competitive advantage are more related to how people are introduced to and experience your brand. Is your brand messaging relevant and compelling? Is your brand's product and service offering meeting and exceeding expectations? Is your brand delivering a superior customer experience? Is your brand reputation one that earns recognition and regard?

This book focuses on the latter, and the premise that, assuming the functional aspects of your offering are competitive, then understanding how people want to feel, and communicating and delivering experiences that feel just right, will be your greatest competitive advantage—one that goes even further to spark desire for your brand. I'll also take a moment to point out that this book refers to customers. Customers is the consistent way I am referring to clients, consumers, and audiences. As you read the word customer, please replace it in your mind with the term you use in your work.

The Power of Emotional Insights

You're about to learn about the influence of emotional insights and, throughout this book, how to discover and unlock them using Limbic Sparks Brand Strategy.

Limbic Sparks Brand Strategy

The non-traditional brand strategy approach that puts emotional insight at the center of how brands attract and retain customers.

Years before creating Limbic Sparks Brand Strategy, I began exploring a wealth of research from top business consulting firms that changed my perspective about what it takes for brands to be most effective at attracting and retaining customers. At the time I had spent the first half of my career working at top New York City advertising agencies, and then most of a decade at a top global brand consultancy, where I led brand strategy development for several global brands, and creation of the company's first-ever global customer experience practice.

During this time, beginning around 2009, I became exposed to Forrester and their extensive research on customer experience, emotion, and brand loyalty. It was the start of the customer experience era, which included company-specific research on the topic and, soon thereafter, what Forrester called the rise of the chief customer experience officer (Forrester, 2011). Their annual Customer Experience Index reported on the relative rankings of hundreds of brands across over a dozen industries. It rated brands on three primary customer experience factors: Effectiveness (value of the experience), Ease (level of ease or difficulty to get the value), and Emotion (how customers feel about the experience).

Year over year, since the early days of this ranking, the results have been consistent about the drivers of brand loyalty. In 2019, Forrester reported that emotion remained a primary area of focus for brands wanting to differentiate from their competitors. They confirmed again in this report that emotion is the biggest driver of brand loyalty—in every industry, how a brand makes people feel has the most impact, followed by effectiveness and ease (Parrish, 2019).

I also became familiar with research from other sources that talk about how the complexity and strength of customer emotions are increasingly impacting the levels of loyalty that people have with brands. For customer interactions to be more successful, they must be contextually appropriate, consistent, empathetic, and responsive. However, most brands are not doing enough to collect or act on emotional insights, which are critical to forging enduring relationships with customers.

After my time at the brand consulting company, I joined a top sonic branding music studio—a studio that creates proprietary music and sounds for brands, products, and entertainment companies. My role was to lead strategy, innovation, and research. One of my first big initiatives was to create a proprietary research capability to help us assess the impact and effectiveness of music and sound, to both guide and validate our creative efforts.

Knowing that our responses to music and sound are first felt instinctively and emotionally, and in the first milliseconds of an interaction, I sought out a research partner that was steeped in neuroscience-based research techniques to be sure we were evaluating responses at the subconscious level. It was then that I partnered with a pioneering behavioral science research company, Sentient Decision Science, and began working with Dr. Cyrus H. McCandless, PhD and Joe Sauer, who became my behavioral science mentors.

This mind-opening work we did together not only confirmed what I had been learning from Forrester and other sources, it also helped me understand why emotions are so powerful and more about their pervasive impact. I was suddenly steeped in decades of neuroscientific research and understanding that rarely makes its way into traditional brand strategy thinking.

Through other sources I became aware of how a lot of this non-conscious activity takes place in the limbic system—the part of the brain that guides emotions and motivation and is central to sparking instinctive connections and a precursor to conscious thought. From reading Gerald Zaltman's book *How Customers Think*, I learned a lot about the interplay between our conscious and subconscious. He breaks down findings from neuroscientists that say our emotions have an outsized influence on our decisions, and that the overwhelming majority of our thoughts occur subconsciously. His book explains that feelings are the conscious experience of emotions, and they are only the small portion of instinctive emotions that we are aware of. Further, this interplay between our conscious and subconscious, and the significant influence of our subconscious mind, is poorly understood by most marketers, leading to inferior approaches to conducting customer research and a lack of reliable data (Zaltman, 2003).

Another source of insight came from Dr. Aaron Reid, PhD, founder of Sentient Decision Science. He co-published a groundbreaking white paper titled "Emotion as a Tradeable Quantity" (Reid and González-Vallejo, 2008). This paper cites studies from neuroscientists who've conducted research on the influence of our emotions, and it shares the implications for more accurately predicting people's preferences. From it I learned about the high correlation between emotion and behavior—firstly, that people's actual preferences are dependent on the emotions they experience and anticipate. It also shares that emotions act as regulators of information processing and are involved in the choice of specific behaviors—that people's judgments and choices are guided by how they feel about something, and that many of those feelings are instinctive and subconscious. Importantly, the paper also makes clear the need for research methodologies to include ways to measure subconscious emotional responses to stimuli, as well as conscious responses, to more accurately predict people's preferences. I'll share specific detail on this type of research in Chapter 10.

It was also around this time that Dr. Daniel Kahneman, referred to as the grandfather of Behavioral Economics, revealed cognitive insights in his book *Thinking, Fast and Slow*. He reenforced that most decisions we make are instinctive and occur in the limbic part of our brain. He also helped us understand that human behavior is far from rational most of the time. Further, his book caught the research community's attention and spurred a lot of discussion, and new entrants, focused on behavioral science (Kahneman, 2011).

When reflecting on all this insight with Joe Sauer on my podcast, he shared: "Every decision has a different blend of rational and irrational influences. And if we're really going to understand consumer behavior, understand why we make the decisions we do, we have to understand each decision in its context" (Limbic Brand Evolution, 2023a).

Cyrus, in an interview article I wrote for *Brandingmag*, emphasized the implications for brand leaders:

> Brand leaders should understand that we aren't subjectively aware of most of what our brain does, but we now have very effective ways of studying the unconscious processes that shape our conscious experience, our behavior, and our choices. What we continue to find is that what really motivates most of us to do most of the things we do, most of the time, has less to do with conscious reasoning than we thought. (Perlmutter, 2020)

Soon after I started working with Joe and Cyrus, it was clear to me that this inextricable link between emotion and desire that is fundamental in human behavior, is not insight that most business or brand leaders apply to their work—it's a big missed opportunity for all kinds of companies. It raised questions for me about the brand strategy approaches and playbooks that I had worked with throughout my career. It confirmed my suspicions that many supposed brand development best practices were sending so many business and brand leaders down the wrong path. Ultimately, I concluded that traditional brand strategy was broken. By and large, as an industry, we were unknowingly ignoring or underleveraging the emotional motivations of the people who we'd like to attract to our brand and missing out on a significant competitive advantage.

> **Emotional Motivations**
>
> The driving forces behind our decisions and behaviors.

What's Wrong With Traditional Brand Strategy

One of the biggest challenges with traditional brand strategy… it's too much about the brand and not enough about the customer. It's guided by what brand leaders want people to know, and not as much on what truly matters to people at an emotional level.

> **Traditional Brand Strategy**
>
> Familiar approaches to brand strategy that are lacking meaningful emotional insights about what matters most to customers.

Despite this wealth of evidence around how much emotion affects people's experiences and impacts business performance, the traditional approach to brand strategy has barely evolved. Its origins come from the persuasion era which dominated 20th-century marketing and advertising—a time when advertising was the primary form of marketing, long before online reviews, customer experience, and social media became significant influencers of buyer behavior. Long before the exponentially increasing number of brand impressions we experience every day became so pervasive and ignorable. Long before the time we find ourselves in now, where people are increasingly prioritizing how they feel, and want to feel, as they evaluate their relationships with people, employers, and brands.

Still in use are terms from the mid-20th century like Unique Selling Proposition, Proof Points, and Reasons to Believe, which all put the focus on the product or offer itself rather than putting the consumer's emotions at the center of consideration, whether that was their intent or not.

Even worse, so many people have more recently jumped on the "What's My Why?" bandwagon—a question popularized in the leadership arena by Simon Sinek (Sinek, 2009). While there's a good argument for business and brand leaders to express their "Why?" it's now often misapplied to brand development. Asking "Why?" in the absence of "Who?" leads to an incomplete brand strategy. In addition to asking "What's My Why?" brand leaders should be spending as much or more time on asking "Who's My Who?" While brand leaders are so focused on expressing the brand's "Why?" they are not going deep enough to understand the brand's "Who?—as in who are our customers and prospects and what do they care about? The fact is, nobody cares about your brand's "Why?" if it isn't relevant to them.

Think about this for a moment. Imagine you're in a club trying to meet someone special. As you go up to people, you start telling them about you— what you do, why you're so passionate about it, why it makes a difference in the world. You spend all your time talking about your Why, but you don't spend enough time getting to know the person you're trying to connect with, and you have no reliable way to say anything that this person will care about. There's a high probability that you're sounding self-centered, boastful, and irrelevant, and the chances of sparking an emotional bond are slipping away. Despite its popularity, this movement to "Why?" is yet another factor sending many brand leaders down the wrong path, limiting the effectiveness of their marketing efforts.

Traditional brand strategy is full of details that the brand wants to tell people, with minimal new insight about the people who the brand is trying to reach. Traditional creative briefs have sections for the primary takeaway, proof points, and reasons to believe, with much less emphasis on customer insights and reasons to care. As a result, most brand messaging gets lost in the weeds of features. It's often guided by internal stakeholders with strong opinions, a lot of confirmation bias, and historical mindsets like "This is the way we've always done it" and "We understand our customers." It's fraught with pressure to meet short-term performance goals that are often prioritized over long-term brand-building efforts. What's missing is an outside-in perspective. What does the customer truly care about?

These traditional brand strategy approaches are not just emanating from business and brand leaders. They are also pervasive across the brand

TABLE 1.1 The Challenges with Traditional Brand Strategy

The Challenges with Traditional Brand Strategy	
Too much...	Not enough...
About your brand	For your customer
Gut instinct	Deep listening
Proof points	Customer insights
Reasons to believe	Reasons to care
Your why	Your who

consulting community that I'm a part of. Have you ever attended a meeting where account managers or consultants shared thick presentation decks filled with data, frameworks, analysis, and the latest buzzwords, but ultimately made ineffective recommendations? It's likely that they only relied on surface-level customer understanding, gut instinct, and made broad assumptions about why people buy. If they used research, it was most likely traditional, survey-based, and less reliable than newer approaches rooted in behavioral science. This behavior is often perpetuated by brand leaders who want quick answers to hard questions, and consultants who may be a bit too confident in their instincts.

These approaches leave brand leaders essentially paying for information overload, and "big idea" recommendations that won't help them build a real connection with customers. Internal confirmation bias, shallow customer understanding, broad assumptions about people, and generic personas should not be the strategic foundation of your brand development investments.

It's why a Chief Marketing Officer client of mine who has led brand development at very big companies, and was always ahead of her time, often challenged rooms full of consultants and advertising executives to back up their ideas by asking, "Where are the insights?"

Misconceptions About Emotional Insights

I'm sure it's no surprise to you that emotion is an important component of brand strategy, marketing, and customer experiences. Focusing on your brand's benefits and connecting emotionally has always been a top priority. I suspect that you're also becoming more aware that an emotionally intelligent approach is not just a nice thing to have—it's necessary for a brand's survival with a sustainable competitive advantage.

So why do these brand challenges persist? Why do most business and brand leaders only have surface-level understanding about their customers, and not deep emotional insights?

Having investigated this topic for years, and having spoken with hundreds of people about it, the answers seem to be rooted in a lack of understanding and common misconceptions about emotion.

The fact is most business and brand leaders are thinking about emotion from the wrong perspective. I still get questions from people like, "What emotion should our brand stand for?" Some brands use emotion in advertising to connect by using humor, sentimentality, or fear tactics. On the other hand, in B2B settings I often hear about business leaders who resist emotion. They say, "I don't want my brand to be emotional, we're a serious business, and our customers are serious people." These common perspectives on emotion have historically been backward.

We need to flip the focus on emotion. It is not about the emotion the brand should stand for. It's about the emotional context of the people who the brand is for. The true power of emotion is not in the brand standing for an emotion or being more emotional. The true power is when brand leaders understand the emotions of the people they are trying to reach—what's going on in their lives, what they are currently feeling, and what they are striving for. When brand leaders discover emotional insights about how people want to feel, then they put their brand out there in a way that meets customers and prospects where they are, by anticipating, addressing, and exceeding those needs, wants, and desires.

Brand Leader

Anyone who is responsible for attracting and retaining customers to what a brand has to offer.

This misconception, however, is not the only reason why more brand leaders aren't benefiting from the power of emotional insights. On my Let's Talk Limbic Sparks podcast, where I talk with brand leaders who are ahead of their peers in understanding and utilizing emotional insight, I always ask this question: "Why do you feel that most brand leaders are still ignoring or under-leveraging emotional insight in their work?" I'd like for you to see these examples of what I often hear.

Slow Adoption

Lisa Richner shared, "I think that there's, in some ways, not widespread understanding of this power of emotion and emotional insights" (Limbic Brand Evolution, 2023b).

Gregg Heard shared, "In the B2B world, I don't think it's something that is top of mind, and I don't think there's a comfort level there. However, there's a lot of research that's happening with that now to suggest that brands that connect emotionally are more successful than brands that connect rationally" (Limbic Brand Evolution, 2021).

Emotions Are Not Logical and Take Work

Liz Engelsen shared, "It's not as easy as looking at the rational and looking at the functional, which are more logical. We all know emotions aren't logical" (Limbic Brand Evolution, 2022a).

Samantha Liss shared, "It's hard to understand your customers, and it takes time, resources and commitment to talk with them. However, you really need to think about how people's emotions relate to what you're delivering to your customers" (Limbic Brand Evolution, 2022b).

Performance Pressure

Joe Sauer shared, "There's a sense of risk. They feel it's something new and prefer that other companies figure it out, with a wait-and-see approach until it become mainstream" (Limbic Brand Evolution, 2023a).

Esther-Mireya Tejeda shared, "It's expected that all our work is deeply quantifiable. A lot of marketing has been reduced to sales enablement, where we're more closely connected than ever to having to drive revenue, improve that return on investment as it pertains to the bottom line. We must be able and willing to take that step back to do the foundational work to set up the insights to really understand the customer, before we start thinking about performance metrics and the growth marketing tactics. Our work must be rooted in a strategic understanding of who our customers are" (Limbic Brand Evolution, 2023c).

Discomfort With Emotion

Maxine Cunningham shared, "I think it's because feelings are scary. Relationships and intimacy can be a lot, right? We don't often think of emotions and intimacy within the business borders. It is a new thing" (Limbic Brand Evolution, 2023d).

Dominik Prinz-Barley shared, "I think it's fear, as simple as that. Emotions are messy. Measuring them is hard, and convincing meeting rooms filled with decision makers, who very often still primarily rely on hard, quantitative data, can be pretty intimidating" (Limbic Brand Evolution, 2022c).

A Missed Opportunity

Kim Christfort shared, "Emotion is often considered to be soft versus hard, a distraction versus a core skill. And I think that oftentimes, people don't recognize the power of emotion and become too intellectual. If you think about the way that we measure success, emotion seems hard to measure. So, people might dismiss it, not realizing the power that it actually has" (Limbic Brand Evolution, 2022d).

Does any of this sound familiar to you? What I keep hearing each time I ask this question is that there's a lack of understanding and hesitation around emotion limiting the effectiveness of brand development work.

Emotional Intelligence for Brands

Here's the good news for you. You don't need to be a behavioral scientist or a neuroscientist to apply this understanding about the interrelationship between emotion and behavior. With what I share throughout this book, you'll be able to think about emotional insights in a whole new way, ask the right questions when doing your work, and gain a competitive advantage, simply by being better at focusing on how people want to feel.

One way to think about this is through the lens of emotional intelligence, a concept popularized, in part, by Daniel Goleman with his bestseller, *Emotional Intelligence: Why it can matter more than IQ* (Goleman, 2005). His book, and most conversations about emotional intelligence, primarily apply to interactions between people. However, what you'll learn about in this book is my perspective on how you can put emotional intelligence at the center of how your brand sparks desire.

For more context on this perspective, I interviewed Kevin Allen, PhD, one of my earliest professional mentors who is now an emotional intelligence expert. He shared:

> Emotional intelligence, as it's been defined by these scholars, centers around how we perceive and express ourselves, how we develop and maintain social relationships, how we cope with challenges, and, most importantly, how we use emotional information in a meaningful way. It's understanding your emotions, and the emotions of others to shape behavior. Goleman documented five core elements of emotional intelligence: Self-awareness, self-regulation, empathy, motivation, and social skills. What's exciting is that everyone has the ability to be more emotionally intelligent. The key to building strong relationships—whether that's person-to-person or brand-to-people—is in your ability to have an ever-present emotional antenna, such that you're constantly in touch and connecting with the emotional states of your constituency, whoever that constituency might be (Perlmutter, 2021).

When I talk about applying emotional intelligence to brand strategy, I'm giving double meaning to the term emotional intelligence.

One meaning relates to my interpretation of how to apply Goleman's principles to relationships between brands and people—in this case, the suggestion that when you are more aware of how your brand make people's lives better, and more in tune with the needs and desires of the people your brand serves, your brand can be more intentional, helpful, relevant, and desirable.

The other meaning relates to the ongoing imperative you have as a brand leader to gather emotional intelligence, referred to throughout this book as emotional insights. Your chances of creating Limbic Sparks, and having customers at hello, improve when you discover and address what people care about the most.

Three Steps to Sparking Brand Desire

Limbic Sparks Brand Strategy is a disciplined approach and mindset. One where you're ever curious about how people want to feel as a central question that we keep coming back to, in all aspects of brand leadership. I created this approach to help brand leaders overcome the limitations of traditional brand strategy.

It's a cure for traditional approaches that are arguably the biggest obstacles to creating a real and meaningful connection with customers and other stakeholders. The foundations of Limbic Sparks Brand Strategy are rooted in all that I learned from my behavioral science mentors, and from what's been documented as the undeniable power of emotional insights.

The methods behind this brand strategy approach emphasize not only listening closely to internal team members, but having an equally important nuanced understanding of what makes customers tick by listening to them directly. The approach requires asking a lot of questions, getting to the root of customer motivation, reserving judgment until insights discovery is completed, and then finding a natural intersection of a brand's "Why?" and "Who?" It does not attempt to force what the brand cares about into people's lives. Instead, it brings fresh and reliable insight into what matters to the people that the brand is for. From there, you can shape how your brand is presented to become more relevant, compelling, and desirable. This approach is not about presentations with big reveals. It is about being insightful and working together to hone compelling narratives that inspire everyone—brand leaders, employees, and customers.

FIGURE 1.2 Three Steps to Sparking Brand Desire

Focus ⟶ Connect ⟶ Evolve

NOTE Throughout this book, you'll learn how to bring Limbic Sparks Brand Strategy into your work to discover emotional insights and spark brand desire using this three-step approach.

Limbic Sparks Brand Strategy includes three steps that this book will explore and illustrate in depth, along with detailed examples of how the approach has been used by brand leaders:

TABLE 1.2 Three Steps to Sparking Brand Desire

Three Steps to Sparking Brand Desire		
Focus ⟶	*Connect* ⟶	*Evolve* ⟶
Discovering the shared emotional motivation that your brand has in common with the people it's for.	Strengthening connections with customers by standing for the emotional benefits they care about the most.	Creating evolved brand expression and experiences to address how people want to feel.

Having worked with business and brand leaders at dozens of companies using Limbic Sparks Brand Strategy, I can tell you that it consistently inspires them to rethink how they've always done things. It puts a new perspective on emotion, and it helps them understand more than they ever knew before about the real reasons that customers buy from them, which are so often very different than they assume, and nearly always emotionally driven.

Once we unlock emotional insights, it helps to reprioritize the core benefits that the brand stands for to attract other people who would appreciate knowing where to find those same benefits. This approach will bring fresh answers about the emotional drivers of your customers, even when ways to create a competitive advantage seem nearly impossible to find.

Looking Ahead

My hope in writing this book is that each chapter that follows will inspire you to unshackle yourself from traditional brand strategy. It will turn you into a believer and practitioner of the idea that addressing what people care about most will give your brand a significant competitive advantage. It will help you become fluent in the exact approach that I use to help brand leaders spark brand desire, and to help their brands become better known for being as good as they are. It will help you bring a new type of emotional intelligence into your work as a brand leader. If you're ready to move beyond traditional brand strategy and do what it takes to spark brand desire, then let's get started.

BRAND LEADERSHIP CONSIDERATIONS

In your own life, what's an example of a brand that you enjoy experiencing again and again, and how does it make you feel?

When we find ourselves consciously desiring to return to a brand experience, it most likely solves a pressing challenge, makes us feel respected and valued, or brings us to a new level of enjoyment. Regardless, it's how that experience makes us feel that keeps us coming back for more.

In your work with brands, how much do you really know about the emotional motivations that drive customer behavior?

Instinctive emotional responses play an outsized role in our conscious customer behavior. However, traditional brand strategy has historically been geared toward persuasion and not guided by emotional insights. When brand leaders prioritize understanding the emotional motivations behind customer behavior, they have a much better chance of igniting their interest and sparking brand desire.

Here are three things you can start doing today:

1 Remember that we gravitate toward what makes us feel good, away from what makes us feel bad, and ignore what's irrelevant.

2 Recognize that focusing on "What's your Why?" in the absence of "Who's your Who?" leads to a lack of relevance in brand messaging.

3 Bring more emotional intelligence into your approach to brand leadership— including insights about what matters most to the people who your brand is for and an ongoing effort to address their emotional motivations.

References

Feltman, R and Elliot, A J (2012) Approach and avoidance motivation. In Seel, N M (ed) *Encyclopedia of the Sciences of Learning*, Springer, Boston, MA. https://doi.org/10.1007/978-1-4419-1428-6_1749 (archived at https://perma.cc/5JZG-2MJW)

Forrester (2011) The rise of the chief customer officer, 24 January, www.forrester.
com/blogs/11-01-24-the_rise_of_the_chief_customer_officer/ (archived at
https://perma.cc/2CPF-5J2P)

Goleman, D (2005) *Emotional Intelligence: Why it can matter more than IQ*, 10th
Anniversary Edition, Bantam, US

Kahneman, D (2011) *Thinking, Fast and Slow*, Farrar, Straus and Giroux, US

Limbic Brand Evolution (2021) Let's Talk Limbic Sparks Podcast – episode
7, Creating Brand Desire Through Design with Gregg Heard, 7 October,
www.limbicbrandevolution.com/podcast/gregg-heard-sage-lets-talk-limbic-
sparks-7 (archived at https://perma.cc/F6RL-PEDW)

Limbic Brand Evolution (2022a) Let's Talk Limbic Sparks Podcast – episode
17, Championing Creativity to Solve Human Challenges with Liz Engelsen,
12 September, www.limbicbrandevolution.com/podcast/liz-englesen-lets-
talk-limbic-sparks-17 (archived at https://perma.cc/W4XC-9HM8)

Limbic Brand Evolution (2022b) Let's Talk Limbic Sparks Podcast – episode
13, Demystifying Consumer Insights for Service Brands with Samantha Liss,
9 May, www.limbicbrandevolution.com/podcast/samantha-liss-lets-talk-
limbic-sparks-13 (archived at https://perma.cc/B4EA-56X7)

Limbic Brand Evolution (2022c) Let's Talk Limbic Sparks Podcast – episode 10,
Prioritizing Brand Purpose and People's Emotions with Dominik Prinz-Barley,
8 February, www.limbicbrandevolution.com/podcast/dominik-prinz-barley-lets-
talk-limbic-sparks-10(archived at https://perma.cc/2JTZ-XPPU)

Limbic Brand Evolution (2022d) Let's Talk Limbic Sparks Podcast – episode 11,
Challenging Brands to Go Beyond Status Quo with Kim Christfort, 14 March,
www.limbicbrandevolution.com/podcast/kim-christfort-lets-talk-limbic-
sparks-11 (archived at https://perma.cc/X4C6-WR7Y)

Limbic Brand Evolution (2023a) Let's Talk Limbic Sparks Podcast – episode
26, Understanding Consumer Behavior with Joe Sauer, 12 June, www.
limbicbrandevolution.com/podcast/joe-sauer-lets-talk-limbic-sparks-26
(archived at https://perma.cc/9XQM-TDY7)

Limbic Brand Evolution (2023b) Let's Talk Limbic Sparks Podcast – episode 29,
Talking with Users to Improve Digital Products with Lisa Richner, 18
September, www.limbicbrandevolution.com/podcast/lisa-richner-lets-talk-limbic-
sparks-29 (archived at https://perma.cc/657A-RNPY)

Limbic Brand Evolution (2023c) Let's Talk Limbic Sparks Podcast – episode 30,
Marketing with Precise Emotional Drivers Insight with Esther-Mireya Tejeda,
16 October, www.limbicbrandevolution.com/podcast/esther-mireya-tejeda-lets-
talk-limbic-sparks-30 (archived at https://perma.cc/F4YV-A4EU)

Limbic Brand Evolution (2023d) Let's Talk Limbic Sparks Podcast – episode 22,
Exchanging Energy Through Conversations with Maxine Cunningham, 13
February, www.limbicbrandevolution.com/podcast/maxine-cunningham-lets-
talk-limbic-sparks-22 (archived at https://perma.cc/JYE6-Q3FF)

Parrish, R (2019) The US Customer Experience Index, 2019: Some small gains, widespread stagnation, no real leaders [blog] Forrester, 11 June, www.forrester.com/blogs/cx-index-2019-results/ (archived at https://perma.cc/S5VR-NAER)

Perlmutter, K (2020) Interview: How instinctive emotion drives behavior, with Cyrus McCandless, PhD, *Brandingmag*, 20 October, www.brandingmag.com/2020/10/20/interview-how-instinctive-emotion-drives-behavior-with-cyrus-mccandless-phd/ (archived at https://perma.cc/BJ98-A2K5)

Perlmutter, K (2021) Interview: Why brands should become more emotionally intelligent, with Kevin Allen, *Brandingmag*, 15 September, www.brandingmag.com/2021/09/15/interview-why-brands-should-become-more-emotionally-intelligent-with-kevin-allen/ (archived at https://perma.cc/U3RL-2NC9)

Reid, A and González-Vallejo, C (2009) Emotion as a tradeable quantity, *Journal of Behavioral Decision Making*, January, www.sentientdecisionscience.com/wp-content/uploads/publications/emotion-as-a-tradeable-quantity.pdf (archived at https://perma.cc/NG3Z-Z6QD)

Sinek, S (2009) *Start with Why: How great leaders inspire everyone to take action*, Portfolio, US

Zaltman, G (2003) *How Customers Think: Essential insights into the mind of the market*, Harvard Business School Press, US

02

Shifting from "About Us" to "For You"

AT&T Performing Arts Center Case Study

"I just wish more people knew about what makes our brand so great, and that I had better words to express it."

This was how my conversation started with Debbie Storey, then CEO and president of the AT&T Performing Arts Center in Dallas. I could feel her heartfelt passion for the brand's mission and for the amazing performances that the Center brings to its stages. Yet she knew something wasn't right. Why couldn't more potential attendees in the greater Dallas area see how wonderful it was? Why was the marketing failing to make the brand more appealing to more people?

Debbie was working with Michelle Holmes, the Center's VP and chief marketing officer, who was leading the project, when they hired me to help them attract more arts lovers. As we started our work together, it became clear that they wished their brand was better understood and more desired.

Both, relatively new to their roles, were frustrated that despite the Center's brand development and marketing efforts to date, many people in Dallas were still unfamiliar with it or weren't compelled enough by what they knew about it to book a ticket to one of its performances. Even more troubling to Debbie, when she stood on stage to introduce performances and welcome people to the Center, she didn't feel like she had the right words to convey what made the Center unique and special. She told me, "I don't feel like what I'm saying is what I feel in my heart."

In one of my many conversations with Michelle about the brand evolution work to be done, she shared the following:

> Our brand challenge is a common one to many performing arts centers. We have a big need to broaden our audience. We have strong loyalty among patrons who frequently visit us for opera, Broadway, and dance performances—they are

people who follow these things and are often older and more affluent. Where we need to do better is in bringing in the new generation of patrons who are younger, family-oriented, more diverse, and looking for entertainment options that feel less formal. We have so much wonderful programming that they will enjoy, in a very welcoming environment, but currently they don't feel connected to our brand.

Although they struggled to articulate it, Debbie and Michelle were seeking more Limbic Sparks—the ability to light up the emotions of more people in the Dallas community they served with a mere mention of the AT&T Performing Arts Center's name. They also knew that they needed to get more return on investment from their ongoing marketing efforts, via more tickets and memberships sold. They were struggling to figure out how.

From "About Us" to "For You"

Until that point, the AT&T Performing Arts Center's brand efforts had been built around an idea that came out of traditional brand strategy. They hinged their marketing on a well-crafted tagline, "Staging the Amazing," and they put lots of support behind it. Yet that approach was letting Debbie and Michelle down.

Like many of my clients, the Center was struggling with one of the biggest challenges with traditional brand strategy… it's too much about the brand, and not enough for the customer. Their messaging told potential audiences too much about what the Center was doing, rather than what it could do for them.

Debbie and Michelle's wish that more people would understand and appreciate their organization is very common among marketers who rely on traditional brand strategy. When brands focus on what they want to tell people about themselves, they are often neglecting the emotional benefits that people are instinctively seeking and are more drawn to.

Their tagline, "Staging the Amazing," inadvertently steered the Center's messaging toward boasting about the quality of their performances, about the beauty of their performance venues, and about their white-glove style of service. Of course, the staff had reason to be proud of showcasing many talented musicians, dancers, actors, and other artists and talking about the amazing performances they staged. However, "Staging the Amazing" was their "Why," and they were coming across to potential audiences like someone who's so excited about their own achievements that they focus only on themselves. All their marketing was "about us" instead of "for you." It showed no curiosity or insight into what potential audiences might care about. For most people encountering those messages, no insight = no relevance = no Limbic Sparks = no connection.

My job was to help the AT&T Performing Arts Center evolve its brand strategy, so that the brand and its marketing could catch up with the actual experience that they wanted more people to know about. How could we better convey, and help people feel, that it was the brand for them?

It was time to put Limbic Sparks Brand Strategy to work, including its three phases—Focus, Connect, and Evolve—that I introduced in Chapter 1 and that you'll learn more about throughout this book.

Focus

Focus is all about Insights Discovery. Importantly, it's about digging into all there is to review and asking a lot of questions, as a basis for strategy development. There are five important components in this phase of brand strategy development that we'll review in detail in Part Two of this book.

For the AT&T Performing Arts Center, this included not only learning about their brand challenges but uncovering what made them so desirable to so many people who already felt like it was a brand for them. To kick off this work, I knew it would be important to see the performance venues and to get a feel for the campus. I scheduled a three-day trip to Dallas, during which time I met with Michelle and Debbie and began the work of Insights Discovery.

As I visited the organization's campus in the heart of the Dallas Arts District, we carried out several research activities:

- I spoke with a variety of people who worked for this brand in various roles, including Chris Heinbaugh, who was leading External Affairs and several years later became the brand's Chief Advocacy Officer.
- I met with other team members who were responsible for preparing for and marketing performances.
- I met with front-of-house guest experience team members at the Center's various performance venues.
- I spoke with Dallas residents who had attended performances, and some who had not.

- We carried out a review of existing customer data, testimonials, and reviews.
- We found a variety of online third-party research reports and case studies about how other performing arts centers had navigated similar brand challenges, and what they learned about expanding their audience base.
- We conducted a thorough review of how the Center was presenting its brand in its marketing.

The objective of all this was to get a deep understanding of what matters most to the people who are part of the AT&T Performing Arts Center organization, and to people the brand was most interested in serving. We were seeking emotional insights that we could use to refocus the brand strategy and brand messaging to help people better understand why it could be a brand for them.

The good news is that many Dallas residents were already feeling Limbic Sparks. Visitors adored the Center, thanks to the quality of the performances and great experiences. No matter who I encountered—affluent supporters with memberships, families who attended community events, or students who came to subsidized performances—they felt welcome and special and walked away with great memories. In their reviews and testimonials, they said things like "I can't believe that I can come into a place like this," "I was made to feel welcome and special," and "It's the best thing Dallas has to offer."

Interestingly, regular attendees didn't all fit into a single demographic category. Some were affluent patrons who paid top dollar for memberships and prime seats; others were middle-class families who attended less expensive community events; some were students who only came to subsidized performances and arts educational activities. The Center is also well regarded for its support of emerging artists who are often getting their first experience on or backstage.

One of the primary outputs of the Focus phase is the Shared Emotional Motivation, which you'll learn more about in Chapter 3. It's the common motivation that both the brand and its customers are driven to achieve. From the Insights Discovery work, we recognized the incredible dedication that the AT&T Performing Arts Center's staff have for their work. They are resilient, hard-working, and love the work they do. They want everyone to feel their enthusiasm for exploring the wide range of performances that they present, and they thrive on making it possible for new performers and stage technicians to get their start. We also found that what united people who frequent the Center was an emotional drive to explore new interests, discover new passions, enjoy memorable moments, and share those experiences with friends and loved ones. Ultimately, we landed on the following Shared Emotional Motivation:

Passion for Entertaining Experiences.

This was not a new tagline to replace "Staging the Amazing." It was a brand strategy insight and a new way to summarize the Center's common mission with its audience, while also describing an audience benefit that would create Limbic Sparks. It's something that is at the heart of what the AT&T Performing Arts Center was committed to delivering, and that people were seeking in their lives.

"Passion for Entertaining Experiences" became the first foundational element of our brand strategy to take us into the Connect phase.

Connect

The Connect phase, as you began to read about in Chapter 1 and will read more about in Part Three of this book, is all about the steps and criteria for developing brand strategy. Core to this phase is developing the Brand Idea. The Shared Emotional Motivation and the Brand Idea are the two bookends of a Limbic Sparks Brand Strategy. Together they ensure that the Brand Idea is a relevant and compelling brand benefit and invitation—criteria that separate Limbic Sparks Brand Strategy from traditional brand strategy.

Our Insights Discovery work helped us better understand why people who know about the AT&T Performing Arts Center enjoy visiting. Even though the marketing was about "Staging the Amazing," people were not pointing to the amazing buildings or the white glove service. As people described what they liked most about visiting the Center, it was less about the high-end aspects of the venues than we anticipated. It was more about the everyday experiences they had while there. Certainly, people had viscerally emotional responses to the performances they saw, but what seemed to be even more powerful was the discovery of new passions, their experiences, and the incredible memories created. For many people, visiting the Center sparked more and more interest in experiencing more of what it has to offer.

With these Insights Discovery findings in mind, we started our Connect phase by listing the emotional insights that we learned about from patrons. These are the things that were most referenced and what consistently rose to the top in our discussions and in our review of testimonials. They describe the feelings people had and how they remembered their experiences. These emotional benefits were also, curiously, absent from the Center's current marketing.

We learned that the AT&T Performing Arts Center is a place where people enjoy:

- discovering new interests
- learning new things
- participating in new experiences
- igniting new passions
- creating memorable moments
- feeling welcome and special

People also spoke about their surprise. Those who were new to the Center were astonished by all they experienced. Their visits were filled with unexpected discoveries. We took note of the fact that people found something that they weren't expecting—experiences that were so enjoyable, memories of events that they wanted to relive—and with so many things to do, every visit led to something new and different.

We reflected on the brand's Mission, which is about being a public gathering place that strengthens community and fosters creativity through the presentation of performing arts and arts education programs. This reminded us that the AT&T Performing Arts Center is a nonprofit that exists in service of the community. It's a vital part of the Dallas Arts District for all of Dallas and the surrounding area to enjoy. It should not feel exclusive or inaccessible. In fact, it should feel quite the opposite.

Further, it became clear that potential patrons, people who had yet to attend an event, were not aware of the emotional benefits that we identified. They were not experiencing the Center's heartfelt mission of being a gathering place for all. Many people who might have enjoyed being there, and possibly felt like it was not a brand for them, were not even aware of what they were missing.

This all led us to a Brand Idea that was directly tied to these benefits and the strategic goal of introducing the brand to a wider audience. After exploring a variety of potential Brand Ideas for the AT&T Performing Arts Center, we all rallied around one:

Yours to Discover

Rooted in that Shared Emotional Motivation, "Passion for Entertaining Experiences," this compelling brand benefit and invitation now opens the doors and welcomes people in. It reminds past attendees that there's always more to discover, and it lets people who are unfamiliar with the Center know where they can find the entertaining experiences that they might enjoy.

"Yours to Discover," which I co-developed with my colleague on this work, Betsy Wise, conveys the passion of the people who work for this nonprofit and their genuine desire to share it. It also evokes curiosity about a place that many people have seen but are not yet familiar with.

One of the most important objectives we were working toward for this overall brand evolution was not just to convey in more inviting detail what the AT&T Performing Arts Center was all about, but to encourage people to explore all there is to experience. However, instead of doing so by talking about what the brand offers and what makes it so amazing, we combined a brand benefit with an invitation based on what we learned about how people want to feel.

By transitioning the Brand Idea from "Staging the Amazing" to "Yours to Discover" as the anchor for all marketing, we can stress that the Center is welcoming to everyone, not just those who already had a well-established habit of attending the performing arts. It's welcoming to younger, more family-oriented people. It's welcoming to those who have a lot of money and those who do not. It's welcoming to those who want to attend a world-class performance, or to those who want to learn how to create one. Regardless of who you are, the AT&T Performing Arts Center is for you to discover and enjoy.

Now that we have our brand strategy, it's time to bring the brand to life.

Evolve

The third phase of Limbic Sparks Brand Strategy is Evolve, which you'll learn more about in Part Four of this book. Evolve is about applying the new brand strategy to Brand Expression & Experiences, such as the brand's visual identity, messaging, and more, in a way that addresses how people want to feel.

Once you've completed the strategy work in Focus and Connect you should assess what needs to be evolved. It's a good moment to pause and consider what's needed next so that the brand comes to life in ways that reflect all you've learned and created to date.

For the AT&T Performing Arts Center, we recognized the need for a significant brand evolution, even though we had a relatively modest budget to work with. The first two priorities were evolving the brand messaging and the visual identity. We created new brand guidelines for each and then applied the evolution to all forms of brand expression.

Brand Messaging

One of the downsides of the prior "Staging the Amazing" brand idea was that it naturally steered brand messaging toward being a bit boastful. We now have a brand idea that is more about inviting discovery. By design, it is more welcoming and inviting. The task at hand was to infuse this new way of communicating into all the brand messaging.

As such, we also introduced new brand messaging and a brand messaging style guide, anchored by three copywriting principles: "Be welcoming and inviting; be enthusiastic and passionate; be friendly and informative."

We began the task of rewriting copy across all touchpoints, including the website, social media, and marketing materials. The new copy made the Center more relevant and inviting by conveying the pleasure of discovery, rather than stressing its quality. Here's an example of this subtle but essential difference:

> **Before:** *On the AT&T Performing Arts Center campus, people from all over North Texas gather to see theatre, dance, opera, rock, comedy, and more. It's a place where new work is premiered, the best performers from around the world stop on their tours, and students take the stage for their very first public performance. Live entertainment is about the experience and human connection.*

> **After:** *When you explore the AT&T Performing Arts Center campus, you'll experience world-class theater, dance, opera, rock, comedy, and more. New works are premiered, nationally touring Broadway shows stop by, and students stage their debut performances. Come, immerse yourself, and find out what moves you. It's yours to discover.*

Visual Identity

As part of our Evolve phase work, we took the opportunity to change the visual identity of the AT&T Performing Arts Center brand. Working with a wonderfully talented designer, we all agreed that the new brand strategy called for a synergistic update to the visual identity.

We identified three core visual identity challenges to overcome: It felt very high-end, it felt corporate, and it lacked cohesion.

The brand logo included the AT&T Performing Arts Center logo type, which was set in a very thin version of the brand's typeface, and often in colors such as brown and gold. It was combined with the words "Staging the Amazing," set in all capital letters. It felt too high-end—like a black tie or formal gown was required. Other aspects of the brand's visual identity took cues from its AT&T sponsor, and it made portions of the brand expression feel too corporate. It included a lot of blue and white, and overall lacked warmth and excitement.

Taking a cue from "Yours to Discover," we sought to dial up the vibrancy and welcoming nature of the visual identity. We made it warmer, lighter, and more inviting by using a bolder weight of the logotype font and by introducing a handwritten typeface to play up the personalized aspect of the new tagline, "Yours to Discover." This also included a warmer and more vibrant color pallet across the visual system, leveraging black, white, and red as anchor colors.

Figure 2.1 shows the before-and-after of the brand logo.

Secondly, we needed to address the issue of a lack of visual cohesion across marketing touchpoints. A big challenge here stems from the fact that when you're a performing arts center with many performers and acts from around the world rotating through your stages—from Broadway performances to international dance troupes, to stand-up comedy, to opera and more—you receive a constant influx of poster art to promote upcoming performances.

Up to this point, the visual identity did not include a systematic solution for using all this artwork, while at the same time giving credit to the AT&T Performing Art Center for presenting the performance. In many cases the received poster art was used with little to no, and certainly not consistent, AT&T Performing Arts Center branding.

To solve this challenge, our evolved visual identity system included a framing device where all outside artwork is housed in a frame that included the AT&T Performing Art's Center logo and tagline, and other copy content, within the frame. The system prioritized use of the new primary brand colors and allowed for secondary color options to ensure that all artwork received from the outside would have a "frame" solution that did not clash or not have enough contrast.

FIGURE 2.1 AT&T Performing Arts Center Logo and Tagline Evolution

Original

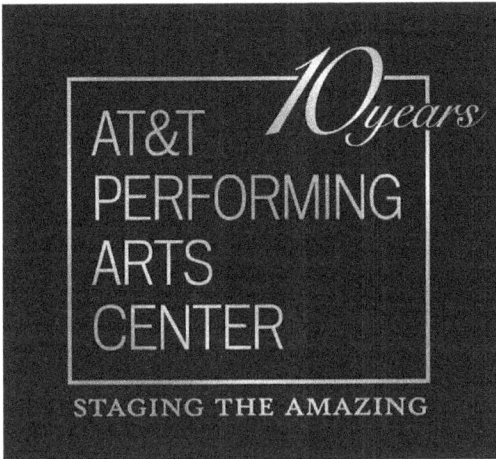

Evolved

NOTE These logos represent the AT&T Performing Arts Center brand evolution. The original logo, using the original tagline, has a brown background and gold type. The evolved logo utilized black type for the brand name and a red handwritten typeface for the tagline, on a white background.

Additional Brand Activation Updates

Now that we had a new style of brand messaging and a new visual identity system, the organization was able to apply it to many brand touchpoints. We continued to support Michelle Holmes in updating marketing materials and the brand website, using all the new visual elements and copy. We also worked with Chris Heinbaugh to create a new Report to the Community—their version of an annual report, using the new visual and copy direction. Further, we worked with the team responsible for securing corporate sponsors for the AT&T Performing Arts Center, a significant source of funding, to bring the new brand strategy and brand expression into their pitches and presentations. As it turns out, this was just the beginning of how this evolved brand strategy was used for years to come.

Enduring Impact

Soon after the brand relaunch, Debbie said to me, "The Limbic Sparks approach opened the doors for us to better articulate what the Center means to us and to the community. It's a brand and brand evolution plan that all of us, from the board to the staff, understand, love, and are excited about."

Sometimes, however, the true test of a brand strategy is unknown at the time it is created. As it turned out, we worked on this brand evolution during the second half of 2019, and it launched in January of 2020.

A few months later, sadly, the AT&T Performing Arts Center had to halt live performances due to the Covid-19 pandemic. As I was writing this book several years later, Chis Heinbaugh sent me this note:

> For the Center, "Yours to Discover" was a critical guidepost, both during the pandemic and emerging from it afterwards. When closed to the public, we shifted to virtual content. We took the same approach to our community and education programs, inviting students and the broader community to continue engaging and discovering through online streamed events. "Yours to Discover" helped us meet the moment, stay engaged with, and expand our community after the pandemic ended. Inviting Discovery continues to be the thread for our brand and all there is to experience at the Center. No matter the change in people and programming here at the Center, "Yours to Discover" reminds us that this is not about us, it's for our community.

Overall, this brand evolution helped many more people feel that the AT&T Performing Arts Center is a brand for them. It inspires them to discover all there is to experience. Debbie and Michelle were happy and enthusiastic about relaunching the evolved brand, as it not only conveyed what they felt in their hearts, but, importantly, it better connected the Center with its patrons and other people in the Dallas community.

Looking Ahead

Next, in Part Two, you'll learn all about the Focus phase, and how to conduct Insights Discovery including five activities, followed by another case study to see how it informed that brand's evolution. Get ready, because now it's time to learn how to Focus.

BRAND LEADERSHIP CONSIDERATIONS

In your own life, have you ever been surprised by a brand that turned out to be more wonderful than you could have imagined?

Sometimes, we stumble onto a brand, having no idea that it will be one we want to experience more often. It's that chance encounter that caught our attention and made us realize that there is so much more to enjoy than we anticipated.

In your work with brands, do you sometimes wish you had a better way to spark interest in your offering?

I most often find that brand leaders don't know exactly why people choose their brand, or why people keep coming back to it. However, if you can discover the top reasons why people keep returning to your brand, you can turn those insights into brand benefits that attract new customers who are most likely seeking the same benefits but are unaware that your brand makes them possible.

Here are three things you can start doing today:

1 Discover why people choose your brand and the specific benefits that they enjoy most.

2 Assume that there are many more people who want to enjoy those benefits, but don't know that your brand makes them possible.

3 Transform your brand messaging from benefits you think people care about, to benefits that your current customers reveal that they value most.

PART TWO

Focus

03

Discovering Emotional Insights

It's tough to get new ideas from old information. Albert Einstein often spoke about the importance of curiosity, saying that it's more important than knowledge. He even claimed that his passionate curiosity was more responsible for his intellect than any special talents (Einstein, n.d.). I'm also of the mind that most effective ideas emerge when you ask the right questions, consider context from a variety of angles, and gather new insights that few others have discovered. Honestly, I'm leery of anyone who starts a brand evolution project with more answers than questions.

Focus, the first phase of Limbic Sparks Brand Strategy, is all about Insights Discovery. During this phase, you'll take time to investigate and bring together a refreshed perspective of what your brand is all about and what matters most to your customers and prospects. It will unlock a treasure trove of insight and, ultimately, lead you to the Shared Emotional Motivation that your brand has in common with the people you serve—one brand strategy bookend. This will set the stage for the Brand Idea, the other brand strategy bookend, which you'll learn about in Chapter 5.

> **Focus**
>
> Discovering the Shared Emotional Motivation that your brand has in common with the people it's for.

What's better—an ok solution that is developed quickly, or a great solution that takes longer?

Honestly, I'm baffled by strategists and brand leaders who set the wheels in motion for attracting customers to their brand when they haven't done the hard work of identifying the emotional insights that influence people's behavior. Despite all the work we do as strategists, businesses, and brand leaders, we often operate with too little insight.

Perhaps you've had an experience like this one, on either side of the table: I was in a pitch meeting where a potential client told me that another group had come into the room with very creative brand ideas. This was our first meeting. They wanted to know if I was going to pitch brand ideas—something I was not prepared for and had no intention of doing. I had to explain why.

As this was happening, my curiosity, as usual, was in overdrive. I was so curious about how the other group had come to the ideas they shared. Were they spit-balling on the fly? Did they study the brand and customer insights, and do the strategy work already, for free, just to try to be impressive during the pitch meeting? Were they just making "educated guesses"? Were they planning to charge for strategy after they proved they had all the answers, or were they going to jump right into creative development? Also, how was the client team going to judge their ideas? Were they going to decide based on their gut instinct, with no new insight and no strategic criteria? Perhaps, I thought, this is why they need a brand evolution in the first place.

I said, "Well, I don't have the answers yet, and I won't be making random strategy or creative recommendations to try and win the project." I politely shared that it would be foolish to play guessing games on something so important. I promised that, if we worked together, they would not hear any brand ideas from me until after Insights Discovery.

As it turns out, they were more interested in fast answers than strategically grounded ones, and we were not a good fit. Personally, I'd never play that game, and if I were on the client side, I wouldn't put my name to recommendations built on such an unstable foundation to evolve my brand.

I urge you to beware of anyone saying "We don't need to develop a robust plan or a strategy," "We don't have time to gather new insights," "We don't need to better understand our customers," "We don't have budget for strategy," "Let's just get started." These statements are a recipe for disaster and a precursor for disappointment. Curiosity is not a step in the process that should be cut short. It's a vital component of brand strategy development.

The most successful brand leaders and strategists are inherently curious. They know that asking the right questions is far more important than having fast answers. They are curious about what matters most to people within their company. They are also curious about what matters most to customers.

They are skilled at connecting the dots to envision new possibilities and bringing these two sets of motivations together. They know that taking the time to do the strategy work, inclusive of refreshed customer insights, solidifies a foundation for brand activations that build strong, long-lasting customer connections.

Brand leader Marcy Ullom put it this way: "You've gotta talk to people. You've gotta talk, talk, talk, talk, talk to people... to try to pick their brain to find out what it is that drives them" (Limbic Brand Evolution, 2024a).

As you read in Chapter 2, we recognized that the AT&T Performing Arts Center was not just a place where there are amazing performances and venues, it is a place where the people who work there and the people who visit can find common ground on a shared mission—"Passion for Entertaining Experiences." It was this understanding that opened the door to a Brand Ideas—"Yours to Discover"—and a more effective way to let people know it was a brand for them. This was directly inspired by insights that our curiosity and the Focus phase approach led us to.

The Risks of Relying on Yesterday's Customer Insights

Have you ever noticed that the most successful brands always seem to know exactly what people want? They serve the customer and discover the unmet needs that no other brand is addressing. The best of the best launch new and better ways to exceed expectations that forever change how people get through their every day.

Their competitive advantage is rooted in understanding the nuances of what motivates people, and how they want to feel, to create meaningful differentiation. This insight may materialize into an incredible feature, a desirable style of service, or a compelling brand promise—something that sparks a strong emotional connection and ongoing brand desire.

Stephan Gans, who leads global consumer insights at PepsiCo, said the following:

> In our business, the drivers of competitive advantage used to be related to physical scale. But those advantages have melted away—not entirely, of course, but competitive advantage no longer rests on physical scale the way it once did. Today, competitive advantage is about who has the most data, and who can leverage it the best for increased consumer understanding and better commercial decision-making (Fleming and Garg, 2024).

This need to constantly refresh insights became very clear during the global Covid-19 pandemic (2020–2023). Typically, the ongoing evolution of customer preferences evolves in small increments and in random patterns across product categories and consumer segments. It's somewhat tough to discern these changes unless you are gathering new insights on a regular basis and observing changing patterns. The pandemic, however, gave us a glimpse into what happens when the world changes, in a big way, all at once. It altered people's everyday routines, shifted their priorities, and disrupted their daily habits, combined with a spike in technology adoption at a pace not often seen.

During that time, we saw the restaurant industry transform to serve more takeout and delivery. Very quickly restaurants needed to adapt their operations to accommodate this shift, including busier drive-through lines, having mobile apps capable of managing curbside delivery, and an overall increase in the proportion of take-out versus dine-in customers. We also saw the healthcare industry adapt to a sudden increase in telehealth, where doctors needed to adjust their practices for video calls versus in-person visits. In both industries, and others, brands that recognized and successfully adapted to the shift in customer needs, and their emotional context, were better able to navigate their business through the pandemic. In late 2020, Cassandra Nordlund, director in the Gartner Marketing practice reported, "For marketing leaders, it's never been more important to anticipate their customer's concerns and to reflect back to them how their brand helps to solve their customer's issues" (Gartner, 2020).

The pandemic was, hopefully, a once-in-a-lifetime global event, but it pointed out something that we don't often see—a massive simultaneous shift in people's preferences, and the need for brands to adapt quickly or fall behind. Not long ago, gathering new consumer insights was an exercise that did not always happen on a regular basis. The pandemic made it clear that brand leaders can't rely on outdated insights. Even when there's no pandemic, or massive simultaneous shifts in consumer behavior, we now know that there's competitive advantage to can be gained and sustained when you're curious about people's lifestyles, motivations, unmet needs, and priorities. When you turn ongoing curiosity into insights, and are on top of shifts in customer preferences, you can be more customer-centric by using that insight to improve brand strategy, messaging, and brand experiences.

When interviewing brand leader Jess Kessler, she shared why it's so critical that brand leaders keep a pulse on their audiences: "Audiences change so fast, and we at times become very comfortable in our approach to things because they've worked, or people have responded well to them. When it comes to creating compelling campaigns, the first step is knowing your audience, and knowing what they want" (Limbic Brand Evolution, 2024b).

The Value of Insights Discovery

The value of insights discovery, especially at the beginning of any new brand development work, is a broader perspective, a deeper understanding, and an opportunity to develop more effective paths forward.

Insights Discovery

A concerted effort to gain a deep understanding of the brand, its context, and the emotional motivations that drive customer behavior, as critical inputs to developing brand strategy, marketing, and customer experiences.

Strategy is often described as a plan of action designed to achieve an objective. I like to think of it as setting the foundation for a future that has yet to unfold. Strategies can have varying levels of uncertainty, but Insights Discovery reduces risk by informing how to adapt along the way, ultimately leading to more effective outcomes. Ongoing discovery can help you go beyond the status quo into new areas of thought and action and guide you to evolve in necessary and relevant ways over time as new insights emerge.

Strategy

A plan of action designed to achieve an objective, or setting the foundation for a future that has yet to unfold.

Specifically, a robust Insights Discovery phase of any brand evolution work can help you improve the results of your efforts in the following three areas.

Avoid Confirmation Bias

Big decisions based on old perspectives and old data are a big risk. The status quo is, if nothing else, predictable, but it's often built on layers and layers of confirmation bias. It's the opposite of curiosity and closes more doors than it opens, because it relies on the pre-existing assumptions rather than seeking new insights.

Confirmation Bias

A behavioral tendency that humans have to interpret new information in ways that confirm existing beliefs.

Think about how you interpret information from social media or the news. If you're like most people, you view information that you agree with as support for your point of view, and you dismiss information that is contrary to your point of view. This happens to all of us, and it takes a disciplined approach to break free of this inherent behavior of believing in our biases and preconceived instincts. Fresh customer insight is the cure for confirmation bias. It causes us to ask: Why are we doing things this way? Is there current data to back up this assumption? Are there new and better ways to move forward?

Gain Deeper Insight

When it comes to sharing feelings, social conformity bias often gets in the way. People only share what they want you to know about, and often they fall into alignment with what other people are sharing or saying. It's another behavioral tendency of humans to adapt what we say and how we behave based on how we want to be perceived. It's why making assumptions based on only observed behaviors and stated preferences, and not asking the right questions in the right way, can lead to unreliable information. Traditional brand strategy often relies on surface-level consumer understanding, and you must go deeper to gain psychographic understanding of what people need, want, and desire.

Social Conformity Bias

A behavioral tendency of humans to adapt what we say and how we behave based on how we want to be perceived.

One of the most challenging things to learn about is people's true thoughts and unarticulated feelings. As Brand Leader Eric Fernandez shared with me:

> People are emotional beings, and our behaviors are the manifestation of our underlying emotions. If you think of this as an analogy and you think of a tree, what we see—the trunk, the branches, the leaves—are the behaviors. The roots—what's underground that we can't see—are the underlying emotion. If you can understand the emotion, then you can better attune to and respond to the behavior" (Limbic Brand Evolution, 2024c).

An ongoing pursuit of gaining deep insight has business advantages as well: According to Forrester's 2024 Customer Experience Index, very few companies, only 3 percent, can be categorized as customer-obsessed. The remainder do not make customers' needs, desires, and satisfaction a top priority when making all business decisions and when taking action. However, organizations that do fall into this category report 41 percent faster revenue growth, 49 percent faster profit growth, and 51 percent better customer retention versus organizations that are not categorized as at customer-obsessed (Forrester, 2024).

Brand leader Ray Li shared, "We talk with our customers all the time. It's shocking how few executives and how few companies really spend time with their customers. They just do things based on their own gut. We just find that there's so much value in talking with people" (Limbic Brand Evolution, 2021).

Spark More Insightful Ideas

Insights Discovery is critical in your work as a brand leader. You spend a lot of time developing marketing, advertising, and brand experiences to attract and retain customers. There's pressure on your creative teams and your agencies is to deliver work that draws people into your brand, ignites their interest, and inspires them to become customers. However, you know the expression—"garbage in, garbage out."

When you jump right into creation without an insight-rich brief, you're bound to get either more of the same, or sub-optimal ideas for the task at hand. Throughout my career I've seen creatives struggle to have successful client presentations, and often it's because the strategy phase was not inspiring. It's a tough task to create new and better ideas when you don't have new insights to work with.

However, when you provide your creative teams with up-to-date, in-depth insights, they can do their best work. I've also been a part of many very successful first-round creative presentations, thanks to a talented creative team who were inspired by learning more about the context of the people who their work was intended for, often through an insight-rich creative brief. New insight about people and what makes them tick is gold for creatives. It helps them develop ideas that are rooted in what matters most to people, and significantly increases the chances that the work will do its job to spark attention and connect with people in relevant ways.

It's Time to Focus

As you read at the beginning of this chapter, Focus involves Insights Discovery—gathering information, hunting for clues, digging for details, and making the most of your curiosity, so that you will have a basis for deciding how to set your brand apart and connect with people. Throughout this phase, your objective is to find the intersection of what's most emotionally motivating for both your brand and for the people who you want to reach—the Shared Emotional Motivation.

Shared Emotional Motivation

The core Limbic Sparks insight identifying what both the brand and customer are most motivated to achieve individually and with each other.

This is the core motivation that your brand has in common with the people you serve, and it's the insight that is central to creating Limbic Sparks. It's also a critical element of brand strategy that sets Limbic Sparks Brand Strategy apart from traditional brand strategy. The Shared Emotional Motivation is one bookend of the brand strategy, with the other bookend being the Brand Idea, which you'll learn about in Part Three.

To discover the Shared Emotional Motivation, you do not want to play the typical brand strategy game of matching the brand's offering with your instincts about customer needs—too much brand strategy is rooted in trying to sell products and services with proof points and reasons to believe and hoping they will persuade potential customers that it's a brand for them.

In contrast, Limbic Sparks Brand Strategy is about discovering reasons to care—outcomes of the brand offering and experience that address your customers' emotional motivation, expressed through messaging that is relevant and compelling. It's done by comparing, side by side, all the things that matter to the brand and to the customer to discover their natural and mutual intersection. This will help you unlock reasons to care, rooted in emotional insights.

Reasons To Care

Meaningful emotional benefits that are intended to ignite customer desire.

Throughout Focus, you'll be gathering emotional insights to shed light on how people want to feel, so that you can present your brand in a way that is instinctively desirable.

Five Limbic Sparks Insights Discovery Activities

The Insights Discovery process will enable your brand to become emotionally intelligent. It will help you understand how to meet people where they are and arm you with emotional insights that improve the effectiveness of your brand development efforts.

This process of gathering information, analyzing clues, digging for details, and following your curiosity will create the basis for determining how to set your brand apart. It involves both qualitative exploration and, sometimes, quantitative research. It requires asking the right questions to get to the heart of what makes people tick, and what drives their perceptions and behaviors.

This investigative work might be more time-consuming than what your organization is accustomed to, but there is no substitute when it comes to uncovering the Shared Emotional Motivation that will enable your brand to create Limbic Sparks. What follows are details about the five Limbic Sparks Brand Strategy Insights Discovery Activities.

FIVE LIMBIC SPARKS BRAND STRATEGY INSIGHTS DISCOVERY
ACTIVITIES

1   Brand Dynamics Review

2   Competitive Audit

3   Category Dynamics Review

4   Brand Team & Customer Interviews

5   Customer Research Study

It's worth noting that throughout this book I'm speaking with you as the brand leader, and I'm suggesting approaches that you should bring into your work. I recognize that you may have people who support you on your team and at outside agencies. If that's the case, then you can use what's recommended in this book to ensure that the approaches your team and agencies use meet the standards of Limbic Sparks Brand Strategy—otherwise, they'll be reverting to traditional brand strategy and you'll be missing opportunities. If you are a brand consultant or student, you can use what's in this book to evolve your skills and approach, and to ensure that emotional insights sit behind your recommendations.

Now, let's review each Insights Discovery activity in detail, so you can see how to bring each into your work.

Understanding Brand Dynamics

Understanding Brand Dynamics, the first step of the Focus process, is a great way to kick off your curiosity.

Brand Dynamics Review

Absorbing existing information about the brand's current business objectives, strategy, messaging, marketing, products, services, customer experiences, long-term ambition, and customer metrics.

As a brand leader, especially if you're new to your team, you'll want to learn from the past. You'll want to understand the context, insights, and thinking behind past decisions, and the biggest challenges and blind spots that exist now. You'll want to gather existing information that can shed light on the current brand strategy, messaging, marketing, product and service details, and existing primary or third-party research. Also, don't forget to scour customer reviews and testimonials, which offer a lot of insight about how customers perceive and experience the brand.

You'll also want to overcome any tendency toward confirmation bias—that tendency to rely on existing data to confirm pre-existing beliefs. I've seen so many brand leaders weighed down by existing internal perspectives that are closing the doors to new ideas and opportunities. It's a big risk to rely on potentially outdated ideas about customers—their attitudes, needs, and buying behavior. Our emotional drivers are not static, and confirmation bias could cause you to miss out on information that can make all the difference in how you create stronger bonds with them. The bottom line for this step is to absorb all there is to absorb, but don't stop there—reserve your judgment, as you'll uncover new, important insights during the later steps of Insights Discovery.

Conducting a Competitive Audit

Following your immersion into brand dynamics, I recommend a competitive audit.

Competitive Audit

Investigating details about primary competitors to see how they differentiate themselves, the language they are using, and what makes them uniquely compelling.

Notably, there's a big difference between the Limbic Sparks approach to competitive audits versus how most people traditionally go about them. More traditional competitive audits are about finding "white space"—literally. The team often plots the conclusions of a competitive analysis on a 2×2 grid, with each competitor's brand positioning and primary messaging points noted. The area of white space on the grid shows where no competitor lives. Many brands then try to shift their positioning to that space.

There are several reasons to avoid this approach. One is that it often leads you to filling the space in a way that is opportunistic and inauthentic—you land on an idea that is different, but not necessarily something your brand fully delivers on. Another is that you are assuming that your competitors have everything figured out and are doing well in their current position. Having worked with many companies, I can assure you that most feel just like you do—that they have many opportunities for improvement. Following their lead is no way to be a leader, and I always suggest spending more time understanding customers versus over-analyzing and chasing competitors.

Remember that your primary objective is simply to understand the language used in the category, and what makes each brand unique in its tone and messaging. A good place to start is company websites, which show exactly how each brand is attempting to set itself apart. You can go further by looking at other marketing materials, auditing their customer experience, and looking at customer reviews to see how people feel about the competitive brands. Something I have no doubt you'll also discover is how many brands are talking about what they do, versus why people should care.

Sparking brand desire is about seizing your own high ground and leadership position regardless of what competitors are doing, rooted in addressing the emotional drivers of your customers and prospects. Doesn't that sound so much better than constantly chasing and trying to one-up the competition?

Category Dynamics Review

Analyzing category dynamics builds on what you learned about your own brand during the first step and what you learned about your competition in the second step.

> **Category Dynamics Review**
>
> Understanding how customers navigate the category, any category-specific peculiarities, and comparing the nuances of product and services offerings across primary competitors.

This is about understanding more specifics of the overall category, how competitive offerings compare to that of your brand, and how customers navigate their journey. In many cases, you'll also want to consider category-specific investigations, such as:

- if it's a highly regulated category like healthcare, financial services, or wine and spirits, you'll want to understand the regulatory constraints that guide marketing;

- if it's a category where there are intermediaries between your brand and the ultimate customer, like real estate, travel, or insurance, you'll want to understand how to create strong connections not only with end-customers, but also with those who sell directly to them;

- if it's a business-to-business product or service and there are two or more tiers of buyer influencers, such as those who use the product and the c-suite members who must approve the capital investment, you'll want to understand the emotional drivers of each group;

- if it's a category where consumers do a lot of research before purchasing or, conversely, purchase very quickly among a lot of seemingly similar choices, you'll want to know about the buying journey and how they gather enough information to make purchase decisions.

The importance of understanding category dynamics can't be underestimated, especially when they impact how your customers and prospects make purchases and build a relationship with your brand.

Brand Team and Customer Interviews

Now that you have a clearer understanding of the brand, the competitive set, and the category, it's time to turn to one of the most important parts of Insights Discovery: Brand Team & Customer Interviews.

Brand Team & Customer Interviews

Discussions with people at all levels of the brand's organization who represent a variety of functions, and hearing directly from customers about their experiences with the brand, their brand perceptions, their emotional motivations, and what it is about the brand that drives the most value.

Insights from these conversations are an essential part of understanding what's driving the feelings and decisions of both internal and external stakeholders. I often speak with 10 or more team members and 10 or more customers during 30–45-minute interviews. I work with my clients to select a set of customers who are representative of the company's customer base across the range of product/service categories, geographies, and company roles. The larger the organization, and the more customers it has, the more interviews you'll want to conduct.

To uncover the most helpful input from your interviews, the Limbic Sparks approach will help you prioritize questions that evoke more emotional responses and deeper insights about what drives decisions. This requires careful advanced thought about how to frame and phrase questions, because our brains respond to different types of questions in different ways. If you ask rational questions, you will get rational answers; you must ask evocative questions if you want emotionally driven answers.

Our autonomic nervous system, which controls our involuntary responses, has two parts called the sympathetic and parasympathetic nervous systems. The sympathetic system is triggered when we feel fear or discomfort, sense a threat, experience concern, or get angry. A trigger causes us to put our guard up instinctively and engages our "fight or flight" response. On the other hand, when something triggers our parasympathetic nervous system, we feel calmer and more at ease, and we tend to speak more freely.

This is why, when developing interview questions, it's important to avoid challenging or very direct questions that make people uncomfortable or on guard. When we feel too vulnerable or defensive, we tend to give post-rationalized responses—meaning that we instinctively modify our verbal responses to align with what we think the other person wants to hear or to say what we feel comfortable saying out loud.

For instance, suppose an interviewer asks you, "What's your biggest flaw in relationships with others?" You might immediately get defensive, with your heart rate increasing and your mind racing to say something that won't make you look bad. However, if the interviewer asks for the same information in a less aggressive way, such as, "If you could instantly change one thing about how you interact with other people, what would it be?", your response will probably be less guarded and more honest. You'd provide deeper and more accurate insights because you'd be thinking about a more positive future scenario, as opposed to revealing something negative from your past or present.

When we ask questions that are more enjoyable, or less threatening, to answer, we get more instinctive, evocative, and forthcoming answers. One thing I like to do at the beginning of an interview is ask a slightly off-topic question that helps the person relax and let their guard down. For instance, I might ask, "What brings you the most joy in the work you do?" A question like this triggers the parasympathetic nervous system, making the subject feel more comfortable and more inclined to trust me. Other steps I take to build trust include not recording interviews, instead simply taking notes, and letting people know that while I'll summarize responses from everyone I'm speaking with, I won't tie specific responses to specific people. This helps interviewees feel comfortable and they become more open with me.

As such, there's an art to framing interview questions that uncover truly insightful nuggets of information. As part of developing Limbic Sparks Brand Strategy, I have a lot of go-to questions that I bring into interviews.

Some of my favorite questions to ask brand team members include:

- What's the best thing your brand does for customers?
- What's the most gratifying customer feedback you've heard?
- If there was one thing that you could improve about the customer experience, what would it be?
- What are three words to describe how you want people to feel after interacting with your brand?

Some of my favorite questions to ask customers include:

- What is the best thing that this brand does for you?
- What have been the biggest surprises when interacting with this brand?
- Which three words describe how you feel when using this brand's products or services?
- If this brand was a superhero, what would be its superpower?

When speaking with your customers and prospects, it's so important to go beyond surface-level questions about what they like and dislike. You'll learn more about why those are not good questions in Chapter 10 about research. Instead, you'll want to explore the deeper context of their lives and keep asking questions to understand what motivations are at the root of their decisions. This includes understanding the aspects and benefits of the brand experience that are most meaningful to them.

Once the interviews are conducted, I encourage you to summarize soundbites from all interviewees on a single page for each question. It will enable you to see the common themes that emerge across interviewees from each question. When you ask the same question to brand team members and customers, you can compare them by listing the responses side by side. Then, create a comprehensive summary page with all the themes that emerged—which creates an incredible insights story all in one place.

Here are some examples of how I like to summarize interview findings, including an example of a question for either the brand team or for the customer, and an example of a question where you can compare the responses from each group side by side. Each page corresponds to a single question and includes a summary overall insight at the bottom of the page. The examples that follow are from a brand that serves as an advisor to manufacturers on product line extensions.

TABLE 3.1 Interview Findings—Brand Team or Customer (example)

Sample Interview Findings—Brand Team or Customer (example)

CUSTOMER INTERVIEWS

When I say [Brand] what comes to mind?

- Knowledgeable
- Trusted
- Very smart people
- Very creative people
- Critical partners
- Proactive
- Personally invested in our success

Summary Insight

Customers have a high level of respect for and feel like they are in good hands with the team.

TABLE 3.2 Interview Findings—Brand Team and Customer Side by Side (example)

Sample Interview Findings—Brand Team or Customer (example)

BRAND TEAM INTERVIEWS	CUSTOMER INTERVIEWS
What do you want people to feel when working with [Brand]?	*How does it feel when working with [Brand]?*
• Relief	• Energetic exchange
• Confidence	• Personalized
• Understood	• Attentive
• Supported	• Extreme expertise
• Involved	• Deliberate
• In good hands	• Very good experience
• Excitement	• Good communication
	• High Trust

Summary Insight

[Brand] delivers a very good and trusted experience that feels energetic, expert, deliberate, and attentive.

Many times, when doing side-by-side comparisons of how the brand team and customer each respond to the same question, you'll find that the things customers care most about are emotional benefits—how the brand experience makes them feel — rather than the product or service features the company's leaders want to talk about. It's often eye-opening to the brand team. Further, once we identify these emotional benefits that draw people to the brand, we know that it's likely there are potential customers out there who will be attracted to those same benefits once they know where to find them.

After you've created the interview findings page for each question, including the summary insight for each, you can bring all the summary insights to a single overall findings page. Reviewing all these summary insights together on a single page is another example of how to distill your findings down to what matters most, and it creates a vibrant picture of what the brand is all about from both the brand team and customer perspective.

When you read the summary in Table 3.3, notice how you start to get a clear sense of what makes this brand unique and compelling. These insights play a big role in developing the brand strategy.

TABLE 3.3 Overall Interview Findings Summary (Example)

Interview Overall Findings Summary (example)

1. [Brand] is driven by creating value from end-user insights and developing new product solutions.

2. [Brand] turns complex challenges and into innovative ideas.

3. Customers have a high level of respect for and feel like they are in good hands with the team.

4. [Brand] delivers a very good and trusted experience that feels energetic, expert, deliberate, and attentive.

5. [Brand] bridges gaps by bringing in resources and talent.

6. [Brand] is a high-energy collaborator that serves as an extension of the team.

7. [Brand] provides customized and unique solutions to help customers envision new applications for or variations of their product offering.

8. The [Brand] personality is collaborative, provocative, inspiring, and insightful.

9. [Brand] enables customers to go from uncertainty to organized to making exponential progress.

10. The [Brand] superpower is SWAT Team-like Precision.

Customer Research Study

Each of the four prior Insights Discovery activities are research—I consider all Insights Discovery to be a form of research. However, there are times when you may want to field an incremental Customer Research Study that goes beyond the first four steps, perhaps using an outside research company.

> **Customer Research Study**
>
> Fielding an incremental investigation of customers and prospects, often using an outside research company, to glean more precise details and new insights about people's lives in the context of your offering, their motivations, and the emotional drivers in your category.

If you don't have the time and resources to collect robust new data across a large and representative group of consumers for your product or service, that's okay—Limbic Sparks Brand Strategy is designed to work with or without incremental research. In many cases, the customer insights you've already collected via the interviews in the previous step, and information that you gathered from customer data and reviews, will be enough to make sound judgment calls on what matters most to your customers.

However, if you do have the time, budget, and staff to conduct incremental consumer research, it's worth considering. In larger organizations, sometimes it's important to have quantifiable data to build consensus internally and to justify recommendations. It's also comforting to have greater statistical significance and more broadly projectable data. In Chapter 10, you'll learn more about a variety of research approaches, and important considerations when designing research studies

Importantly, because I just can't wait until Chapter 10 to say this, before you launch a research study, it's important to use the right methodology for the task at hand. Not all research is the same, and newer methodologies rooted in behavioral science will often be more appropriate for uncovering reliable emotional insights than traditional, survey-based methodologies. As Dr. Cyrus H. McCandless, PhD, puts it, "Behavioral science research measures attitudes, and determines the causes of choice behavior, rather than relying solely on respondents' self-reported evaluations, and predicts real-world purchase behavior much more accurately than self-reported data alone" (Perlmutter, 2020).

Focusing Your Insights Discovery Findings

Once your curiosity is piqued, it may be tempting to keep working on the five Insights Discovery activities indefinitely. While this should be an ongoing activity in the background of your day-to-day work, at some point during a brand strategy evolution, you need to transition from curiosity to analysis. By completing these five steps, you will most likely have plenty of information to turn data into insights and find the intersection between what really matters to your customers and what really matters to your organization. Plus, you'll have a sizable amount of detail that you can draw from for later stages of brand strategy development during the Connect phase, and strategy activation in the Evolve phase.

When it's time to summarize and focus your findings, start by reviewing and reflecting on everything you've learned from the Insights Discovery steps. When I'm doing this work, I'm keeping notes on things I want to remember. I'm summarizing findings from all the five activities and referring to those summaries. Then, it's time to boil down all that matters most, both to your brand and your customers, by creating a single side-by-side chart like the one shown in Table 3.4. This is a sample for the brand above, where I shared interview findings, that is an advisor to manufacturers on product line extensions.

TABLE 3.4 Insights Discovery Finding Summary Chart (Example)

Insights Discovery Finding Summary Chart (example)	
What's most emotionally motivating for the Brand? **[Brand] cares about...**	*What's most emotionally motivating for customers?* **Customers care about...**
Challenging assumptions	Focusing on their core competencies
Simplifying complexity	Minimizing investment risks
Taking responsibility	Having trusted collaborators
Creating energy & enthusiasm	Uncovering and minimizing risks
Being curious	Practical solutions to complex problems
Earning trust & fueling confidence	Improving on the status quo
Being detail-oriented & deliberate	Speed to market
Developing new and valuable ideas	Quality in workmanship
Turning chaos into viable new offerings	Long-term investment value
Having exponential impact	Driving growth with new offerings

This chart makes it easier to look at each group's emotional drivers independently and spot the areas of intersection. It will help you avoid the common trap of trying to force-fit a brand's benefits onto consumers, whether they really care about those benefits or not. Also, having a confining chart like this and committing to only use the allotted space on the page will help you focus your findings to highlight what matters most. I'm a big fan of distilling information down so the insights are clear and concise.

Developing the Shared Emotional Motivation

Now, finally, we can return to the primary objective of the Focus phase and develop the Shared Emotional Motivation. You'll remember from earlier that the Shared Emotional Motivation is the core Limbic Sparks insight identifying what both the brand and customer are most motivated to achieve individually and with each other.

I love the way Jeremy Goldman, a technology analyst, described it to me once, using his own words: "The Shared Emotional Motivation is akin to finding the shared heartbeat of the brand and its audience. It's where genuine connections blossom, as people sense the brand is an extension of their own values and desires" (Goldman, 2024).

To brainstorm language for the Shared Emotional Motivation, you can start by listing possibilities, then refine the list until you get to the highest-order shared motivation that meets the criteria above. Play with the language until you have a phrase that captures the Shared Emotional Motivation in just a few words that carry emotional punch. Sometimes it has one meaning when looked at from the Brand perspective and a slightly different meaning when looked at from the Customer perspective.

These are the three criteria I look for in Insights Discovery findings when trying to summarize a brand's Shared Emotional Motivation.

SHARED EMOTIONAL MOTIVATION CRITERIA

1   It must convey something that both the brand and its customers feel strongly about.

2   It must convey an objective or ambition that both the brand and its customers are driven by.

3   It must convey the most valuable thing the brand makes possible for its customers.

For the example brand above, when looking at the Insights Discovery Findings Summary, we considered a variety of potential Shared Emotional Motivation Ideas. After much ideation and discussion, we landed on the following Shared Emotional Motivation:

Extraordinary Marketplace Value.

This is what both the brand and their customers are trying to achieve individually and with each other. Have a look at the Insights Discovery finding summary chart again (Table 3.4) with this Shared Emotional Motivation in mind. You'll see how it represents what both the brand and its customers are striving to achieve, and how it delivers on the Shared Emotional Motivation criteria.

Below are a few other examples of Shared Emotional Motivations that I've developed for brands. You'll continue to see more of these throughout the case study chapters.

TABLE 3.5 Shared Emotional Motivations Examples

Example Shared Emotional Motivations

Business Type		Shared Emotional Motivation
Performing Arts Center	→	Passion for Entertaining Experiences
Online Mental Healthcare Provider	→	Compassionate Mental Health Care
Law Firm Specializing in Divorce	→	Everything Will Be Okay
Cloud-based Staffing Software	→	Reducing the Burden and Uncertainty of Staffing

Throughout the cases in this book, you'll learn more about how Insights Discovery led us to both the Shared Emotional Motivation, and the Brand Idea that we develop in the Connect phase. It's also worth noting that the deep reservoir of findings and emotional insights gathered in Focus will be used throughout brand strategy development and activation. Think of Focus as a "V" where you distill a lot of data and insights down to the Shared Emotional Motivation. The Brand Idea and Strategy sit at the bottom of the "V" and on top of an upside-down "V" that represents Evolve, where all that insight turns into customer-facing brand expression rooted in your in-depth understanding of how people want to feel, and how you will help them feel that way.

FIGURE 3.1 Discovery and Activation of Emotional Insights

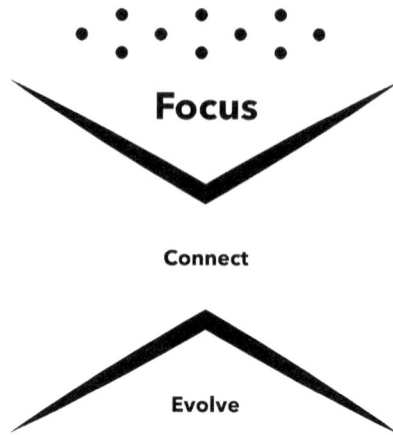

NOTE In Focus, our objective is to gather a lot of information that can be distilled into insights for strategy development that happens in Connect.

Setting Brand Strategy Success Criteria

For our brand strategy to be successful at sparking desire, I like to take a moment between Insights Discovery and strategy development to set several Brand Strategy Success Criteria based on what we discovered about the brand and its customers.

> **Brand Strategy Success Criteria**
>
> Internal alignment on the magnitude and specific objectives of the brand evolution, determined after Insights Discovery and before Brand Strategy development.

I'll often include a draft of these criteria in the Insights Discovery Findings Review and discuss them with my clients to be sure we're seeing the same opportunity for what the brand strategy can do for the brand, and how we should judge the recommendations I'll make during the Connect phase.

Here's an example set of criteria for one of my clients:

1 Emphasize the transformational impact the brand has on staffing challenges.

2 Prioritize the most compelling emotional benefits vs. product features.

3 Connect emotionally with an invitation to solve their biggest stresses and challenges.

4 Connect emotionally with everyday language, not business jargon.

5 Be bold—lead a rallying cry that is focused on C-suite need.

These criteria are different for every brand, and sometimes they are designed to gain stakeholder alignment on the bold evolution that I anticipate we'll be recommending. As a brand leader, these criteria can also prepare your internal team for the recommendations you'll ask them to consider later. I always find that it's easier to get buy-in on the ideas if there are agreed criteria for what the ideas are designed to accomplish.

Looking Ahead

The next chapter will share in detail how we evolved the Sundless brand, including our Focus phase, which was pivotal to uncovering the emotional drivers that matter most to customers and prospects. Then, you'll move on to Part Three, Connect, where you'll learn how to create each component of a Limbic Sparks Brand Strategy. Keep reading to see what it takes to get to a durable competitive advantage.

BRAND LEADERSHIP CONSIDERATIONS

In your own life, how often do you make big decisions with very little information?

Think about big investments of your money and time—buying a house, buying a car, taking a new job, entering a new significant relationship. I suspect that you don't do it with blinders on. It's more likely that you get very curious and consider a lot of variables before getting in too deep.

In your work with brands, do you sometimes wish you understood your customers better?

If so, you're not alone. Way too much brand work is done with way too little customer insight. More often, brand leaders settle for broadly understood details about their customers, in the absence of a deep understanding of what makes them tick. Sometimes agencies and consultants come back with slick presentations and shallow insights that are more style than substance, and their strategic recommendations are either like what another competitor is saying, or built on an unstable foundation.

Here are three things you can start doing today:

1   Insist on an approach to Insights Discovery that includes hearing directly from customers—whether through interviews, a scouring of reviews, or a robust research study.

2   Before developing a brand strategy, tagline, or campaign, be sure to understand the intersection of what your brand does well for people and what people are seeking in their life.

3   Once you understand your customers better and see the opportunity to better connect with them, set criteria for what your brand evolution must achieve before you move into Connect and Evolve.

References

Einstein, A (n.d.) BrainyQuote.com, www.brainyquote.com/quotes/albert_ einstein_174001 (archived at https://perma.cc/MD8L-VC2L)

Fleming, T and Garg, V (2024) Reimagining Consumer Insights at PepsiCo, Strategy + Business: a PwC Publication, 25 March, www.strategy-business.com/ article/Reimagining-consumer-insights-at-PepsiCo (archived at https://perma.cc/ VLC9-BK3L)

Forrester (2024) Forrester's 2024 US Customer Experience Index: Brands' CX quality is at an all-time low, Forrester Newsroom, 17 June, www.forrester.com/ press-newsroom/forrester-2024-us-customer-experience-index/ (archived at https://perma.cc/D74X-X5PJ)

Gartner (2020) Gartner says marketing leaders must prioritize four core competencies to survive and thrive in 2021, Gartner Newsroom, 1 December, https://www.gartner.com/en/newsroom/press-releases/2020- 12-01-gartner-says-marketing-leaders-must-prioritize-four-c (archived at https://perma.cc/7E26-SJ4B). This Gartner content is archived and is included for historical context only. GARTNER is a trademark of Gartner, Inc. and/or its affiliates.

Goldman, J (2024) Conversation with Kevin Perlmutter

Limbic Brand Evolution (2021) Let's Talk Limbic Sparks Podcast – episode 9, Crafting an Insight-Driven Lifestyle Brand with Ray Li, 15 December, www. limbicbrandevolution.com/podcast/ray-li-sene-lets-talk-limbic-sparks-9 (archived at https://perma.cc/A25R-J4RL)

Limbic Brand Evolution (2024a) Let's Talk Limbic Sparks Podcast – episode 35, Meeting People Where They Are with Marcy Ullom, 15 April, www.limbicbrandevolution.com/podcast/marcy-ullom-lets-talk-limbic-sparks-35 (archived at https://perma.cc/VQ7D-48YD)

Limbic Brand Evolution (2024b) Let's Talk Limbic Sparks Podcast – episode 32, Staying One Step Ahead to Create Brand Value with Jess Kessler, 15 January, www.limbicbrandevolution.com/podcast/jess-kessler-lets-talk-limbic-sparks-32 (archived at https://perma.cc/W4Y5-WCTQ)

Limbic Brand Evolution (2024c) Let's Talk Limbic Sparks Podcast – episode 36, Uniting Brands and Fans with Eric Fernandez, 15 July, www.limbicbran devolution.com/podcast/eric-fernandez-lets-talk-limbic-sparks-36 (archived at https://perma.cc/YLU9-7JWC)

Perlmutter, K (2020) Interview: How instinctive emotion drives behavior, with Cyrus McCandless, PhD, *Brandingmag*, 20 October, www.brandingmag.com/2020/10/20/interview-how-instinctive-emotion-drives-behavior-with-cyrus-mccandless-phd/ (archived at https://perma.cc/AVG3-3RU5)

04

Finding a Durable Competitive Advantage

Sundless Case Study

"How do we convince manufacturers that our new product is better, stronger, and safer than the well-known brands that they've used and trusted for years?"

This is the challenge that Lin Sang shared with me when we first met, and it was a steep one. Lin is a senior marketing leader at ZZDM, the China-based creator of Sundless, a newly patented, unbreakable material used by manufacturers to make products incredibly durable and bulletproof. As revolutionary as the product was, ZZDM had learned that it was a hard sell.

Breaking Through in a Competitive Category

Sundless was launching in an industry with brands that have been around for decades: DuPont's Kevlar, Honeywell's Spectra, and Avient's Dyneema. Those materials are each well-known and respected by manufacturers, who use them as components in their products. With powerful brand-name recognition, these materials are also trusted by individual customers seeking extremely durable and strong products. They are used to make ropes that hoist the heaviest of objects, to protect mountain climbers, and to secure large ships to docks. They can also bulletproof clothing, vehicles, or body armor used by law enforcement and military personnel. Even for people who don't shop for these kinds of products, the Kevlar brand name is almost synonymous with the category.

By taking on these strong rivals, Sundless was betting it could change the competitive landscape. But could it? I told Lin that the task ahead was to develop a strategy to launch his brand in a way that gives manufacturers a compelling reason to consider Sundless over materials they already knew and trusted. We had to make Sundless not just another option, but what marketing manager Xiran Liu called "the most influential new material brand." With anything less than that level of influence, Sundless just wouldn't break through.

The good news was that after years of research and development, their team was ready to demonstrate to manufacturers, and the world, that Sundless was significantly better than any competitive material. They recognized the need for a way to succinctly convey why Sundless was a better choice, and they set out to establish their brand positioning in the global market. It was at this point that Lin and Xiran decided to work with me and my collaborators on this project, Vincent Fatato and Remo Strada, President and Creative Director, respectively, of GreyBox Creative. The Sundless team was excited to get started using Limbic Sparks Brand Strategy to set the foundation for how the brand would come to life, using emotional insights, and then to use the strategy to create brand messaging, a visual identity, a website, and other assets that they could use for marketing and tradeshows.

From the outset, the Sundless team knew that we would be digging deep for insights and the motivations of their customers to set the brand apart. We explained during one of our first meetings that if we were applying traditional brand strategy, we would be able to move quickly into positioning Sundless around levels of strength and durability in contrast to those of rival brands. We would then try to persuade manufacturers—rationally—that Sundless was a better material. We would highlight what the brand does well and the statistical evidence for how much stronger and more durable the material is for certain use cases, hoping that the rational minds of manufacturers would lead them to switch to Sundless for its superior features and benefits.

Instead, we took an entirely different approach. My job was to help the Sundless team find a way to position their brand so that it would catch the attention of manufacturers in an already crowded space with long-standing competitive brands.

We recognized that the only way Sundless could succeed in a crowded B2B market was if it could motivate manufacturers to change the preferred material they chose to use in their own branded products. To do that, we needed to understand the underlying motivations that drive the feelings and decisions of key people at manufacturing companies. We needed to uncover insights that would help us ignite interest in Sundless, so much so that manufacturers would consider switching to the brand.

The Sundless team understood securing new manufacturing customers is a tough process, and the first crucial step is to generate interest—to open a conversation and invite trial. To support the sales process, Sundless has a program that enables manufacturers to try the product using samples that can be tested in their production facilities. However, without the right words to say to start the conversation, it was even difficult to get manufacturers to try the product.

The big challenge was that their manufacturing customers and prospects were inherently risk averse; they didn't like to change things they were already comfortable with unless there was a truly compelling reason to change. Trying a new material is a time-consuming process, and seemingly a waste of time if they feel that what they are already using is good enough. Just getting them to try Sundless was a task unto itself.

Lin and Xiran recognized the need to create Limbic Sparks by finding the intersection of the emotional motivations of their prospective customers and the benefits of the Sundless brand. They wanted to generate enough interest, and trials, knowing that making the sale would be much easier after that point.

Focus

During a kick-off conversation with the Sundless team, we outlined all the important steps for Insights Discovery. We talked about their product, its use cases, and competitive products. They shared details about the sales process and the challenges they were having. We talked about specific conversations they have with prospective customers and challenges they often hear that slow down the road to trial. I let them know how crucial it was that our Focus phase included having interviews with current customers, to understand not only why they chose Sundless, but also their thought process along the way. Following the meeting we started down the path of Insights Discovery.

Brand Dynamics Review

We began our Brand Dynamics Review by studying Sundless's existing product brochures and fact sheets. We learned about a wide range of use cases, manufacturing processes, and the factors that made Sundless's new material a technological breakthrough compared to those of its competitors.

We also learned how challenging it had been for the company's marketing team to convey the nuances of their innovation—and to inspire potential customers to care about those nuances.

Not surprisingly, the original marketing materials were very much about the product, and it wasn't yet clear whether they addressed what matters most to manufacturers.

Competitive Audit

Next, for our Competitive Audit, we reviewed everything we could find out about the competitive set that Sundless competes against, and how their rival materials were made and marketed. We learned that the well-established brands all had similar positioning around strength, safety, durability, and reliability. Kevlar, the dominant brand in the category, talked about being "better, stronger, and safer." Dyneema's messaging focused on "never compromising strength, comfort, performance, and protection." Spectra stressed its "lightweight strength."

Kevlar had a big advantage with a strong reputation among end consumers, not just among B2B purchasers. Made from a material called Aramid fiber, Kevlar first became commercially available in the early 1970s. It became famous because the military and law enforcement widely adopted Kevlar bulletproof vests, which gave the brand mainstream visibility in movies, books, and other media. One important aspect of Aramid fiber, we learned, is that it's incredibly flexible, which makes it somewhat better for certain use cases than Sundless, but for other use cases, Sundless was far superior. Conveying the nuances of these details makes marketing a challenge in this category (OTEX Specialty Narrow Fabrics, 2022).

Category Dynamics Review

Auditing the competitive set led naturally to our Category Dynamics Review. It became clear that every company in this category threw around impressive-sounding statistics about product quality and superiority, but none of them seemed to stand out significantly when you compared those statistics side by side. While Kevlar was made from Aramid fiber, Dyneema and Spectra were made from with the same raw material used to make Sundless, Ultra High Molecular Weight Polyethylene (UHMWPE). The key difference was that these brands were produced using a woven fiber technique that had been around since the late 1970s. Sundless, in contrast, uses a newer, patented process that creates a solid film instead of a woven fiber (Google Patents, 2011).

This solid film variation makes Sundless much stronger, safer, more durable, and more reliable for a variety of use cases. This was important information for manufacturers to know but challenging to convey simply and emotionally. The category was already confusing for manufacturing customers to navigate, and even more confusing for end-users of the products that are strengthened by these materials, because every brand cites the same basic messaging of "stronger, safer, and more durable." If we simply tried to claim product quality superiority ("Trust us, for real, we have the best product!") that messaging would be unlikely to break through in a differentiated or credible way.

Our digging into Category Dynamics led to another obstacle to stressing innovation in our messaging. Since UMHWPE fiber had been used for decades and the Sundless film version was new to the market, widely available product charts that compared various materials referred only to UHMWPE, not to "UHMWPE fiber." Thus, even people who are familiar with the difference between Aramid and UHMWPE will not be familiar with the difference between UHMWPE fiber and UHMWPE film.

This complexity made it extra hard to differentiate between traditional fiber products and the new Sundless film alternative. For example, when companies or customers seek a durable rope, they would review a chart that explained the differences between types of materials used in rope manufacturing, ranging in strength from nylon and polyester on the low end, to the Aramid in Kevlar, to the UHMWPE in Dyneema and Spectra. As Sundless entered the market, our concern was that prospects would accidentally lump Sundless with the other UHMWPE products, despite the unique advantages of Sundless's new solid film version of UHMWPE. If we hadn't investigated category dynamics, we would have missed this detail, which soon became one of several crucial insights behind our brand idea.

Brand Team & Customer Interviews

Our next step was conducting Brand Team & Customer Interviews. At first, we had to navigate how to best conduct these interviews, because all the people we wanted to interview were in China, and most of them did not speak English. However, the idea of not doing the interviews was not an option, and as you'll read, these interviews had a significant impact on our brand strategy. To overcome the language barrier, we created a list of interview questions, and with the help of my clients, we translated them into Chinese. We also adapted the questions to account for cultural language nuances and references. For example, one of my favorite questions, "If Sundless were a superhero, what would their superpower be?" could not be used because, I learned, the superhero reference would not be easily understood in their culture.

Once the questions were crafted and the translations were completed, we used a combination of sending the questions to the interviewees, and my clients and I conducting the interviews together. Our set of Sundless interviewees included brand team, marketing, product development, the CEO, and other senior executives. Among other things, we asked:

- What are the best things Sundless does for its users?
- Why is the world better now that Sundless is available?
- Describe the ideal user of products that contain Sundless.
- What's the best feedback you hear from manufacturers who have started using Sundless?
- What are the toughest questions that manufactures ask before agreeing to try Sundless?
- What are manufacturers who use Sundless most surprised by after trying it?
- How does Sundless help manufacturers become more successful?

From these internal team interviews we learned that the Sundless team was driven to create and launch next-level innovations that can increase value for manufacturers. They were very proud of their new product because it had so many advantages over the competition. They revealed that manufacturers who tried Sundless were surprised by the many benefits it offered for their products. We also learned that the biggest challenge was simply getting manufacturers' attention and getting them to try Sundless—because once they tried it, they were usually very interested in adopting it.

We also crafted customer interview questions for manufacturers who had become early adopters of Sundless. Here are a few of the questions we asked:

- What's most important to you in manufacturing your product?
- What's at stake when it comes to choosing the material you use in manufacturing?
- What would prevent you from using Sundless?
- What was your number one reason for agreeing to try Sundless?

- What have been the biggest surprises after trying Sundless?
- What would you lose if you stopped using Sundless?
- How does it make you feel to know that Sundless is part of your products?
- How does Sundless help you be more successful?

As often happens during Insights Discovery, we found that the reasons customers shared for why they liked Sundless were not only different from what the brand team expected them to say, but also gave us a roadmap toward compelling new messaging that could draw interest among potential new customers.

Manufacturers who had started using Sundless were happily surprised by the quality and value. They shared a need to offer the highest-quality products to their own customers, and they wanted to improve production time and decrease their costs. They acknowledged that Sundless was new and innovative, but they were risk averse. Trying Sundless was a big step since, to date, they had been comfortable and secure with the materials they were already using. They also made it clear that their products protect people's lives, and if a new material didn't do what it was supposed to, their own brand reputation, and people's lives, were at stake.

This meant that the manufacturers' emotional drivers had less to do with the Sundless brand than with their own situation, challenges, and motivations, which is also very common in my experience. People are indifferent to a brand unless the brand gives them a compelling reason to care. For Sundless to break through, capture manufacturers' attention and interest, and get them to try a new material, the benefits had to be more compelling than simply one-upping the typical category claims of stronger, safer, and more durable materials.

Summarizing Our Insights Discovery Findings

Now, as we moved from all the insights discovery activities into a narrow set of clear emotional insights, we used the Insights Discovery Findings Summary chart to get a clear picture of what the brand cares about and what its customers care about, side by side.

When we filled in the left and right columns of our findings summary, it looked like Table 4.1.

You can see how what the brand team was most motivated by differs from what their manufacturing customers were most motivated by. The Sundless team wanted to be known for their innovative new material. They

TABLE 4.1 Sundless Insights Discovery Findings Summary

Sundless
Insights Discovery Finding Summary Chart

What's most emotionally motivating for the Brand?	*What's most emotionally motivating for customers?*
Sundless cares about...	**Customers care about...**
• Bringing New Innovation to the World	• Protecting Their Brand Reputation
• Being Known for Endless Innovation	• Comfort in What They've Always Done
• Having the Most Influential New Material	• Improving Production Time & Cost
• Demonstrating a 0-to-1 Improvement	• Using the Highest-Quality Materials
• A Commitment to the Environment	• Having the Highest-Quality Products
• Increasing Value for Customers	• Product Safety & Durability
• Collaboration with Customers	• Having a Competitive Advantage
• Working with R&D-Savvy Customers	• Being Good to the Environment
• Feeling Innovative & Impactful	• Feeling Confident in Their Choices

also had a heartfelt mission to help their customers with benefits that went beyond what they could get from competitive material brands.

Customers, on the other hand, were seemingly indifferent to the material itself when they described what mattered to them. Their emotional drivers were mostly around having a competitive advantage for their own branded products. They needed their products to be safe, durable, and made from the highest-quality material. They also wanted to improve production time and cost. Most importantly, we learned that they were risk averse, and it would take benefits beyond the ordinary to get them to try something new.

Our task was to find the real and relevant intersection of their respective motivations.

Crafting the Shared Emotional Motivation

The Shared Emotional Motivation, as you'll recall, articulates what both the brand and customer are most motivated to achieve individually and with each other.

After a fair amount of ideation, refining, and conversations with my clients, we landed on the following Shared Emotional Motivation:

An Uncompromising Advantage

This came out of our understanding that the Sundless team were all about improving on the status quo with a material that brings improvements, without trade-offs, while their customers were looking for a competitive advantage for their own products, which they'd like to get without giving anything up or spending more in production.

"An Uncompromising Advantage" brought together their mutual ambition of having the best of all worlds—the most innovative, best-performing, most cost-effective materials that will improve the products being manufactured for end users. It summarized what motivates both Sundless and its customers on an emotional level: A competitive advantage without sacrifice.

This Limbic Sparks Insight was the real and relevant intersection of what matters most to both the Sundless team and manufacturers, and now becomes the first bookend of the brand strategy.

We checked against the three criteria identified in Chapter 3 for a Shared Emotional Motivation, and "An Uncompromising Advantage" passed all three:

✓ It must convey something that both the brand and its customers feel strongly about.

✓ It must convey an objective or ambition that both the brand and its customers are driven by.

✓ It must convey the most valuable thing the brand makes possible for its customers.

The final step of Focus was to align with the Sundless brand team on the Brand Strategy Success Criteria. You may recall from the last chapter that we said that these criteria help to create internal alignment on the magnitude and specific objectives of the brand evolution that we are striving to achieve.

We agreed on the following Sundless Brand Strategy Success Criteria, which guided us into our Connect phase work:

1 Reintroduce the Sundless brand.

2 Introduce and differentiate this new category of material.

3 Emphasize the emotional benefits for manufacturers.

4 Overcome initial concerns about how and why it is better.

5 Create interest and desire for manufacturers to try Sundless.

These criteria gave us guideposts to judge the brand strategy work that was to follow and hold ourselves accountable to these ambitions. Without these criteria, set in advance, those reviewing the brand strategy might be tempted to fall back into traditional brand strategy and rely on a brand idea that was too much about the brand, and not enough about customers.

Connect

After Focus, we continued to guide Sundless through the Connect phase of strategy development—a phase you'll hear a lot more about in Part Three.

Connect is where you create the Limbic Sparks Brand Strategy and iden-tify the most compelling brand benefits to ignite interest and spark desire for your brand. It includes determining the Core Brand Benefits, the Brand Personality & Voice Traits, the Brand Idea, and the Brand Positioning Statement.

For Sundless, when identifying the Core Brand Benefits, we knew from the beginning that a traditional brand strategy approach, relying on nuances about the product, would not be enough to attract the interest of manufac-turers.

As such, we focused our attention on the most compelling qualities of Sundless that could be turned into emotional benefits that address what's most important to manufacturers. If there was a chance of them trying a new material, we knew we'd need to share how it gave them an uncompro-mising advantage.

We knew that Sundless is:

- a revolutionary innovation
- a solid monolithic film, not a weaved fiber
- a material that increases strength and durability
- a material that offers manufacturers new benefits without sacrifice
- a material like nothing else out there

Ultimately, we got specific with three Core Brand Benefits that our Insights Discovery work revealed would capture their interest:

- Superior material: Film. Not fiber.
- Advanced performance: More durable.
- Better for manufacturers: Higher quality and environmentally friendly.

When thinking about the Brand Personality & Voice Traits, it was important that we came across in a way that imbued both the strength and reliability of the product. We wanted to accurately reflect what it felt like to not only work with the Sundless team, but also to use the Sundless material.

We landed on the following Brand Personality & Voice Traits:

- Sundless is *Bold*, and as a result, its brand voice should feel Provocative, not uncertain.
- Sundless is *Innovative*, and as a result, its brand voice should feel Compelling, not weak.
- Sundless is *Dependable*, and as a result, its brand voice should feel Helpful, not vague.

It was now time to develop the Brand Idea, which would also serve as the Brand Tagline. The Brand Idea is the compelling brand benefit and invitation. While every component of the brand strategy, and how that translates into Brand Expression & Experiences, plays a role in whether people have interest in the brand or not, the Brand Idea is a super-critical component that can make or break your efforts. In a few words, it needs to set your brand apart and cause someone to take an interest in it.

For Sundless, we considered a variety of territories and possible Brand Ideas. One territory referred to the innovative aspects of Sundless—that it's revolutionary and innovative versus anything else available. Among others, we considered "Revolutionary by Design" as the leading Brand Idea for this territory. Ultimately, however, we rejected it because it felt like a cliché—it's an idea we'd all heard before, and it would not be as distinctive as other options. In the end, it was not a durable competitive advantage.

Another territory we considered was related to the fact that Sundless is film, not fiber. This is what makes Sundless different than any other material out there and what leads to many of its competitive advantages. For this territory, we considered the Brand Idea "The Solid Choice." While there was a lot of heart for this Brand Idea, we rejected it in the end because it was too much about the brand, and not enough about the customer. Yes, it's a compelling brand benefit and a jumping-off point to many other benefits we can talk about, but it was not as much of an invitation as we were striving for. While this idea did not become the Brand Idea, it's included in the Core Brand Benefits and is used in brand messaging.

Our third Brand Idea territory was focused on Sundless being so different that you need to experience it. We wanted the Brand Idea to play a key role in attracting interest and trial. This territory led us to the Brand Idea:

A Material Difference.

Recall the original challenge we were presented with by Lin Sang: To break through an established competitive landscape, get the attention of manufacturers, and shatter the norms of the category with a new type of material. We ended up with a Brand Idea and Tagline that communicated how Sundless is different than anything else available, in language that considers the emotional drivers of risk-averse manufacturers. "A Material Difference" became the other bookend of the Sundless brand strategy. It is the brand's response to manufacturers who are seeking "An Uncompromising Advantage."

The final step of creating the brand strategy is the Brand Positioning Statement—the statement of distinct customer promise, and a summary of the overall brand strategy.

For Sundless, we brought together all that the brand makes possible for the people who it serves. The Sundless Brand Positioning Statement is:

Sundless is the revolutionary ultra-high molecular weight polyethylene film— materially different from fiber or anything else—so manufacturers have an uncompromising advantage.

Throughout Connect, we continually went back to our Insights Discovery findings to bring emotional insights into the brand strategy. We also reflected on the Brand Strategy Success Criteria that we set at the end of Focus. Let's see how we did.

Sundless Brand Strategy Success Criteria:

✓ Reintroduce the Sundless brand.

✓ Introduce and differentiate this new category of material.

✓ Emphasize the emotional benefits for manufacturers.

✓ Overcome initial concerns about how and why it is better.

✓ Create interest and desire for manufacturers to try Sundless.

Once we complete the Connect phase, we summarize the brand strategy components, which you'll learn more about in Chapter 5, into a single chart.

Evolve

The Evolve phase for Sundless came when we applied the new brand strategy to both brand messaging and visual expression—work I did in collaboration with Vincent and Remo of GreyBox Creative. I was responsible for Brand

TABLE 4.2 Sundless Brand Strategy Summary

Sundless
Brand Strategy Summary

Shared Emotional Motivation	An Uncompromising Advantage
Core Brand Benefits	Superior Material
	Advanced Performance
	Better for Manufacturers
Brand Personality & Voice Traits	Sundless is Bold, and as a result, its brand voice should feel Provocative, not uncertain.
	Sundless is Innovative, and as a result, its brand voice should feel Compelling, not weak.
	Sundless is Dependable, and as a result, its brand voice should feel Helpful, not vague.
Limbic Sparks Brand Idea & Tagline	A Material Difference
Brand Positioning Statement	Sundless is the revolutionary ultra-high molecular weight polyethylene film—materially different from fiber or anything else—so manufacturers have an uncompromising advantage.

Messaging, and they developed a new Visual Identity and created the brand's new website.

With the brand strategy as a guide, Vincent and Remo developed a variety of options for the Sundless brand logo. They explored various colors, type styles, and logo marks. While all the brand strategy components played a role in their thinking, it was the Brand Personality & Voice Traits—Bold, Innovative, Dependable—that they were working to convey clearly in the logo. You can see in Figure 4.1 how this logo reflects those traits.

Also, there's the logo mark, which is made up of lines that represent an "S" for Sundless, and strips of film, to nod to the fact that Sundless is made of a solid film, not fiber.

For development of the Sundless website, they carried through the visual style with colors and imagery that feel Bold, Innovative, and Dependable.

FIGURE 4.1 New Sundless Logo and Tagline

The website is also where we brought the Brand Messaging to life, leveraging the Brand Personality & Voice Traits to inform the writing style, and the Core Brand Benefits to inform messaging. We also went back to the deep well of Insights Discovery findings to reflect on emotional insights about benefits that will ignite interest and provide even greater detail on why manufacturers should care about this material brand.

As you can imagine, the home page reflects much of the language that's part of the brand strategy, and other pages of the website get more specific for different Sundless use cases and their audiences.

For example, the top of the Sundless website home page is a direct reflection of the brand strategy and says:

The Most Advanced UHMWPE Material

Sundless is the revolutionary ultra-high molecular weight polyethylene film— materially different from fiber or anything else.

Sundless. A Material Difference.

It includes core benefit sections with the following headlines, supported by a few sentences with more detail:

Superior Material: Film. Not Fiber.

Advanced Performance: More Durable.

Better for Manufacturers: Higher Quality and Environmentally Friendly

The center of the home page shares specifics for each of the two audiences that Sundless serves:

Sundless is for Bulletproofing: The revolutionary UHWMPE monolithic film material formed as a single piece without joints or seams that gives you a safer product.

Sundless is for Ropes & Netting: The revolutionary UHWMPE monolithic film material that gives your ropes and netting 30% more abrasion resistance, longer life and they are easier to manufacture.

Further down the page it says:

> *Sundless is the solid choice for product manufacturers who want a competitive advantage for their products. It is an exceptional new material without sacrifice.*

You can see how so much of the language we considered for components of the brand strategy, whether it was used there or not, was used to bring the brand to life in the Evolve phase.

One of the great things you'll find with Limbic Sparks Brand Strategy is that the effort you put into Insights Discovery pays off well beyond the initial brand strategy. It yields a lot of emotional insight that you can put to work when you activate your brand.

Launching the Brand

Without knowing what manufacturers really cared about, we might have felt it was enough to rely on product claims and to compare Sundless to rivals based on its features—the rational benefits that most traditional brand strategy relies on. However, that wouldn't be enough to ignite interest, because manufacturers are also emotionally driven by concern about their reputations and are hesitant to try new materials that might hurt product quality, regardless of whatever statistics Sundless threw at them.

Instead, Limbic Sparks Brand Strategy challenged us to seek a deeper understanding of why the key decision makers would care about this brand if we gave them messaging tied to the right emotional drivers.

About a year after the brand re-launched, Xiran Liu of Sundless emailed me an update: "*A Material Difference* has been successful in capturing manufacturers' attention. They are curious about Sundless. It's doing exactly what we hoped for to give us an opportunity to share how Sundless is a new and innovative material that will give them better performance without sacrifice."

Looking Ahead

Now that you have a good grasp of Focus, it's time to move to the next phase of Limbic Sparks Brand Strategy: Connect. This next part of the book demonstrates how the Shared Emotional Motivation serves as a critical insight to help you develop your Brand Idea and other brand strategy components. You'll read how Connect builds on what you've discovered about your brand and your customers to create emotionally compelling brand messaging. Are you ready? I hope so, because you're on your way to creating Limbic Sparks.

BRAND LEADERSHIP CONSIDERATIONS

In your own life, do you avoid things that are inconvenient?

Most people do. We instinctively and most often choose the path of least resistance. It's why we sometimes stick with things we don't like, because the time and effort to make a change feels more daunting than staying the course.

In your work with brands, do you understand what may be preventing your potential customers from switching to your brand?

Logic does not always prevail. Just because something is better, doesn't mean it's easy or convenient. Sometimes there are risks involved in making a change. By understanding the emotional motivations of your prospective customers, you can address them head-on with messaging that ignites their curiosity to learn more.

Here are three things you can start doing today:

1 Don't assume that product or service superiority claims are enough to get customers to switch to your brand.

2 Discover what's causing customers to stay with the status quo, what the limitations of the status quo are, and what would motivate a customer to consider a new option.

3 Bring emotional insights into your brand strategy work so that you can position your brand as a competitive alternative—one that will overcome any objections by addressing emotional motivations and decision drivers.

References

Google Patents (2011) US Patent 7976930 B2, Non-fibrous High Modulus Ultra High Molecular Weight Polyethylene Tape for Ballistic Applications, 7 December, patents.google.com/patent/US7976930B2/en (archived at https://perma.cc/2JCN-HHBM)

OTEX Specialty Narrow Fabrics (2022) The Core Differences Between UHMWPE & Kevlar [blog] 4 April, www.osnf.com/uhmwpe-vs-kevlar/ (archived at https://perma.cc/BF83-2PQ6)

PART THREE

Connect

05

Developing Brand Benefits
& Invitations

Most brand leaders are on a quest to increase love and loyalty for their brands. All want promotors to significantly outweigh detractors—with many more people enthusiastic about their brand than those who actively dislike it. The main challenge, however, is not one of brand advocates vs. brand haters, it's one of capturing people's attention and interest. This reminds me of something that Elie Wiesel spoke about when he said the opposite of love is not hate—it's indifference (Sanoff, 1986). While he was not talking about business or brands, I find his insight to be extremely relevant to developing an effective brand strategy.

Over the years there have been many reports and estimates tossed around about how many advertising and digital marketing impressions people are exposed to every day—from hundreds to thousands. Regardless of what number is accurate today, it's fair to say that every day we are inundated with marketing that just passes us by, and we don't remember or even consciously notice the large majority of what we are exposed to.

The important thing to remember is that we ignore that which does not spark our attention. "Our brains are brilliant summarizers of information. We instinctively choose the path of least resistance, and we tend to dismiss or embrace new ideas or products based on first impressions," says Dr. Cyrus H. McCandless (Perlmutter, 2020). For many things that don't ignite our interest, we are either unaware or indifferent.

What do you think is better, a Brand Idea that tries to be a persuasive soundbite, or one that is a highly relevant benefit and invitation?

Here's the thing. People are not eagerly waiting for your brand to arrive on their doorstep. They're going about their day, actively skipping ads whenever possible, scrolling past your brand in the feed, or deflecting an onslaught of spam email sales pitches. They are consciously or subconsciously ignoring anything that doesn't stand out as relevant to them. They're busy, distracted, and focused on their own life and business. They're seeking happiness, less stress, the ability to overcome challenges, and looking for ways to be more successful at whatever they are trying to achieve. The last thing people want is to be interrupted by irrelevant brand messages.

Behavioral science tells us that while customers may scrutinize factual details before a purchasing decision, we first need to capture their interest, and that often means tapping into their emotion. Cyrus goes on to say, "When we understand why customers really choose a brand over competitors, we very often find that the most powerful reasons are emotional or intuitive. Emotion is a powerful driver of our choices, perceptions, conscious considerations and the narratives we construct about them" (Perlmutter, 2020).

It's why understanding what people care about and turning those emotional insights into relevant and compelling brand strategy is so important. Leveraging emotional insights to ignite interest is the way to break through indifference.

Connect, the second of three phases of Limbic Sparks Brand Strategy and the one we'll explore in this part of the book, is all about strengthening connections by tapping into meaningful emotional benefits. In this chapter you'll read about how to develop the Brand Strategy and in the next chapter I'll share how it was done for a specific brand that's been through the process.

Connect

Strengthening connections with customers by standing for the emotional benefits they care about the most.

Why Should People Care About Your Brand?

In your own life, you've probably had the feeling that a brand is attempting to convey product or service details enthusiastically, but its message is completely irrelevant to you. It feels like selling rather than solving. This often happens because the messaging was created without fully understanding what's most motivating to you and other potential customers.

Buying is an evaluation process. The process varies for different types of products and services, for different price points, and for every individual. However, there is no doubt that our instinctive emotional response to our initial exposure to a brand has a significant impact on the strength of our interest in and desire for that brand.

This is why one question every brand leader must always ask themselves is: "Why should people care about this brand?"—with the important word being "care." If you want to move people from indifferent to aware to interested to customer, uncovering their underlying motivations—what they care about—is the crucial first step. When you put emotional insights at the center of brand strategy, you will have a much better chance of creating Limbic Sparks and having customers at hello.

This is especially true when brands operate in very crowded competitive environments—whether they are selling sneakers, computers, insurance, online mental healthcare, professional services, or B2B cloud-based software solutions. Often, on the surface, what a brand offers may seem just like what competitors offer. In many categories brands are at risk of being seen as undifferentiated unless they find a way to convey how they are different beyond the specific services and features that they provide, and unless they find a way to convey value at an emotional level. When brands rely on lists of features, proof points, and familiar category language in their marketing, they often struggle to be understood for what makes them unique. They also risk being outdone by competitors if they have not established a more sustainable competitive advantage rooted in emotional benefits.

In complex sales situations like B2B where there are sometimes many layers of decision makers, brand leaders and sales teams can support each other to bridge the gap between a differentiated brand and sales tactics. I've seen companies invest heavily in managing a substantial lead generation capability, a skilled and savvy sales team, content marketing, and customer relationship management tactics, yet the impact of these efforts is undercut when they don't have something compelling to say to spark desire for what the brand has to offer.

It's true that people will ultimately go through a conscious evaluation process before making an important purchase for their business, or an out-of-the-ordinary purchase for their family. They'll want to understand all the services and features. They'll want to have confidence that it's a worthwhile use of money. They'll need to be convinced that there will be an acceptable level of ROI or bang for the buck. They'll want to trust the service provider and the quality of the product. That said, how you ultimately close the sale is different from how you stand apart as a brand. Standing apart starts with being real, capturing an individual's attention, igniting interest, and sparking desire.

Brand Strategy Watchouts

Brands significantly increase their chances of earning customers' attention and business when they feel that their personal and professional motivations are in alignment with the brand's motivation. Brands have the best chance of piquing someone's interest when someone's first impression is that the brand will be life-enhancing in some way, and when the brand's presentation gives potential buyers the answer they are seeking to "What's in it for me?"

Traditional brand strategy, however, often misses the mark with potential customers due to a focus on benefits or the use of language that does not connect. Two big watchouts are to avoid meaningless brand benefits and avoid clichés and jargon.

Avoid Meaningless Brand Benefits

The first important watchout is to avoid benefits that may sound good to you, but will have little, or negative, impact on prospective customers. All too often, brand messages focus on "what we do" instead of "so you can," or benefits that are prioritized by the organization but not so important to the people you're trying to reach.

Whether in our work or personal lives we are emotional beings. We are moved by things that we care about or that capture our instinctive attention. When we encounter a brand, we are evaluating, often instinctively and subconsciously, "What are the risks?" and "What's in it for me?" It's in those first moments, when interest is either piqued or not, that we move forward, sometimes without a conscious thought. It's this tension between our unconscious instincts and conscious decisions that is so important for brand leaders to understand, and why the work we do in Focus to discover emotional insight into what people truly care about is so valuable.

Further, it's important to be sure the benefits you choose not only are the most meaningful, but that they don't go in the opposite direction and spark negative connotations. One example of an idea that went poorly is from the Pretzel Crisps brand—a type of pretzel that is known for being thin and crunchy. Unfortunately, in 2010 they had a misstep with the "thin" benefit and launched a campaign using two headlines: "You can never be too thin" and "Tastes as good as skinny feels." The campaign received backlash because, as CBS News reported, "A simple Google search would have revealed to the company that those are slogans bandied about in a creepy section of the blogosphere inhabited by 'pro-ana' anorexic girls who encourage each other to become ever-thinner" (Edwards, 2010). This is an extreme example, but it reinforces why it's so important to choose benefits and words carefully, and be sure that they are coming across as intended to capture the good kind of attention.

Avoid Clichés and Jargon

Another important watchout is to avoid generic language that has, over time, lost distinctiveness and impact due to excessive repetition.

I was once working with a client who came to me with a positioning territory of "Human Potential Optimized." Unfortunately, it was a B2B brand in a very niche category, and this brand idea did nothing to help people understand what they did, or why they should care. It could have been for any type of company in almost any category of product or service. Their brand name was equally non-descriptive, and their website was loaded with many all too familiar generic phrases, such as "break down barriers," "one and done," "illuminate new possibilities," and "your success is our business." Very little of this, however, shed light on the incredible benefits that this brand makes possible for its customers. In speaking with the CEO, she said, "We're still not seeing the human connection we were hoping for, and we're struggling to attract customers that would benefit from our services."

Think about the landscape of B2B brand messaging, and how often you see undifferentiated language. While brands try to project themselves in a business-like way that they believe will be appealing to other businesses, they often forget that there are people on the other end who respond instinctively and emotionally before they do anything else. Not only is this kind of language familiar, but it's also not what people respond to. Jargon and clichés in marketing create distance between the brand and its desired customer, because when something feels so familiar and so inauthentic, it is either completely ignorable, or even worse, a turn-off.

Brené Brown often talks about authenticity. She calls it a choice, suggesting that we can choose to show up as our true selves, in a real and honest way, or we can choose to project ourselves in some other way (Brown, 2018). I think the same can be said for brands, and my behavioral science mentor, Joe Sauer, explained it this way: "If you're going to be successful, you have to be genuine and honest. Your communications have to really truly represent the brand" (Limbic Brand Evolution, 2023).

Avoiding clichés and jargon helps you be more authentic and real, and helps your brand come across as more natural. This idea, being real, is so important and central to the Limbic Sparks approach that it's why we put so much effort into Insights Discovery to uncover the insights that matter most for both the brand and the customer.

An overuse of clichés and jargon is a direct result of traditional brand strategy that lacks specific emotional insights about what people truly care about and what sets your brand apart. When you don't know the specifics of what matters to people, your brand messaging is more likely to be broad and undifferentiated. Without specificity, you hurt the chances of your brand standing out as uniquely different or personally desirable. Limbic Sparks Brand Strategy is all about being specific.

In Focus, you learned how to discover emotional insights about what matters most to people. In Connect, we turn those insights into benefits that will spark interest and desire.

Iconic Brand Ideas

"Think Different"—Apple

"The Ultimate Driving Machine"—BMW

"Intel Inside"—Intel

"Be All You Can Be"—The U.S. Army

"When it absolutely positively has to be there overnight"—FedEx

"Just do it"—Nike

"Everywhere you want to be"—Visa

"Save Money. Live Better."—Walmart

Successful Brand Ideas draw you in. They ignite a feeling. They make an ambition seem possible. They make you feel like you want what they have to offer. The most memorable and long-lasting Brand Ideas ignite our emotions, connect with us in a very real and visceral way, and are an invitation to something you realize you would like to bring into your world.

This doesn't happen by chance. It happens because the brand leaders did what it takes to be a desired brand—they did the hard work of discovering emotional motivations. They identified what the people they are trying to reach care about at a deep level. They used emotional insights to develop a relevant and compelling Brand Idea, recognizing that the most engaging and sustainable brand benefits are emotional ones. They prioritized getting real, to create strong customer connections. They got very clear on what it is they do that makes people's lives better and presented their brand in a way that answers "What's in it for me?"

Brand leader Joe McCambley once said to me, "Long-term emotional appeals deliver short-term results better than short-term tactics. You're going to see more and more brands working to strike a balance between the rational and the emotional, with an understanding that the emotional is a lot more powerful than we ever gave it credit for" (Limbic Brand Evolution, 2021).

When it comes to iconic brand ideas, also called slogans and taglines, there's research that points to why some are more effective than others. An article titled "The Psychology of Slogans: What Are They and How Do They Work?" summarized qualities of effective slogans—the ones that positively predispose us to a brand. It shares that slogans are more effective when they appeal to our innate human motivation to meet basic psychological needs (Cobalt Communications, 2019). Further, the article shared the following five ways slogans are made more effective:

1 Clean and clear: Studies showed that the most-liked slogans are 4.9 words long, and the most recalled slogans are 3.9 words long. Overall, message clarity and brevity make for an effective, memorable slogan.

2 Use of music or poetry: Slogans can be made more effective when paired with a melody. This is something I can vouch for from my days working at a sonic branding music studio. For example, think about memorable slogans like, "Like a Good Neighbor, State Farm is There" or McDonald's "I'm Lovin' it."

3 Make customers feel something: Emotional appeal can go a long way in reaching your audience. You can construct your slogan around a particular curiosity or appetite, which makes for high relatability. You could also focus on making your slogan a challenge, which can motivate consumers.

4 Work with the brain: Understanding how the brain works, ease of comprehension, memorability, and mentioning a benefit are all surefire ways to increase your slogan's impact.

5 Written in the first person: Hearing an effective slogan feels like you're being spoken to directly, even though slogans are engineered for mass appeal.

Think about these qualities of effective slogans—they all point to capturing someone's attention in an emotional way. They're not suggesting that the brand gets more emotional. They're suggesting that your best bet is to appeal to how our brains process and respond to things.

Many factors impact how people will respond to your brand, from taglines and other messages people see in marketing, to the brand's visual and sonic appeal, to reviews from other people who have already experienced the brand, to whether you can make the case to your leadership team that brand investment is worthwhile. Your job in Connect is to set the strategic foundation for how your brand all comes to life cohesively to generate interest and spark ongoing desire for what you're selling.

It's Time to Connect

The Connect phase is about creating that strategic foundation for how your brand comes to life at every touchpoint to create Limbic Sparks. Together, the Shared Emotional Motivation that we developed in Focus, and the Brand Idea that we'll explore in Connect, become the bookends of the brand strategy. These brand strategy components, along with the Core Brand Benefits, the Brand Personality & Voice Traits, and the Brand Positioning Statement, set the foundation.

Michael Porter, who is an academic professor, one of the world's most influential thinkers on management and competitiveness, and generally regarded as the father of the modern strategy field, put it simply, emphasizing that strategy is about differentiation and making choices (Porter, n.d.).

Limbic Sparks Brand Strategy will help you make strategic choices rooted in emotional insights, so you can differentiate your brand based on what people care about the most.

FIGURE 5.1 Discovery and Activation of Emotional Insights

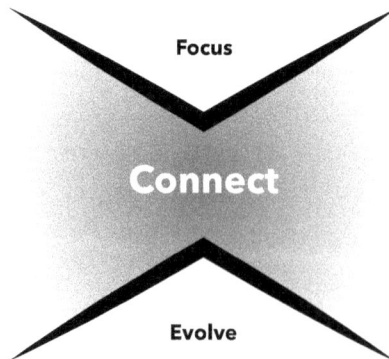

NOTE In Connect, our objective is to distill Insights Discovery down to the most important insights and turn those into very thoughtfully crafted brand strategy language.

For the AT&T Performing Arts Center, we arrived at "Yours to Discover" as the Brand Idea, because we discovered the Shared Emotional Motivation of "Passion for Entertaining Experiences." This led to a strategic choice to be welcoming and invite discovery to ignite interest among people who previously did not consider the brand when seeking new sources of entertainment. For Sundless, we arrived at "A Material Difference" as the Brand Idea, because we discovered that both the Sundless team and their customers are motivated by "An Uncompromising Advantage." The strategic choice to differentiate, not on comparative claims about the product quality, but on the fact that Sundless is a material like nothing else available, is specifically designed to ignite interest among risk-averse manufacturers who want a competitive advantage without sacrifice.

Ideas like these are clear and specific, leveraging the benefits that we've identified are of most interest to customers and most differentiating for the brand. We leverage this understanding to set the brand apart and attract new customers who crave the same benefits, whether they know it yet or not.

Five Limbic Sparks Brand Strategy Components

This complete set of brand strategy components will help your brand come to life in a unique and compelling way. Each component of the strategy should be thought about carefully and scrutinized as you make deliberate choices rooted in a solid set of emotional insights. Your strategy should also be designed to accomplish the Brand Strategy Success Criteria that you set at the end of Focus.

FIVE LIMBIC SPARKS BRAND STRATEGY COMPONENTS

1 Shared Emotional Motivation

2 Core Brand Benefits

3 Brand Personality & Voice Traits

4 Limbic Sparks Brand Idea

5 Brand Positioning Statement

Shared Emotional Motivation

In Chapter 3 you read about how to conduct Insights Discovery and how to develop a Shared Emotional Motivation. While this primary Limbic Sparks insight is a deliverable of Focus, it's also one bookend of a Limbic Sparks Brand Strategy that you carry forward into Connect.

> **Shared Emotional Motivation**
>
> The core Limbic Sparks insight identifying what both the brand and customer are most motivated to achieve individually and with each other.

This insight is what's often missing from traditional brand strategy, it's how you will ensure that the work you do in the Connect phase is rooted in what matters most at an emotional level to your customers and prospects. It sets the stage for the other brand strategy components that follow, serving as an ambition to be addressed, so that they are so on point, so relevant, and so compelling that they address the motivations of the people your brand is for, and spark their desire.

Core Brand Benefits

During Insights Discovery, you tapped into your curiosity and developed a robust understanding of what your customers care about. You learned about their personal and/or professional responsibilities, their priorities, their stresses, their motivations, and their ambition. These insights include a treasure-trove of details that will help you create Limbic Sparks by concentrating on the most emotionally desirable benefits across all customer segments. Once you identify reasons why people desire your brand, you can then turn them into the Core Brand Benefits that you use to attract new customers.

> **Core Brand Benefits**
>
> The most emotionally desirable and sought-after benefits across all customer segments. They answer the questions "What's in it for me?" and "Why should people care?"

It's at this point that I like to look back on the Insights Discovery Findings, including specific answers to customer 1x1 interview questions such as, "What's the best thing this brand does for you?" "What's the biggest impact this brand has on you/your business?" "If this brand no longer existed, what would you miss most?" "What are the three most important benefits you get from this brand?" and others.

When you review the answers to these questions, you'll start to see themes emerge. My go-to approach is to list benefits on a whiteboard and then bucket them into categories. I like to stick with three categories so that in the end there are three Core Brand Benefits. I prefer three because of the rule of three principle which suggests that people have an easier time recalling things in groups of three versus larger sets. Also, strategy is about making choices, and it's good discipline to get your ideas down to a list of three distinct benefits.

As you group like ideas together and ladder each set to one Core Brand Benefit, it will enhance focus and clarity of your messaging. Once you land on your three Core Brand Benefits, take a moment to be sure that they are distinctly different from each other and from what competitors are saying. When you look at them side by side, collectively they should represent the most sought-after benefits your brand has to offer.

As you read in the last chapter about Sundless, we had a variety of benefits and the following three categories emerged: Benefits related to the material being different than other materials available, benefits related to quality of the material, and benefits related to how the material gives manufactures a set of advantages that they can't get from other materials. This led us to our three Core Brand Benefits for Sundless:

- *Superior material: Film. Not fiber.*
- *Advanced performance: More durable.*
- *Better for manufacturers: Higher quality and environmentally friendly.*

Later, during the Evolve phase, you'll have the opportunity to get even more specific by identifying sub-benefits for each of the core benefits that are more directly related to individual customer segments. This will be part of the Brand Messaging Hierarchy, which you'll learn how to develop in Chapter 6 of this book.

Brand Personality & Voice Traits

Next, I turn my attention to developing the Brand Personality & Voice Traits that will guide brand expression. I do this second, because these traits will inform language and tone choices for the Brand Idea. They will also help your brand feel consistent and authentic across all aspects of Brand Expression & Experiences.

> **Brand Personality & Voice Traits**
>
> The humanistic traits that guide the feel of Brand Expression & Experiences.

The Brand Personality traits are the humanistic traits of your brand, and they translate into the Brand Voice as follows: Brand is (Personality Trait) and as a result, its Brand Voice should feel (Brand Voice Trait), not (opposite of the Brand Voice Trait).

Your objective is to choose a set of words to represent three distinct aspects of the Brand Personality, that when combined paint a very specific picture of what this brand feels like to interact with.

Here are two examples:

Let's say a brand you're engaging with is "Trailblazing, Confident, and Relationship-focused." Close your eyes, say the words and imagine it feels like interacting with this brand.

Now, close your eyes and imagine interacting with a brand that is "Caring, Expert, and Proactive." Can you feel how experiences with a brand that has these personality traits will be different from the brand above it?

It's this kind of specificity that we want to get to, so that Brand Messaging and all forms of Brand Expression & Experiences have a consistent feel. Importantly, you want the Brand Personality Traits to be authentic to the brand. It's not a good idea to attempt to stretch the Brand Personality into areas that are inauthentic. However, you may discover during customer interviews that they feel the brand personality a bit differently to people internally. This gives your brand permission to define itself that way, knowing it will be completely believable to customers because it's what they are currently feeling. This will then better represent the actual brand experience that prospective customers can anticipate, and it may do a better job of generating interest. Most importantly, select a set of Personality Traits that feel true to the brand and distinctive enough to guide copywriters and designers who will bring your brand to life.

When choosing Brand Personality Traits, you can go back to the Insights Discovery findings to source ideas. I like to think about conversations I had with people who work for the brand to understand their style and values. I also like to look at answers to questions from 1x1 interviews with brand team members and customers, such as, "How does it feel to work with/use this brand?" "If this brand were a person, what three words would you use to describe its personality?" and "If this brand was a superhero, what would be its superpower?" and others.

As you do this, start listing possible Brand Personality Traits and bucket them into categories of like words. It's ok to have a primary word and a set of synonyms that enrich the meaning and intent of the category. For example, Caring, Empathetic, and Dependable are all traits that fit into one category, and you can choose one to be the anchor, such as Caring, with the other words providing more context. Then you can have another category of traits such as Expert, Well-Informed, and Resourceful, that can be anchored by the word Expert. The third category can be Responsible, Intuitive, and Proactive, anchored by Proactive.

Once you have your three anchor Personality Traits, you can develop the corresponding Voice Traits, which inform how the brand should feel when people interact with it, using the construct below. If it's helpful to you, you can include the Personality Trait synonyms to bring further clarity to those who will be referencing the brand strategy.

Brand is (Personality Trait), and as a result, its brand voice should feel (Voice Trait), not (opposite of Voice trait).

Here are examples:

- *Brand is Caring (Empathetic, Dependable) and as a result, its brand voice should feel Friendly, not inauthentic.*

- *Brand is Expert (Well-Informed, Resourceful) and as a result, its brand voice should feel Knowledgeable, not vague.*

- *Brand is Proactive (Responsible, Intuitive) and as a result, its brand voice should feel Reassuring, not inaccessible.*

Limbic Sparks Brand Idea

Now, we're ready to develop and select a Brand Idea—the other bookend of the brand strategy. For it to qualify as a Limbic Sparks Brand Idea, it must be a compelling brand benefit and invitation—one that is an overt benefit combined with an overt or implied invitation to potential customers—that provides a way to achieve the Shared Emotional Motivation.

Brand Idea

The Limbic Sparks Brand Idea is the overarching compelling brand benefit and invitation. It can also serve as the customer-facing brand tagline.

The Brand Idea should feel real, not jargony. It should be written in words people say in everyday conversation. It should feel like your brand is talking directly to the people who encounter it. It should be informed by customer insights and the Shared Emotional Motivation that your brand makes possible and that the people your brand serves aspire to achieve. The Brand Idea's primary job is to move people from indifference about your brand to interest ignited. That's all, admittedly, a high bar, but it's what Limbic Sparks Brand Strategy is all about.

Unlike traditional brand strategy, where many brand ideas are a statement about the brand, a Limbic Sparks Brand Idea lets people know that your brand is where they will experience the emotional benefits they are craving. Also, in this approach, the Brand Idea sets the foundation of the creative brief. You may be used to strategists or account planners developing brand ideas as a part of a brand strategy brief, and copywriters developing brand taglines. Limbic Sparks Brand Strategy is designed to bring these two tasks together no matter who is involved in developing the final set of customer-facing words.

Developing the Brand Idea is a mix of art and science. It's work that takes time and lots of ideas. Without the investigative work that was done in the Focus phase, it would be so much harder to get there, and quite frankly, it would be guesswork. Throughout your ideation, you'll want to vet your ideas among some people who can serve as good sounding boards and give you honest feedback on their initial responses. You may even want to consider customer research to evaluate the strength of ideas, using a research approach that I describe in Chapter 10. Importantly, you'll want to check ideas for any alternative meanings or cultural sensitives. Further, you'll want to search online for the ideas to see if they've been used by other brands, and then check the U.S. Patent and Trademark Office (uspto.gov) website to see if any other brand has trademark rights to ideas on your consideration list, as a preliminary search that should be followed by a complete search using a trademark attorney, for any Brand Idea you would like to use.

My approach to ideation begins early. As soon as I start having conversations with my clients and their customers, I'm listening for soundbites and nuggets of detail. I keep a running list of ideas that I add to throughout the process. As I said earlier, Focus is all about collecting information, developing insights, and reserving judgment until later. It's also a time when ideas are coming at me and I'm sure to capture those thoughts in a notebook for later consideration. Anyone who looks at one of my lists of random ideas would be shocked by just how many ideas I have, most of which are not at all good enough for sharing. However, this list means that I'm not starting with a blank page when the strategy work in Connect begins.

All that said, when it comes to developing the Brand Idea, there is no exact way to do it—you need to start listing ideas that come to you when you set aside time to work on it, or at any other random times during brand development. You'll want to refine and prioritize your options based on the Brand Strategy Success Criteria. You'll want to consider language that feels reflective of the Brand Personality & Voice Traits. You'll want to refer to the Core Brand Benefits, as your Brand Idea is both a summation of and invitation to those benefits. While you most likely won't be able to communicate all the benefits in one Brand Idea, you're trying to the answer "What's in it for me?" and "Why should they care?" in one most compelling brand benefit and invitation that will ignite interest and spark desire for your brand.

Here's how I approached ideation for a brand that offers a cloud-based software platform to help companies better manage their staffing (with some details changed). They work with companies that have a lot of variability in staffing needs. For the people who are responsible for staffing, predicting staff requirements in advance is always a challenge to do manually—it's incredibly time-consuming, and often not as accurate as it needs to be. There are risks to inaccurate staffing levels—they either do not have enough staff to take care of customers as well as they would like, or they have too much staff on hand, which reduces profitability.

During the Brand Idea development stage of this project, we identified three emotionally motivating brand benefit territories to focus on for developing the Brand Idea: Transformation (this software platform transforms staffing operations and has significantly positive impact on staffing' levels, the quality of service, and profitability); Control (this software platform gives you greater predictability and puts you in better control of staffing operations and cashflow); and Simplification (this software platform brings tremendous simplification to your staffing operations, so you can increase profitability and focus more resources on customer service). From these territories here are a few of the Brand Ideas that rose to the top of our consideration list:

Simply Transformed

Take Control

Remarkably Simplified

We considered each of these options and others, reflecting on all the emotional insights, the Shared Emotional Motivation (which was "Reducing the Uncertainty and Burden of Staffing"), and the following Brand Strategy Success Criteria:

1 Emphasize transformational impact the brand has on staffing challenges.

2 Prioritize the most compelling emotional benefits vs. product features.

3 Connect emotionally with an invitation to solve their biggest stresses and challenges.

4 Connect emotionally with everyday language, not business jargon.

5 Be bold—lead a rallying cry focused on C-suite need.

In the end, we chose the "Remarkably Simplified" idea. We preferred that over "Simply Transformed" because we recognized that transformation is never simple, and we did not want the idea to be ignored because it did not seem to be feasible or believable. We did not choose "Take Control" because we didn't think it was broad enough or in as good alignment with the Brand Personality & Voice Traits as the "Remarkably Simplified" territory. We chose "Remarkably Simplified" because we deemed it to be a more compelling emotional benefit and invitation given the Shared Emotional Motivation and the previously agreed Brand Strategy Success Criteria.

One other consideration that came into play for this client was that we decided to create a Brand Descriptor, which is a way to succinctly explain what a brand does using descriptive language.

> **Brand Descriptor**
>
> Succinct statement to bring clarity to what brand does, sometimes paired with a non-descriptive brand name.

Since this brand's name was somewhat abstract, making it difficult to know what the brand does from just the brand name, and it had relatively low awareness and familiarity, we paired the brand logo with the descriptor "Workforce Platform." Doing this provides greater clarity on what the brand offers at the highest level, and it removes the need to convey that detail in the Brand Idea, which is purely focused on the benefit of "Remarkably Simplified."

Brand Positioning Statement

The final component of the brand strategy is the Brand Positioning Statement—the statement of distinct customer promise. While the sentence structure is flexible, it's important to ensure that it is written to convey not just what the company does, but why people should care.

Brand Positioning Statement

The statement of distinct customer promise, identifying the brand, who it's for, and what it does to make their life better.

Going back to Sundless from the last chapter, we landed on the following Brand Positioning Statement:

> *Sundless is the advanced monolithic UHWMPE film that provides manufacturers with revolutionary innovation at great value, so products have an uncompromising advantage.*

While there's no exact formula for a Brand Positioning Statement, I suggest they include the following components:

- Brand Name: *Sundless*
- What the brand is: *Advanced monolithic UHWMPE film*
- Who the brand is for: *Manufacturers*
- Sub-benefits: *Revolutionary innovation at a great value*
- Overarching brand benefit: *An uncompromising advantage*

You can see how this statement brings together what the brand is with the most compelling emotional benefits for the people who the brand serves.

Your Brand Strategy on a Page

Congratulations! Earlier, you completed Insights Discovery, and now you've come to the end of creating the foundational brand strategy. Once I get to this stage, I like to create a Brand Strategy One-Page Summary, like the example you saw in the last chapter for Sundless, so that all the Brand

Strategy components are on a single page. This can be a great reference guide for yourself and for anyone else who will need to refer to it as brand development continues into Evolve, which you'll read about in the next part of this book.

TABLE 5.1 Limbic Sparks Brand Strategy One-Page Summary

Limbic Sparks Brand Strategy One-Page Summary	
Shared Emotional Motivation The Limbic Sparks Insight	
Core Brand Benefits Why People Should Care	
Brand Personality & Voice Traits Traits that Guide Brand Expression	
Limbic Sparks Brand Idea Compelling Brand Benefit & Invitation	
Brand Positioning Statement Distinct Customer Promise	

Looking Ahead

That was a lot, but now you have a true sense of what separates Limbic Sparks Brand Strategy from traditional brand strategy. In the next chapter you'll see an example, with specific details, of developing a brand strategy that connects directly with the emotional motivations of the brand's customer, including all the steps we took to get there. Then, in Part Four, we'll explore how to Evolve, by applying the brand strategy to the various ways your brand comes to life. You'll learn how to activate your brand strategy so that it becomes the orientation point and guide for all aspects of the Brand Expression & Experience. But first, check out the next chapter to see how a Brand Idea can position your brand as delivering on the most compelling benefit a brand can offer in its category.

BRAND LEADERSHIP CONSIDERATIONS

In your own life, how much do you enjoy talking to salespeople who come at you with an elevator speech and familiar sales pitch?

Me, not so much. We can smell these one-sided pitches coming from a mile away. Lots of familiar introductions, lots of jargon, and an inauthentic desire to get to know us. When this happens, we put our guard up, and we hope they go away soon. Nobody wants an irrelevant sales pitch.

In your work with brands, are you making a first impression that is so relevant that it ignites the interest of the people your brand is for?

First impressions set the tone for everything that happens next. When we encounter a brand, we instinctively sense if it's something we want to bring into our life. That's why your most prominent brand messaging should address what matters most to the people your brand is for. It should feel like the brand understands its customers and is inviting them to come and get the benefits they desire.

Here are three things you can start doing today:

1 Assume that people are ignoring your marketing unless it answers, "What's in it for me?"

2 Avoid using cliches and jargon in your brand messaging, as this kind of language reveals that your brand has nothing unique to say, making it ignorable, and possibly a turn-off.

3 Be sure that your Brand Idea is not an "about us" sales pitch, and that it is, instead, a compelling benefit and invitation for customers to enjoy benefits that they are craving.

References

Brown, B (2018) *Dare to Lead: Brave work. Tough conversations. Whole hearts.*, Random House, US

Cobalt Communications (2019) The psychology of slogans: What they are & how they work, 18 December [blog] cobaltcommunications.com/cobalt-60/the-psychology-of-slogans/ (archived at https://perma.cc/7NMV-K6M2)

Edwards, J (2010) A thin line: Pretzel company uses anorexics' mantra as ad slogan, CBS News, 9 August, www.cbsnews.com/news/a-thin-line-pretzel-company-uses-anorexics-mantra-as-ad-slogan/ (archived at https://perma.cc/2XSB-SH3S)

Limbic Brand Evolution (2021) Let's Talk Limbic Sparks Podcast – episode 6, Breaking Through in a Competitive Category with Joe McCambley, 13 September, www.limbicbrandevolution.com/podcast/joe-mccambley-saatva-lets-talk-limbic-sparks-6 (archived at https://perma.cc/MKD4-4YQS)

Limbic Brand Evolution (2023) Let's Talk Limbic Sparks Podcast – episode 26, Understanding Consumer Behavior with Joe Sauer, 12 June, www.limbicbrandevolution.com/podcast/joe-sauer-lets-talk-limbic-sparks-26 (archived at https://perma.cc/PD2K-K44V)

Perlmutter, K (2020) Interview: How instinctive emotion drives behavior, with Cyrus McCandless, PhD, *Brandingmag*, 20 October, www.brandingmag.com/2020/10/20/interview-how-instinctive-emotion-drives-behavior-with-cyrus-mccandless-phd/ (archived at https://perma.cc/C3L7-BPPM)

Sanoff, A (1986) One Must Not Forget: Elie Wiesel Interview, *US News & World Report*, 27 October

Wikipedia (n.d.) Michael Porter, en.wikipedia.org/wiki/Michael_Porter (archived at https://perma.cc/R53P-SLK6)

06

Turning Customers into Heroes

Blue Ridge Case Study

"We need a bold way to set our brand apart and to differentiate ourselves in a very crowded category."

This was the challenge I heard from Kyle Pexton, CEO of Blue Ridge, and his team, during our first meeting. Their company is a big player in the very crowded supply chain management software space. They have many very happy customers in the United States and Europe, yet they were struggling to succinctly clarify what makes them different and better than the competition, and it was limiting the success of business development efforts.

Blue Ridge has a SaaS, cloud-based software solution in a category of companies that helps businesses with warehouses full of goods to always have the right amount of inventory. They serve manufacturers, distributors, and retailers in industries such as food service, wine and spirits, automotive, furniture, HVAC (heating, air conditioning, and ventilation), hardware and home supply stores, and more. If a company has a warehouse, or multiple warehouses, Blue Ridge and its competitors have software solutions to make managing and maintaining the right inventory levels easier for all those involved.

Competitors range from those that are very niche, specializing in serving specific industry segments, to conglomerates like SAP and Oracle that have massive enterprise-level software solutions for supply chain management and many other aspects of business operations. The challenge for companies looking to use an inventory management solution is that there are so many choices, all of which seem, on the surface, to have very similar offerings. As companies are looking to shift from manual spreadsheets to a robust software inventory management system, the process of selecting a provider can be overwhelming.

This sea of sameness among providers is made even more challenging by a slew of undifferentiated brand messages that range from "about us" statements like "We are the Supply Chain Experts" and "The Market-Leading Supply Chain & Retail Planning Platform" to generic statements such as "Inventory Optimization Solutions" to cliché statements like "Move Forward Faster" and "Confidence in an Uncertain World." Brands are using terms like "Smart" and "AI" to come across as more advanced. There are also a few brand ideas that stood out to me, such as "Make Better Inventory Decisions" and "Fulfill Your Potential" because they are benefit-oriented. Blue Ridge, when we met, was using the line, "We Put You at the Center of Supply Chain Success." While this positioning territory certainly leaned in the right direction, it was not doing enough to differentiate the brand.

My job was to help Blue Ridge stand out in this crowded and confusing space. When I first met them, we talked about how the Limbic Sparks approach was different than traditional brand strategy and how we needed to uncover emotional insights to create stronger connections between the brand and its desired customers. Kyle later revealed, "We brought you in for your emotion-centric approach." The more I spoke with the Blue Ridge team, the more it became clear that they are a very well-regarded brand, and we needed to find their unique Brand Positioning and Brand Voice.

Focus

During the first phase of strategy development, Focus, we conducted Insights Discovery to uncover the Shared Emotional Motivation between Blue Ridge and the people they serve. Before having any answers for how to differentiate Blue Ridge, there was a lot of Insights Discovery to be conducted, utilizing the five primary activities that we reviewed in Chapter 3.

Project Kick-off and Brand Dynamics

First, it was important to understand brand dynamics by absorbing all the existing information that we could. What often happens at this moment is we set up a file-sharing folder where clients drop things for review related to business strategy, product/service offering, customer profiles and data, current marketing materials, and so much more. We also conducted a meeting with someone who presented a demonstration of the Blue Ridge software, so that we could understand its functionality and the user interface firsthand.

Another always important moment is the project kick-off meeting, which we held with about seven key players from the Blue Ridge team. It included

Kyle, heads of sales, marketing and client experience, the head of their Europe division, and other people who were part of the project's core team.

During this meeting, I shared an overview of the overall project and the Limbic Sparks Brand Strategy approach for those I was meeting for the first time. I also asked a handful of questions, including some of my top kick-off curiosities:

- Why is brand evolution so important for Blue Ridge?
- What's your biggest concern about how Blue Ridge presents itself today?
- What do you wish more people knew about Blue Ridge?
- What do you believe will be the most challenging part of this brand evolution?
- Please share a bit about Blue Ridge today, vs. your vision for Blue Ridge in the future.
- What else should I know as we get started together?

Throughout this discussion, I could feel the energy of the team and their passionate commitment to their work and the role they play in their customers' businesses. They also started recognizing that they all shared similar feelings about what's less than ideal about how the brand currently presents itself externally, and their anticipation was piqued for all that would come next in our work together.

In one of my favorite moments of the meeting, Kyle's closing statement to the team was that he understood how busy they all are, but he asked them to please include this project among their top priorities, as it would be one of several core aspects to fueling the next stage of the company's growth.

Competitive Audit and Category Dynamics

Next was the competitive audit, primarily looking on company websites to understand the depth of their offerings, how they were positioning themselves, and their core talking points. As I shared earlier in this chapter, this category, like many others, especially in the B2B space, suffers from a lot of generic brand messaging, a lot of brands expressing their Why, and a lack of emotional benefits rooted in deep customer understanding.

I sought to understand category dynamics through conversations with my clients and desktop research where I was able to learn more about supply chain management than I ever knew before. I even kept a glossary of terms and acronyms in my notes so that I could be more fluent in the language of the category and fully understand the discussion in meetings when these terms were used.

Interviews and Customer Research

Then came the Brand Team & Customer Interviews, which included over 20 one-on-one discussions that I conducted among a mix of brand team members, US-based customers, and Europe-based customers. We ensured that these customers represented different industries that Blue Ridge serves, and levels from the C-suite to supply chain managers. As you read about in Chapter 3, these interviews included questions to provide deep insight into what sets Blue Ridge apart, why customers choose Blue Ridge, why they continue to be customers, and how it makes them feel to have Blue Ridge as part of their day-to-day work.

The final Insights Discovery activity for this project was to review incremental customer research—quantitative data about how customers felt about their relationship with Blue Ridge. Fortunately, we did not need to field a new research study, as we had access to 77 reviews that customers contributed to a website for B2B company reviews. We found that Blue Ridge had a 4.7 out of 5 stars rating, with 79 percent 5-star reviews. Even better, our analysis revealed a goldmine of insight from these reviews beyond knowing they were nearly all very positive. The biggest value came from the comments that customers left to answer the review questions—including the review headline, what they like best about the company, what they dislike about the company (25 percent of reviewers left this space blank or said "nothing"), and how the company is benefiting them. When customers are asked questions like these and have a small space to answer, they reveal the things that matter most to them. With 77 reviews, we were able to rank the feedback by themes and know with reliability what topics were thematic for this brand.

Once all these activities were completed, we pulled together an Insights Discovery Findings session with the core team, and we began to paint a picture of what differentiates Blue Ridge from its competitors, and why customers continue to work with this brand. We discussed how the emotional drivers we uncovered form the basis of customers' mindsets and how they approach their work. We also came to clarity on what drives the Blue Ridge team and what they prioritize in their relationships with customers.

We discovered that the Blue Ridge team cares deeply about providing high quality and great value to their customers. They strive to make people's jobs easier, empowering them with data and insights. As industry insiders, many of whom have deep forecasting expertise and have held roles at other companies managing inventory, they uniquely understand their customers. This inspires them to be incredibly empathetic and supportive to ensure their customers' success.

Concurrently, we learned a lot about the people served by Blue Ridge. They are people who have a high-stakes job. They are responsible and under pressure to predict inventory levels accurately, often with too little information. Sometimes this includes many thousands of SKUs across multiple locations with seasonal variations. Their work has a direct impact on the financial health of their company. They would like nothing more than to have better data that makes their internal recommendations more accurate more often.

We also discovered why customers enjoy their relationship with Blue Ridge so much—what's currently creating Limbic Sparks for them. Consistently, we heard that customers are incredibly happy with Blue Ridge. Blue Ridge has a program called LifeLine where former practitioners help clients maximize the use of the software—a service that is ongoing and that no competitor offers. LifeLine was mentioned in 25 percent of the online reviews and in most customer interviews. This combination of the robust yet intuitive software and the LifeLine team are both very appealing and, in combination, highly differentiating as part of the customer experience. Further, customers like the confidence-inspiring data that helps them do their job better—they feel better prepared, more in control, and less stressed. Overall, we learned that Blue Ridge brings a tremendous amount of value to its customers, some of which is intangible and not coming through in their sales and marketing efforts. This was a missed opportunity that we were on track to fix.

To conclude our Insights Discovery work and the Focus phase, we developed the Shared Emotional Motivation. As you may recall, the Shared Emotional Motivation is one bookend of the brand strategy that authentically connects the brand and its audience. It conveys what both are striving to achieve and sets us up to develop the brand idea, which is a highly relevant benefit and invitation.

The Shared Emotional Motivation

For Blue Ridge, we landed on the following Shared Emotional Motivation:

Improving Planning Precision

This is the common motivation that both Blue Ridge and their customers are striving to be better at, every day. We found that Blue Ridge is incredibly successful at helping customers improve planning precision, and in the Connect phase we'll use the details learned in Insights Discovery to bring the brand to life in a highly relevant and compelling way.

Connect

Where Focus is all about gathering information and distilling it into insight, Connect is all about developing a strategy that sets the foundation for how the brand should come to life across all touchpoints.

Before jumping into this phase of ideation work, it's important to reflect on what's been learned thus far and to have conversations about what it suggests, and what should be prioritized in the work ahead. When you set criteria before beginning the Connect phase you will have strategic objectives in mind when judging brand strategy options.

For our brand strategy to be successful at sparking desire, we took a moment as the last step of Insights Discovery to agree on several Brand Strategy Success Criteria based on what we discovered about the brand and its customers.

For Blue Ridge, the criteria we set were as follows:

1   Bring out the heartfelt human motivation of the Blue Ridge team
2   Lean into the differentiating fact that Blue Ridge = software + people
3   Recognize and address the emotional motivations of customers

These criteria will guide us as we develop the Brand Idea, as well as the Brand Positioning, and when we set the Personality & Voice Traits to guide brand expression.

Identifying Core Brand Benefits

In this work, the first step we took to developing the brand strategy was to identify and prioritize the most compelling benefits that people get from the brand. As we considered how to prioritize a short list of three brand benefits, we reflected on conversations with customers. There are many benefits of working with Blue Ridge that customers talked about, but we wanted to focus on the ones that were repeated most often and that were rising to the top as the drivers of choice and loyalty. Not surprisingly, these benefits had a lot to do with the software itself, and even more to do with the way it feels to work with Blue Ridge.

We landed on three benefit territories:

1 *Eliminate guesswork*. Blue Ridge helps customers be more precise, so they can accurately predict the demand of each item in your inventory.

2 *Maximize inventory performance*. Blue Ridge helps customers right-size their inventory, so they can improve cashflow and increase profitability.

3 *Unmatched partnership*. Blue Ridge stands by their customers in a way that no other competitor does by providing LifeLine industry expertise, so they get the most value out of their software.

This list of benefits, you should know, was not the first draft. A similar initial set of ideas was developed and shared. These higher-level ideas were backed up by a list of sub-benefits that fell under each conceptual category. Then we had a series of discussions among people from the marketing team, the sales team, and the customer support team to fine-tune language. This helped us all be comfortable with the three core benefit territories so that we could use them as a foundation to the brand strategy language. Then, we continued to fine-tune and bring more dimension to all the benefit language in the Evolve phase where we finalized the Brand Messaging Hierarchy.

Determining Brand Personality & Voice Traits

The next thing we worked on was the Brand Personality & Voice Traits. As you may recall, these are the traits that guide brand expression. They set the tone for how the brand should come to life and serve as a guidepost for the kind of language we use in the brand idea, and all other forms of brand expression to be developed.

When thinking about the Brand Personality & Voice Traits, it was important to reflect on the Insights Discovery work. Specifically, we reviewed our findings for questions like "How does it make you feel to work with Blue Ridge?" and "If Blue Ridge was a person, how would you describe its personality?".

This led us to the following Brand Personality & Voice Traits:

- Blue Ridge is *Confident*, and as a result, its brand voice should feel Expert, not vague.

- Blue Ridge is *Enthusiastic*, and as a result, its brand voice should feel Supportive, not inaccessible.
- Blue Ridge is *Empowering*, and as a result, its brand voice should feel Motivating, not complicated.

These words, which were carefully chosen through a process of ideation and refinement, are great to have in place as we develop the other strategy components. They serve as a guide for what it feels like to work with Blue Ridge, which we want to convey in the Brand Idea.

Creating the Brand Idea

Now, we're ready to develop and select a Brand Idea—the compelling brand benefit and invitation. It's where we needed to focus our thinking on how we want people to feel when they encounter Blue Ridge. This brand idea, which will also serve as the brand tagline, would soon become the first and most prominent message that customers and prospects would see when they encountered the brand—on their website, at conferences, in sales materials, and on social media. It needed to be a real reflection of how current customers are made to feel when they work with the brand, and how prospects want to feel when they do their work. Further, we needed to recognize that prospects seeing the brand tagline is only one, often the first, step in the sales process. There are many steps to go to close the deal. That said, the tagline is the door opener, it's the first impression, it's the way you initially create Limbic Sparks—with a relevant and compelling brand benefit and invitation.

Now, I'm in brand idea generation mode. It's quite a scene with both a notebook and a whiteboard, each filled with ideas. Parts of the process include blocks of time for idea generation, and other ideas come at all moments and hours of this weeks-long period. I've been known to go for walks and suddenly stop to jot down an idea. I've been known to pop out of bed at 2 am to write down an idea. My mind is wandering during other activities. My family and I will go for a road trip, and I'll turn off the music in the car to conduct a spontaneous focus group and ideation session. When working with collaborators, we have multiple conversations to bounce ideas. Most of all, I'm generating and collecting ideas, highlighting those that feel most right, and letting them marinate. I like to see if they still feel good a few days later, and what other, hopefully better, ideas emerge.

Finally, I'm ready to share ideas with my clients. Often that first brand idea discussion is a nail-biter for me, because I've spent weeks preparing for the meeting, and I'm revealing all my cards—all my best ideas to date.

Should we have a meeting where my clients don't like what I'm presenting, I'm not just back to the drawing board, I'm back to a blank slate.

Here's the good news. Time and time again, Limbic Sparks Brand Strategy does not let me down. Whereas traditional brand strategy leads to ideas that are not rooted in a deep understanding of customer insights, including their motivations and decision drivers, this approach is coming from a wealth of reliable detail about what matters most.

The day had finally arrived and we were discussing brand ideas for Blue Ridge. On that day I presented six potential ideas. All met the criteria of being a brand benefit and an invitation. All reflected the core benefit that customers feel from Blue Ridge and that prospects want to feel. Some were more conservative, such as "Buy Better" and some were leaning more into the Brand Personality & Voice Traits—confident, enthusiastic, and empowering—like "Be a Supply Chain Wizard."

This presentation was well received for its range of ideas and led to a lot of conversation about options. This conversation lasted a couple of weeks, because I suggested that the Blue Ridge team sit with the ideas for a while to let them marinate. As self-described left-brain, rational thinkers, I wanted them to have all the time they needed to get comfortable. Simultaneously, they challenged me to improve upon territories that felt close, but not exactly there yet. I love this part of the process, and I always keep in mind that no matter how much heart I have for a Brand Idea or anything I'm ever recommending to a client, it's not about what I like. It's about what my clients like. While I always encourage my clients to take some time to consider initially uncomfortable ideas, especially when they are backed up by insights, if, ultimately, they're not feeling it, then it's not for them.

With this work, one of our key discussion points was around how "bold" we wanted to go with the Brand Idea. It was universally agreed that a line like "Buy Better" and later adapted to "Plan Better. Buy Better." was good. But was it good enough—did it truly go far enough to differentiate the brand? It was also agreed that a line like "Be a Supply Chain Wizard" put the brand in a bolder space and would stand out among the competitive positioning territories. However, we wanted to be careful about word choice, and the word "wizard" was not sitting right with everyone. I kept thinking and we kept talking. In a later meeting, I shared, and we rallied around, an evolved idea, one that we ultimately selected to be the Brand Idea:

Be Supply Chain Invincible

However, it took some conversation, time, and thought to officially choose the idea as final. We agreed that this is the high ground in the category that

Blue Ridge had earned, but the team wanted to be sure that it was true to the brand, and that it would feel real to customers and prospects.

Fortunately, we were able to reflect on all the Insights Discovery work to give us comfort. Not only would it stand out from all the competition, but it is also true, rooted in what we heard from Blue Ridge customers—in one-on-one interviews, in brand testimonials, and throughout 77 customer reviews. This is how Blue Ridge makes customers feel and how prospects want to feel. It was supported by all of the work we'd done to date, and it was specifically inspired by a soundbite I'd heard weeks earlier during a customer interview: "I used to be the person who got in trouble at work for having less than accurate inventory levels, and now I'm the person people rely on so that our inventory level is right and our cashflow is better. Blue Ridge makes me feel like a hero at work."

We had ourselves a Brand Idea!

Articulating the Brand Positioning Statement

The final step of Connect is to bring it all together with a Brand Positioning Statement—the statement of distinct customer promise. For Blue Ridge, we landed on the following:

> Blue Ridge is the supply chain software that improves planning precision with an unmatched partnership to help you eliminate guesswork, maximize inventory performance, and be supply chain invincible.

Here is how that Brand Positioning Statement breaks down into core components that we outlined in Chapter 5:

- Brand Name: *Blue Ridge*
- What the Brand is: *the supply chain software*
- Who the Brand is for: *(Implied: people responsible for supply chains)*
- Sub-benefits: *Improves planning precision with an unmatched partnership to help you eliminate guesswork, maximize inventory performance*
- Overarching brand benefit: *Be supply chain invincible*

See is how it all comes together on the Limbic Sparks Brand Strategy one-pager in Table 6.1.

TABLE 6.1 Blue Ridge Brand Strategy Summary

Blue Ridge
Brand Strategy Summary

Shared Emotional Motivation The Limbic Sparks Insight	Improving Planning Precision
Core Brand Benefits Why People Should Care	Eliminate Guesswork Maximize Inventory Performance Unmatched Partnership
Brand Personality & Voice Traits Traits that Guide Brand Expression	Blue Ridge is Confident, and as a result, its brand voice should feel Expert, not vague. Blue Ridge is Enthusiastic, and as a result, its brand voice should feel Supportive, not inaccessible. Blue Ridge is Empowering, and as a result, its brand voice should feel Motivating, not complicated.
Limbic Sparks Brand Idea & Tagline Compelling Brand Benefit & Invitation	Be Supply Chain Invincible
Brand Positioning Statements Distinct Customer Promise	Blue Ridge is the supply chain software that improves planning precision with an unmatched partnership to help you eliminate guesswork, maximize inventory performance, and be supply chain invincible.

Let's review against the Brand Strategy Success Criteria:

✓ Bring out the heartfelt human motivation of the Blue Ridge team.

✓ Lean into the differentiating fact that Blue Ridge = Software + People.

✓ Recognize and address the emotional motivations of customers.

Success. We now have the strategic foundation to evolve the brand!

Evolve

You'll read a lot about the Evolve phase of brand evolution in the next part of this book. It's when we move from brand strategy to company-wide and customer-facing brand activation. You'll learn how to apply and activate your brand strategy so that it becomes the orientation point and guide for all aspects of the brand experience inside and out. You'll see not only how brand strategy guides marketing, but how it can be the catalyst to achieve business objectives through customer-centricity.

For Blue Ridge, we took a few next steps to bring this evolved brand strategy to life. Throughout the Focus and Connect phases, we included a core group of stakeholders who represented many parts of the company in both the United States and Europe. Now it was time to not only evolve the brand, but to share the evolution with everyone in the company, and soon, customers and prospects outside the company.

For all the Evolve work, our primary emphasis was to infuse the new strategy, messaging, and Brand Personality & Voice Traits. Most importantly, we wanted people to know this is a brand that will help them feel invincible. With our bold new positioning territory and Brand Idea, we needed to be sure that the look and feel of the brand felt as bold as the brand language.

Refreshing the Visual Identity

Once we landed on the new Brand Idea, we recognized that it brought an energy to the brand that was not yet reflected in the current visual identity. Working with a wonderful graphic designer, we all agreed that a big change was unnecessary, but some enhancements would serve the brand well.

Blue Ridge already had an established color palette, anchored in blue, and it included a mango (yellow-orange) secondary color. We dialed up the use of mango as a more prominent accent to bring more vibrancy to the brand. Using carefully selected stock imagery, we created a photography library of curated images to represent customers-in-action, in a range of scenarios such as offices and warehouses. We ensured that they were all in a cohesive look and feel and did not look like typical stock photos. We also licensed the use of an illustration style to represent features and benefits of Blue Ridge's offering. With both the photography and illustrations, we customized them to include hints of yellow and orange to subtly bring the brand's accent color to life in a way that feels completely natural.

One more significant enhancement to the visual identity was the creation of a consistent look for the new tagline—*Be Supply Chain Invincible*. We designed it using a newly introduced typeface, in bold and all caps, and using the brand's core colors. This tagline is now able to be prominently displayed across brand touchpoints as a hero image. As part of our work, we updated the brand's visual identity guidelines and provided some templates for marketing materials so that the Blue Ridge marketing team and any other partners they work with can consistently use and build upon the evolved visual identity.

FIGURE 6.1 Blue Ridge Logo and New Tagline

NOTE This is the Blue Ridge logo and the new Brand Tagline. There are various color combinations that can be used, such as a blue background, white "Be Supply Chain" type, and mango "Invincible" type. Alternatives include using mango as the background color, with "Be Supply Chain" in white, and "Invincible" blue, or a white background, with "Be Supply Chain" in blue, and "Invincible" mango.

Evolving Brand Messaging

As part of our Evolve phase, we also developed the final Brand Messaging Hierarchy, a core component of any brand evolution project, which you'll learn more about in the Evolve section of this book. For Blue Ridge, this work included taking the three Core Brand Benefits that we identified in the Create phase and building out sub-benefits of each for each of the brand's primary target audiences: C-suite Decision Makers and Users of the Software. This Brand Messaging Hierarchy becomes a single page to guide copywriting and talking points for the brand.

Using this Brand Messaging Hierarchy, we rewrote or edited copy across a variety of brand touchpoints—the website home page, sales presentations, product one-pagers, and more. This all enables the Blue Ridge marketing team and any other partners they work with to consistently write brand messaging with focus on the brand benefits that we know matter most to customers. It's also a living document that can and should be updated over time as new insights emerge and new brand benefits need to be introduced to customers.

After the evolved brand was launched, the new *Be Supply Chain Invincible* tagline was front and center on the company website. Below it was the following copy:

Supply chain software that improves planning precision.

Faster, more accurate planning to right-size your inventory and improve cash flow with an unmatched LifeLine team, made up of industry experts who provide you with coaching to get the most out of your software.

Eliminate Guesswork

No more buying on spreadsheets, gut instinct, or educated guesses. Gain a comprehensive overview of your entire inventory and associated forecasts, with the ability to drill down to SKU-level details by specific location or across all locations. Predictive insights, proven reliability, and data-driven analytics mean you're always prepared and in control to make fast, accurate decisions.

Maximize Inventory Performance

Ready to save money while improving customer fill rates? Our software ensures you have the right inventory, in the right place, at the right time. It's flexible, with an out-of-the-box platform that allows for rapid implementation. You'll realize ROI in months, not years.

Unmatched Partnership

You won't find a partnership like this anywhere else. Our unmatched LifeLine team, made up of industry experts, provides regular coaching to help you accelerate software adoption and performance. We'll stand by you so you can Be Supply Chain Invincible.

Relaunching the Brand

One of the final pieces of my work with Blue Ridge, and on the day that the evolved website went live, I had the wonderful opportunity to join the leadership team launch as they launched the brand evolution internally as part of a monthly online town hall meeting for all global employees. I was so proud as Kyle, the Blue Ridge CEO, opened the meeting and introduced the presentation titled "Blue Ridge Brand Evolution: Bringing to Life What Makes Us Different and Better." From there I had the opportunity to present a summary of the brand evolution, including how it is rooted in customer insights about what matters most to them and why they choose Blue Ridge.

Soon after that, a Blue Ridge employee proudly posted an image of the new tagline on LinkedIn with the following message:

When I first heard our tagline at Blue Ridge, "Be Supply Chain Invincible," the phrase immediately struck a chord.

Being invincible doesn't mean that bullets won't fly in your direction.
Being invincible means the bullets that fly won't hurt your business.

Props to the marketing team. This tagline is a great representation of what Blue Ridge can do for your supply chain.

Around the same time, Blue Ridge held its annual customer conference. I was so thrilled to see the posts starting to flood LinkedIn from Blue Ridge and from their customers, with people standing in front of the *Be Supply Chain Invincible* signage. A few customers even referenced the tagline in the messages of their posts, as they raved about the event.

At the beginning of this project, Kyle challenged us to lean into our right-brain and be bold. When the work concluded, he said to me, "I've done brand strategy work before, and it was a challenging process. But with your Limbic Sparks approach, it was more enjoyable, and I'm thrilled with the results for our brand."

Looking Ahead

Are you feeling it? You're probably starting to recognize the difference between brand strategy with and without deep customer insights. Now, in Part Four, Evolve, we'll take this strategic foundation and turn it into a brand that people are instinctively attracted to. This section will also include two case studies—one related to transforming brand messaging rooted in the most compelling customer benefits, and one related to differentiating a brand with very appealing customer experience. It's time to get into the details of Brand Expression & Experiences

---

BRAND LEADERSHIP CONSIDERATIONS

In your own life, have you ever felt a lack of confidence or like you have imposter syndrome?

We all do, sometimes. We know down deep that we're good enough, that we have what it takes, and that our quality level is high. However, without hearing it from others, and without that positive reinforcement, we may feel insecure in putting ourselves out there.

In your work with brands, do you sometimes feel like you're placing risky bets on campaign ideas?

Sometimes brand leaders are reluctant to stake a big claim. Perhaps it's for fear of not living up to it or that customers won't find it to be believable. It that's true—that the brand can't live up to it or customers won't find it to be believable—then certainly don't stake that claim. However, when your brand delivers and customers have revealed that they experience these sought-after benefits, it's time to own the high ground and use it to attract new customers.

Here are three things you can start doing today:

- Discover what specific benefits make your brand better than any other competitive option by hearing directly from your customers.
- Turn those insights into messaging that will elevate your brand above competitors by standing the most emotionally appealing brand benefits.
- Be bold in staking your claim when you know it's rooted in what customers already believe to be true.

PART FOUR

Evolve

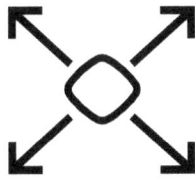

07

Designing Brand
Expression & Experiences

The Eames Lounge Chair is an incredible piece of furniture that epitomizes the mid-century modern era. Its iconic design and impeccable craftsmanship create an ergonomically perfected leather seat with a baseball mitt look that you just sink into, surrounded by molded wood veneer and shock-absorbing cast aluminum. This chair was originally designed in 1955 by Charles Eames and his wife and professional partner Ray Kaiser Eames. It's still made today using the same exquisite design details, offering buyers a variety of leather and wood combination options that don't take away from its unique look. For decades, it's been premium-priced and sought-after (Portale, 2021).

When you think about what it takes to make something so iconic, so premium, and desired, you must consider what drives such a high level of emotional appeal. I'm nearly positive that luck has nothing to do with it. If you were to ask Charles Eames, he most likely would have said it's about paying attention to the details. Famously, he is said to have referred to the details as not just the details, but the most important part of design (Eames, n.d.).

This notion that the details are the most important part of design gets to the heart of what Limbic Sparks Brand Strategy is all about. A brand's ability to have a discernible competitive advantage is getting slimmer and slimmer. Choices are unlimited and digital experiences are lowering the barriers to entry to most anything. This is why it's so important for you as a brand leader to now turn your attention to the details in all aspects of how your brand comes to life, using the brand strategy as a foundation. When it comes to attracting and retaining customers, you'll find that good enough is rarely good enough, and small details have a big impact.

Evolve, the third of the three phases of Limbic Sparks Brand Strategy, is all about creating evolved Brand Expression & Experiences, by applying the strategy to the ways in which people interact with your brand.

> **Evolve**
>
> Creating evolved Brand Expression & Experiences to address how people want to feel.

In Focus, your insights discovery work led you to a robust understanding about what's most important to your customers. You came to a Shared Emotional Motivation—what your brand and your customers are most motivated to achieve individually and with each other—and you set criteria for what your successful brand evolution is meant to accomplish. During the Connect phase of brand strategy development, you put so much work into articulating just the right words to set the foundation for how your brand will come to life, with a relevant and compelling Brand Idea rooted in the most emotionally desirable Core Brand Benefits. You developed an over-arching Brand Positioning Statement, and you articulated Brand Personality & Voice Traits.

All these brand strategy components set the foundation of a future that has yet to unfold. They are the real and relevant reflection of what your brand is all about and why people should care. It's now time to activate your Limbic Sparks Brand Strategy using the emotional insight-rooted words that you've carefully chosen and turning that foundation into customer-facing Brand Expression & Experiences.

> **Brand Expression & Experiences**
>
> How your brand comes to life through visuals, sounds, words, and all forms of interaction at every touchpoint, leading to an overall brand impression.

Informing Tactics With Strategy

What do you think is better—investing your scarce resources in brand strategy development or brand activation?

In my experience, the answer must be both. One without the other is insufficient. The most successful brand evolutions happen when the strategic foundations are strong and when the activation of that strategy cascades across how the brand comes to life across all touchpoints. A strategy is only worth the paper it's printed on. However, once you turn the emotional insights you've discovered into Brand Expression & Experiences that represent brand benefits that are meaningful to your customers, as well as your unique and sustainable competitive advantage, you'll have a great new way to spark brand desire.

From *The Art of War*, originally written in the 5th century BC, by Chinese military strategist Sun Tzu, "Strategy without tactics is the slowest route to victory. Tactics without strategy is the noise before defeat." This idea conveys that strategy and tactics must work in tandem and either one without the other will lead to failure.

While I personally feel that developing and activating a brand strategy is a whole lot more fun and optimistic than war-gaming, I do see the wisdom in his words. The most successful brand evolutions that I've experienced are the ones that start off with more questions than answers, that lead to a strategy using emotional insights to set the brand apart, and that bring all that strategy and insight into how the brand presents itself going forward.

The least successful brand evolutions are the ones that happen with a traditional approach to strategy development plagued by a lack of customer understanding, or when brand evolution efforts do not fully embrace all that is discovered to improve connections with prospective and current customers. While few and far between, I've had experiences where there was a respectable investment in brand strategy development, and then the brand leaders or their leadership team lost momentum, and activation efforts were not prioritized. It's disappointing and wasteful, to say the least. Even worse, these brand leaders did not give themselves the opportunity to experience the results they were hoping for.

Recognizing the Big Impact of Small Details

The more you get to know me, the more you see how much I'm into details. I like to ask questions. I'm curious about why things are the way they are and how they can be better. This trait has been with me since I was a kid—taking things apart just so I can see the inside and then figure out how to put them back together.

Also, for as long as I can remember I've been a woodworker, building furniture and doing other light construction projects. I've designed and built much of the furniture in my home—a kitchen island, an armoire, a rustic dining room table with benches and chairs, a toy chest and bins for my once-young children, and many other pieces. I enjoy planning and construction equally.

Throughout the process, I'm considering the needs that what I'm about to build will solve. I'm soliciting input from my family about desired functionality, about how it should look, and about how it will fit into or evolve the environment of our home. With joy, I scrutinize every detail, from the type of wood I'll use, to the methods I'll use to join wood together with as few screws and brackets as possible, to the finishes I'll use to bring the grain of the wood to life in the perfect color and amount of sheen. Inspired by Charles Eames, I know that the details make the difference between a piece of furniture I'm indifferent to, versus one that I do not want to live without.

I've carried this attention to detail into my professional life, and I'm a big fan of both meanings of "the golden rule." As a woodworker, the golden rule is "Measure twice and cut once." Applying this definition to brand development, it means you should think about strategy before activation. The other golden rule is "Treat others the way you would like to be treated," which I believe should be everybody's mantra, and that brand leaders should channel this principle into the experiences people have with their brand.

It's this attention to details that most likely led me down the path of shifting from a career in advertising to one more centered in brand strategy and customer experience. I recognized that brands could no longer hide bad experiences behind good advertising. Throughout my journey, I've asked questions that go beyond the surface, I've prioritized time for gathering input from a variety of perspectives, I've built a career on connecting the dots in unexpected ways, and I've leaned into facts proven by research and known to behavioral scientists that establish how a brand experience makes us feel has an outsized impact on our desire for that brand.

Throughout this book, you've come to understand why the ongoing pursuit of emotional insights matters so much, and that our instinctive emotional responses triggered subconsciously in the limbic part of our brain often have a cascading effect on what we feel and do next. Naturally, we gravitate toward things that make us feel good, and away from things that make us feel bad. This means that the smallest details of how a brand presents itself can have a substantial impact on whether we are interested in, or ignore, that brand going forward.

You may recall from Chapter 3 that Limbic Sparks Brand Strategy is all about the collection and distillation of emotional insights. In Focus, we collected insights. In Connect, we distilled insights into a specific and thoughtful brand strategy. Now, in Evolve, we dig back into the well of insights to activate the brand strategy by using specific details that we discovered to evolve Brand Expression & Experiences.

FIGURE 7.1 Discovery and Activation of Emotional Insights

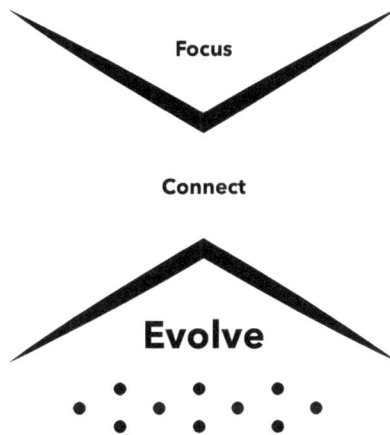

Focus

Connect

Evolve

NOTE In Evolve, we build on the foundation we set in Connect, and bring back specific details that we discovered in Focus to support development of Brand Expression & Experiences.

It's Time to Evolve

Brand Expression is how your brand communicates through visuals, sounds, and words. Each of these areas of focus must be thoughtfully designed and informed by your brand strategy so that they come together as one cohesive Brand Experience.

As brand leader Gregg Heard once said to me, "Behind every great brand experience is strong design." (Limbic Brand Evolution, 2021) That's why it's always a good idea to set aside resources and budget for evolving your Brand Expression when you're evolving your Brand Strategy. You'll want to work with professionals who you can trust to bring your brand to life—writers and visual and sonic identity designers. My favorite people to work with in these fields are those who are wonderfully talented, who respect brand strategy, who are collaborative, who are willing to carry over brand equity that is working, and who come up with ideas for how to activate brand strategy in ways I couldn't have imagined on my own.

Brand leader Amy Belledin, who grew up on the creative side of the business, once said to me, "If you want a creative team to develop amazing creative ideas, you have to let them do what they are best at, and trust that they are going to come back to you with some really incredible ideas and approaches to solving the problem or challenge that you've outlined" (Limbic Brand Evolution, 2022).

Your primary objective now should be to Evolve the three pillars of Brand Expression so they are in sync with your evolved brand strategy and lead to Brand Experiences that will ignite people's interest in what your brand has to offer.

Three Pillars of Brand Expression

THREE PILLARS OF BRAND EXPRESSION

1 Visual Identity

2 Sonic Identity

3 Brand Messaging

These three pillars guide the way your brand communicates through visuals, sounds, and words. The brand guidelines and assets that come out of Evolve will help you activate your brand so that it feels like it was designed for the people it is for and increase the odds of catching their attention and earning their business. What follows are important considerations for each.

Visual Identity

Your brand's Visual Identity is the guidelines and assets for how your brand looks—including your brand logo, colors, fonts, icons, illustrations, photography, and more. It's the core elements of a cohesive system that enable your brand to have a flexible, yet consistent look and feel.

Visual Identity

The guidelines and assets for how your brand looks.

Your Brand Idea and your Brand Personality & Voice Traits play a large role in informing your brand's visual identity. When creating or evolving your Visual Identity, you'll want to consider, along with your designer, the best way to express the brand so that it sparks positive feelings and conveys details about your brand that are consistent with your brand strategy. This includes retaining visual equities that are currently working well and evolving what needs to evolve so that it better reflects where you're taking the brand.

For the AT&T Performing Arts Center, the Brand Idea shifted from "Staging the Amazing" to "Yours to Discover." As such, we shifted the Visual Identity of the brand from one that felt high end and corporate, to one that is warm and welcoming. We introduced warmer colors, friendlier fonts, and fleshed out the Visual Identity system to solve a variety of brand and marketing challenges.

For Blue Ridge, the "Be Supply Chain Invincible" Brand Idea and the Brand Personality Traits—Confident, Enthusiastic, and Empowering—helped us know it was time to evolve the brand's Visual Identity. We recognized that the current identity was a solid foundation, but we evolved it to better reflect the brand we now wanted to project. We dialed up the use of their orange-yellow accent color to bring more vibrancy and energy. We introduced a bold typeface for the Brand Idea and other top-level headlines to convey more confidence and enthusiasm. We evolved the photography style, so that stock photo selections felt more cohesive, authentic, and proprietary.

Sonic Identity

Your brand's Sonic Identity is the guidelines and assets for how your brand sounds. It includes your sonic logo (an audio complement to your visual logo), a sonic anthem (a brand theme that gives you an overall feeling for the brand's story and personality), user experience sounds (sounds that correspond to actions in a digital environment), and guidance for non-proprietary music selection, such as licensed music for ads, in-store music, or call center on-hold music.

> **Sonic Identity**
>
> The guidelines and assets for how your brand sounds.

You may be thinking, I don't have a Sonic Identity. The fact is, most brands don't—and, for many types of businesses, it's a mistake not to have guidelines and assets to inform how your brand sounds. Sound has an impact on how people feel during their experience with your brand, whether you pay attention to these details or not. It's also true that sound affects us subconsciously first and we may not even realize the positive or negative impact it's having.

In your own experience, I suspect you play music to put yourself in a certain mood or state of mind. For me, sometimes it's high-energy music, and sometimes it's calming music. I like to say that I play music to match or take me to the mood I want to be in. Next time you're waiting on hold too long, pay attention to the sound being playing while you wait. Is it mindless and calming? If so, you probably wouldn't have consciously thought about it, and it helps you pass the time. On the other hand, is it high-energy and chaotic? If so, and you're eager to resolve whatever you're calling about, then it's probably triggering some level of anxiousness and impatience. Or is what you're listening to a short loop of music and announcements that repeat over and over? If so, then it's probably causing you to think about how long you've been waiting—every time it loops, you're reminded that you're still waiting. Is it silent? Then you're probably wondering if you've been disconnected. These small details—what sound plays while you wait on hold—have a significant impact on how you feel while waiting, and perhaps the mood you're in when you finally speak with a person.

Whether it's your customer service on-hold music, the overhead music people hear in your branded spaces, the sounds that come from your product or mobile app, or the music and sounds in your ads, these are important details that you want to consider as part of your brand evolution, to ensure that they set the right tone for how you want people to feel.

Brand Messaging

Brand Messaging is the words and language style your brand uses to communicate with people. This includes everything from the brand tagline to the press release boilerplate copy. It includes every word on your brand's website and every word in your brand's social media posts. It includes what's said in the new employee onboarding presentation and what salespeople say to prospective customers. It includes your advertising copy and your customer service communication protocols. The more interactions and touchpoints your brand has with people, the more you'll want to be sure that your brand messaging is consistently conveyed and reflects your brand strategy.

> **Brand Messaging**
>
> The words and language style your brand uses when communicating with people.

This is not to say that every word said needs to be scripted. No one wants your brand language to be unnatural or feel like it was written by a robot. In fact, completely the opposite—your brand language should feel human, real, relevant, and engaging. Your interactions with people should feel natural, one-to-one, and they should demonstrate that you care. To achieve this, there needs to be a combination of brand guidelines and flexibility, and there needs to be an understanding of what the people who you are communicating with care about.

Your objective for Brand Messaging is to evolve the current words being used across your brand touchpoints with words that are a better reflection of your evolved brand strategy. Whether that entails edits to what you already have or complete re-writes depends on the gap between your brand strategy and your current brand messaging.

When I'm doing this work, I'll often go back to my detailed Insights Discovery findings presentation, print pages, and pin them to the wall as reference. It helps me recall the many nuggets of detail that will now make their way into the words a brand uses to spark desire.

Writing Brand Messaging starts with developing tools to compile details you or your copywriters should reference so that the words and writing style your brand uses consistently reflect the brand strategy.

Brand Messaging Toolkit

> **Brand Messaging Toolkit**
>
> - Customer Personas
> - Brand Messaging Hierarchy
> - Brand Messaging Style Guide

Customer Personas

The first step when creating your brand messaging toolkit is to create your primary Customer Personas. You may have worked with customer personas in the past, and perhaps it was a bit daunting. Many times, when working with clients, they share with me customer persona work they've done in the past. It often includes six or more customer types, fake names, a stereotypical stock photo, and made-up profile details. Often there's a list of products and services that would appeal to them, and sometimes a list of their concerns and priorities.

This outdated style of personas come out of a traditional brand strategy approach that includes surface-level and broadly known details about customer types that lack the kind of deeper-level emotional insights that you get from Limbic Sparks Brand Strategy.

Customer Personas

Insightful descriptions of like-minded customer segments that highlight the emotional motivations of each in the context of your offering.

Limbic Sparks Brand Strategy is all about the refining of ideas to get them down to the most specific and important details, especially when it comes to emotional insight. This includes removing layers of information that are not helpful. As such, when it comes to Customer Personas, I'm a proponent of fewer personas that aggregate what we've discovered about segments of people who have similar motivations.

For Blue Ridge, the brand you read about in Chapter 6, you may recall that we identified two primary Customer Personas: C-Suite Decision Makers and Users of the Software. We could have created many more customer personas, including the variety of C-suite executives (CEO, CTO, CFO, etc.) and the variety of Users of the Software (Demand Planners, Supply Planners, Procurement Specialists, etc.). However, in the spirit of simplifying complexity, we agreed to focus on two personas: The C-Suite Decision Makers who need to approve the capital investment for the purchase based on an anticipated return on investment to the company, and the Users of the Software, who we want to advocate for the benefits it will bring to their work and the company at large.

Once there's agreement on the primary Customer Persona segments, my approach is to write a short paragraph for each that reveals a very deep understanding of what makes them tick. I pack it with insight and leave out a lot of obvious or generic information that is more of a distraction than it is helpful.

For Blue Ridge, this is what we wrote about each of their primary Customer Personas:

C-Level Executives are focused on increasing revenue and profits and reducing expenses for their company. They recognize the importance of always having items in stock to serve customers, but they question the amount of cash tied up in inventory. For some, the cashflow challenge is a threat to their company's existence. If anyone has a proven solution that can solve this challenge, their ears are wide open—especially if it will pay for itself. Nothing would make them happier than having optimal inventory levels to never disappoint customers while the cost of inventory decreases and cashflow increases.

Users of the Software are tasked with estimating optimal inventory levels to meet demand. They are in the unenviable position of having to be right all the time and often missing the mark. They must anticipate demand of thousands of SKUs across multiple locations and with seasonal variations. It's a no-win situation. They would like nothing better than to be as accurate as everyone wants them to be. They want to have greater insight and confidence in their purchase recommendations so they can meet demand without going way overboard. If there's a way to get this right so they can always deliver good news, not bad, they're interested.

You can see how these personas are written concisely and include very specific emotional insights that should be top of mind when writing brand messaging for either of these audiences. For example, when discovering emotional insights about the C-level executives we heard their concerns about company cashflow and profitability. Some shared that before working with Blue Ridge they were on the verge of bankruptcy. We also found out that they are reluctant to sink more cash into capital expenditures that will take a long time to have a return on the investment. Through our understanding of those significant emotional concerns, we were able to address them head on, and in specific detail, as opposed to touting vague or broader benefits that would not capture their attention as well.

Similarly, for the Users of the Software, we discovered their emotional challenge of being in a "no win" situation and being wrong more often than they are right. This specific emotional insight played a big role in us moving toward a message to convey how, with Blue Ridge, they can eliminate guesswork and be right much more often.

It's this detailed understanding that led to "Improving Planning Precision" as the Shared Emotional Motivation, and the "Be Supply Chain Invincible" Brand Idea. Customer Personas written with this depth of insight will enable you to write Brand Messaging that directly addresses emotional drivers to capture the attention of the customers you want to attract.

Brand Messaging Hierarchy

As you're figuring out, Limbic Sparks Brand strategy is packed with insight, yet it should not be complex or verbose. It's all about distilling a lot of information down to the most essential components. When developing your brand strategy in Connect, you distilled a lot of Insights Discovery information down to three Core Brand Benefits. Even if you serve multiple audiences, those same benefits are designed to apply to each. Now, as part of creating your Brand Messaging toolkit, we'll bring further dimension with sub-benefits that apply more specifically to each of your primary Customer Personas.

To build out the details of the messaging, I suggest that you create a Brand Messaging Hierarchy with segment-specific brand benefit details. Once completed, it serves as a very concise reference to guide development of Brand Messaging across all touchpoints.

> **Brand Messaging Hierarchy**
>
> The overarching and Core Brand Benefits and sub-benefits that are most emotionally motivating for each Core Customer segment.

It's important to remember that this hierarchy is to outline emotional benefits, not the product or service offering features. Certainly, the benefits are a result of those offerings, but the style of writing here is in the form of benefits that matter most to the people your brand serves—the "reasons to care."

The Brand Messaging Hierarchy format includes references to the Shared Emotional Motivation and the Brand Idea. It includes the Core Brand Benefits across the top, and the Customer Personas down the side.

Going back to Blue Ridge, and to share that as an example, we identified three Core Brand Benefits and two primary Customer Personas:

- Eliminate Guesswork, Maximize Inventory Performance, Unmatched Partnership
- C-Suite Decision Makers and Users of the Software

TABLE 7.1 Limbic Sparks Brand Messaging Hierarchy

**Limbic Sparks
Brand Messaging Hierarchy**

Shared Emotional Motivation: _____

Brand Idea: _____

	Core Benefit #1	Core Benefit #2	Core Benefit #3
Customer Persona #1	• Sub-benefit • Sub-benefit • Sub-benefit	• Sub-benefit • Sub-benefit • Sub-benefit	• Sub-benefit • Sub-benefit • Sub-benefit
Customer Persona #2	• Sub-benefit • Sub-benefit • Sub-benefit	• Sub-benefit • Sub-benefit • Sub-benefit	• Sub-benefit • Sub-benefit • Sub-benefit

Those are the three benefits that are consistently highlighted across brand touchpoints—the ones you'll most likely feature on the website home page and in other prominent places. However, those benefits alone are not enough to communicate all the specific details of what will be emotionally motivating to new customers. Now it's time to be more specific about sub-benefits in each of those categories.

The next step entails filling in the hierarchy with specific emotional benefits for each customer segment that corresponds to each Core Brand Benefit. It's also where you'll want to go back to all your Insights Discovery work to mine for what's most important in support of the Core Brand Benefits.

Table 7.2 shows a portion of what's included in the Blue Ridge Brand Messaging Hierarchy so you can see how the sub-benefits bring further dimension to the core benefit, and are specific to each segment.

It's likely that when developing the original set of Core Brand Benefits, you had many of these sub-benefits in mind. Often during brand strategy development, I'll have all these benefits listed, categorize them, and give each category an all-encompassing overarching benefit. I'll then save my notes for developing the Brand Messaging Hierarchy later. Many times, I'll also run workshops with my clients to share drafts of the sub-benefits and get their feedback, until we all agree that the full set of primary and sub-benefits is the best representation of what people appreciate most about how the brand makes their life better. Again, it's not about what the brand team wants to say, it's about what is most relevant and compelling for customers.

TABLE 7.2 Blue Ridge Brand Messaging Hierarchy (abbreviated)

Blue Ridge Brand Messaging Hierarchy (abbreviated)

Shared Emotional Motivation: *Improving Planning Precision*
Brand Idea: *Be Supply Chain Invincible*

	Eliminate Guesswork	Maximize Inventory Performance	Unmatched Partnership
C-Suite Decision Makers	• Faster More & More Accurate Planning • Empower Teams to Make Better Decisions	• Right Sizes Inventory • Fast ROI Pays for Itself	• Simplifies Buying Complexity • Deepens Buying/ Planning Knowledge
Users of the Software [*Partial list of Benefits for Illustration Purposes Only*]	• Actionable Insights & Buying Recommendations • Always Be Prepared & In Control	• Feature-Packed & Flexible • Frees up time	• One-to-One Training & Support • Makes Job Easier

The Brand Messaging Hierarchy becomes a great reference tool for anyone writing for your brand. As part of my work with clients, I've written or re-written entire brand websites using a one-page Brand Messaging Hierarchy as a guide for what to say. It can be used as a reference for all forms of brand messaging.

Brand Messaging Style Guide

Your Brand Messaging Style Guide should include a set of writing dos and don'ts, informed by your brand strategy. Beyond the specifics that are related to your brand, I suggest including two things that should be part of any brand messaging style guide: "Write in the first person" so you're talking to your reader, not about them, and "Avoid cliché language and business jargon" that just makes your brand sound like so many other brands.

Brand Messaging Style Guide

The dos and don'ts that guide your brand messaging.

Here are two examples of Brand Messaging Guidelines for brands that you have become familiar with in this book.

For the AT&T Performing Arts Center, with the Brand Idea "Yours to Discover," we created the following Brand Messaging guidelines:

Do:

- be welcoming and inviting—to reinforce that everyone is welcome
- be enthusiastic and passionate—to convey passion for all there is to enjoy and discover
- be friendly and informative—to appeal to all audiences by speaking in plain language

Don't:

- be too formal
- be too distant
- be too much about us

For Blue Ridge, here are some examples that we included:

Do:

- Focus on positive outcomes—ex: "Go from educated guesses to meeting demand without going over."
- Write in the first person—ex: "We'll stand by you, so you can Be Supply Chain Invincible."

Don't:

- Focus on the negative or use fear tactics—ex: "We know how disruptive the implementation of a new software platform can be."
- Write in the third person—ex: "Relentlessly focused on customer success."

When you write your Brand Messaging Style Guide, be sure that it includes specific details that you want writers to focus on so that your brand messaging is clear, consistent, and reflective of your brand strategy.

Prioritizing Desirable Brand Experiences

Beyond evolving your Brand Expression, you also want to look for ways to improve your Brand Experience. Brand Experience is the overall impression that people have with your brand. It's the coming together of your brand's visuals, sounds, and words at every brand touchpoint.

You should consider the individual details of your Brand Experience and think about how they all work together cohesively to help people feel the way they want to feel in every interaction. What follows are some examples of Brand Experiences I've had where the details set them apart, for better or for worse.

How Are You Treated?

In your own experience, I suspect there are brands you actively engage with that bring both value and enjoyment to your life, and others that bring frustration. Think about the relationship you have with some professional service providers—accountants, lawyers, financial advisors. Like many brands, there are many choices of people who can do the work they do. Certainly, their level of skill and experience is an important factor, but how they communicate with you is another. Whether through conversation or written correspondence, they may come across as friendly, helpful, interested in you, and that will make you feel cared for and valued. Some of these professionals are cold, seem disinterested, perhaps have a bit of an attitude, and make you feel more like a burden than a valued customer. How they communicate with you, your experience with them, and how that makes you feel, has a big impact on your desire to do business with them again.

I probably shouldn't reveal this, but sometimes when looking for a professional to work with, I meet someone and immediately there are Limbic Sparks. From that point forward my mind jumps to "I hope their fee is reasonable," because I already know I'm going to hire them. After that point, my day-to-day experience working with them lets me know if my initial instincts were right, and if there are still Limbic Sparks.

More Sell Than Solve?

Sometimes our experience with a brand takes a negative turn when they have not fully considered the effect of their Brand Messaging. One example that comes to mind for me is when I was purchasing my second pair of a popular running shoe. To save a bit of money, I was checking out several on- and offline stores to buy them, including the manufacturer's online store. While on their website, I opted into a prompt for "free shipping and offers" and put the shoes in my cart. Before making the purchase, I wanted to see what offers I'd get over the next few days. Regardless, I was inclined to buy directly from the manufacturer because the prices were similar everywhere. Limbic Sparks ignited for me with this brand when using the product, so I wanted them to benefit directly from my purchase of a second pair.

Then, over the next week, I got two emails a day, as if the previous day's reminders weren't enough. They contained pressure-filled messages with the following subject lines: "The item in your cart can sell out," "Last chance to get free shipping," and "Your cart is waiting." These emails included details about discounts, but unfortunately not ones that were valid on the shoes I was considering and had put in my shopping cart. Throughout the week they did not send me a single email that tried to be helpful—only typical sales tactics, twice a day. This was such a turn-off that I unsubscribed from their emails. Then, I bought the same exact shoes at Zappos for the same amount of money, including the free shipping that Zappos always offers.

Zappos, always known for attention to detail in their customer experience, sends emails that are friendly and helpful. Once, when I left an item in my cart at Zappos, their no-pressure follow-up email had the friendly subject line, "We see what you did there…" followed by the question "Looking for something?" and a message reminding me of their free shipping and free 365 day return policy, with a phone number to call for assistance if needed. After I made this purchase at Zappos, emails came with enthusiastic messaging that made me feel valued and excited. The subject lines included the following messages: "Hey, thanks for your order," "Ship, Ship, Hooray. Your order has shipped," and "Beep Beep! Your order's been delivered."

The Zappos brand purpose is simply "to live and deliver WOW." They certainly live up to that in their Brand Experience, and for me, there are Limbic Sparks. Now, Zappos is my first stop for buying shoes (Zappos, n.d.).

Is It Annoying?

Another example of how details impact brand desire is in the home appliance category. They all have sounds—some are pleasant and some are annoying. Now, on the rare occasion when my wife and I shop for appliances, we pay attention to the sounds they make, as those sounds become the soundscape of our home. I can tell you that there are appliance brands we did not buy because of their sound.

This question "is it annoying?" can extend to so many other product and service categories and impact our desire to do business with a brand. I'll bet you can think of a few instances of brand experiences that became annoying enough to walk away from.

Do the Details Make You Smile?

Are you familiar with Cutco? Their Brand Idea is, "American-Made Knives. Guaranteed Forever." I've had a set of Cutco knives for a long time. Years after purchase, I learned that they offer free knife sharpening to Cutco knife owners—included in their "Forever Guarantee." All you need to do is set it up on their website, mail the knives to them, and they come back sharpened a couple weeks later. I was a bit reluctant to send my beloved knives through the mail, and I was pleasantly surprised that Cutco anticipated my emotional concerns and addressed them in their Brand Experience (Cutco, n.d.).

After registering, I received an email that included confirmation, shipping details, and a video showing how to pack the knives safely. A few days after shipping the knives I received an email with the subject line "Your Cutco is now being serviced!" The email included a visual that resembled a postcard and an illustration of a Cutco knife sitting on a lounge chair on a sandy beach. The message on the postcard said, "I'm enjoying all the attention!" and the rest of the email provided confirmation that my knives were received along with contact details to reach the product care supervisor if needed.

The next day I received another email with the subject line, "Your Cutco is on its way home!" It included a tracking number and nice note about how the product care team took care of my knives, and a video titled, "What happened during your Cutco's visit?" This adorable video, shot from the knife's perspective, shows the knife being packaged, arriving at Cutco and being unboxed, sharpened, and repackaged. The video ends with a title card that says "Home Sweet Home" and the sound of a doorbell. Talk about a brand that has thought through every detail of the experience. Limbic Sparks ignited, even more than before!

Does Your Experience Re-Set Your Expectations For the Category?

Have you experienced Trader Joe's? This US grocery store chain is known for its emotionally appealing brand experience. It starts with their curated selection of private label unique and high-quality food items spanning many international cuisines. It continues into their meticulously designed use of language, signage, overhead music, product packaging, and signature Hawaiian shirts.

In store, their signs are most often on a chalkboard look with colorful handwritten messages, prices, and pictures. For example, I've seen a sign that says, "Feeling adventurous? Check out our NEW ITEMS? We search high and low to bring you exciting new products!" It included an illustration of a hot air balloon to bring forward the adventure theme. One other example, promoting feta cheese, had an illustration of a block of feta cheese wearing sunglasses, lying on a towel on the beach with a palm tree. The headline said, "It doesn't get feta than this!" On their website, the About Us page says, "Simply put, every time a customer shops with us, we want them to be able to say, 'Wow! That was enjoyable, and I got a great deal. I look forward to coming back!'" (Trader Joe's, n.d.).

For my family, going to Trader Joe's is not just going grocery shopping, it's a family event. It's something we look forward to and enjoy doing together. Their attention to detail not only leads to an enthusiastic customer base, but one that grows through word of mouth and social media communities, not advertising. Trader Joe's is a wonderful example of a brand that creates Limbic Sparks for so many people, thanks to consideration of so many details that make for a category-redefining experience. It's also clear that if your brand is about delivering "Wow," you're setting an expectation among your customers, and for the way you approach Brand Experience.

It's About How You Make People Feel

As you think about evolving the experiences people have with your brand, it's important to consider the emotional context of each interaction. You can ask the following questions when evaluating how to design and improve specific Brand Experiences:

- How are people feeling as they enter the experience?
- How do they want to feel at different moments during the experience?
- What is the feeling that you want to be sure people have at the end of the experience?

An Ongoing Evolution

I'm hopeful that you've been inspired by the opportunities ahead for your brand. If you're feeling this way, know that this book is having an impact on you, and that you'll be even better able to lead your team to ignite Limbic Sparks for your brand. Limbic Sparks Brand Strategy is not just a set of frameworks and steps, it's a philosophical approach that can become muscle memory for how you continue to evolve your brand over time. You can use that muscle memory to stay in tune with customer motivations and how the details of your Brand Expression & Experiences can continue to be fine-tuned.

"It's the responsibility of any brand leader to constantly try to improve, to make your product and experience remarkable, and to try and express what you do in a better way, each and every day." That's what brand leader Jonathan Rosen once said to me, and I couldn't agree more (Limbic Brand Evolution, 2023).

For a brand to consistently be relevant and desirable, it takes a brand leader who is always curious and responsive to new consumer insights and marketplace dynamics as they emerge, and applying those insights to how their brand ignites interest and sparks desire.

Once you truly understand what matters most to your customers and prioritize how they want to feel, there might be many things about your Brand Experience that you'll want to evolve. Remember that brand development is an ongoing evolution, and Rome, as they say, was not built in a day.

Looking Ahead

We're setting high standards for Brand Expression & Experiences, and I have no doubt that you're seeing how small details can have a big impact. In the next two chapters I'll share in detail about how Limbic Sparks Brand Strategy helped two brands evolve and differentiate themselves. As you keep reading, you'll read about a variety of ways in which evolved Brand Expression & Experiences can be specifically designed to ignite interest and spark ongoing brand desire.

Brand Leadership Considerations

In your own life, are you more open to buying something when it fits with your personal sense of style?

We all have a personal sense of style. It's why there are so many choices in the world, why we don't always wear a uniform, why our homes all look different on the inside, and why we have so much variety in retail stores and restaurants. We bring things into our life that meet our personal criteria for what's good, and we avoid what doesn't feel like it's right for us.

In your work with brands, do you experience the brand from your customer's perspective?

It's the smallest details that have the biggest impact. Perhaps it's the music playing while people wait on hold. It could be how easy or difficult it is to return a purchase. It could even be how people feel when they read the subject line of an email from your brand. When it doesn't feel right, we are not eager to return. However, when you pay attention to the details, and design every interaction to appeal to the sensibilities of your customers, it will go a long way toward endearing them to your brand.

Here are three things you can start doing today:

1   Consider your brand experience from the perspective of a customer.

2   Only work with consultants, agencies, designers, and writers who are more focused on creating highly desirable customer interactions, versus winning creative awards.

3   Set high standards for the brand experience you're responsible for.

References

Cutco (n.d.) The Forever Guarantee, www.cutco.com

Eames, C (n.d.) Brainy Quote, www.brainyquote.com/quotes/charles_eames_169188 (archived at https://perma.cc/6UVG-4B2R)

Limbic Brand Evolution (2021) Let's Talk Limbic Sparks Podcast – episode 7, Creating Brand Desire Through Design with Gregg Heard, 7 October, www.limbicbrandevolution.com/podcast/gregg-heard-sage-lets-talk-limbic-sparks-7 (archived at https://perma.cc/G7QB-FJK4)

Limbic Brand Evolution (2022) Let's Talk Limbic Sparks Podcast – episode 16, Elevating Creative Leadership in Marketing with Amy Belledin, 15 August, www.limbicbrandevolution.com/podcast/amy-belledin-lets-talk-limbic-sparks-16 (archived at https://perma.cc/NC6G-CLX8)

Limbic Brand Evolution (2023) Let's Talk Limbic Sparks Podcast – episode 24, Guiding Brand Evolution with a Relational Mindset, 10 April, www.limbicbrandevolution.com/podcast/jonathan-rosen-lets-talk-limbic-sparks-24 (archived at https://perma.cc/66XF-H9HP)

Portale, E (2021) I tried it: How much hype does the iconic Eames chair really deserve?, *Architectural Digest*, 1 November, www.architecturaldigest.com/story/eames-lounge-chair-review (archived at https://perma.cc/VQ4U-LCDH)

Trader Joe's (n.d.) About Us, www.traderjoes.com/home/about-us (archived at https://perma.cc/9YKA-2PNY)

Zappos (n.d.) About Us, www.zappos.com/c/about (archived at https://perma.cc/4454-XYNH)

08

Amplifying the Most Compelling Brand Benefits

Scratch Event DJs Case Study

"If you need a female punk rock DJ in Albuquerque, we have two. But we need to do a better job of attracting new customers and we're not sure how."

When Rob Principe and I first met, he shared that with me. We talked about how current customers are very loyal, but customer acquisition efforts could be better. Rob is Founder and CEO of Scratch Music Group, the world's leader for DJ Booking and Education, which he co-founded in 2002 with the late and legendary Jam Master Jay of Run-D.M.C. (Scratch Music Group, n.d.). The Scratch Music Group includes Scratch DJ Academy, which has taught over 500,000 aspiring DJs and producers worldwide. It also includes Scratch Event DJs, with over 7,600 highly screened DJs. They have DJ'd over 125,000 events in 35 countries on six continents, for over 1,500 corporate customers. Many of their customers work in sports, retail, hospitality, or any other corporations that put on events, or for ad agencies and trade show producers that support corporate brands (Scratch Event DJs, n.d.).

Even though Scratch Event DJs has such a vast scale and is unmatched competitively, they faced the same brand challenge as many other service-based businesses. Rob and his team were eager for more corporate customers to recognize and appreciate the unique value of their services, and to think of Scratch whenever they produce an event. Rob's ambition for our brand evolution work was to be able to convey more clearly and compellingly why Scratch Event DJs should be seen as the resource for any corporation putting on an event.

My job for Scratch Event DJs was to help them refresh their Brand Strategy and Brand Expression so that they could become an instinctively desirable partner among corporations that entertain guests. As with many brand leaders who I work with, the Scratch team already had a great product and service offering, but they were not getting the broad recognition that we all knew was possible.

Focus

We started our work together in a way that you're probably becoming familiar with. It began with a kick-off meeting that included the Scratch leadership team, me, and the GreyBox Creative team, Vincent Fatato and Remo Strada. We talked about the Limbic Sparks Brand Strategy approach, and how we use emotional insights that come from the brand team and customer to shed light on how to set the brand apart. We also used our first meeting to discuss topics such as "Why is this brand evolution so important?" and "What do you wish more people knew about Scratch?"

Brand and Category Dynamics

Throughout Insights Discovery we considered the Brand and Category Dynamics. We understood that DJs can be found everywhere, and that with the technology that exists, anyone can call themselves a DJ. That said, quality levels vary greatly. There's a big difference between someone who can DJ off a playlist, and someone who can guide and change the energy of a room. We came to understand that not all DJs are qualified to be part of the Scratch DJ network, and how high their quality standards are.

For years, their primary brand messaging was focused on the ROI of hiring a DJ for events. The logic behind this brand messaging was based on research that proves that the right music makes events more enjoyable for guests, increases the time they stay at the event, encourages guests to spend more, and fuels their desire to return. Thus, the investment in hiring a DJ

We also learned a lot about how Scratch had been approaching Brand Messaging. Marketing materials and their website emphasized the size of their DJ network, that they've been around since 2002, and the return on investment (ROI) of hiring a DJ. Their Brand Idea was *Growth Through Music*, which was supported by the following at the top of their website: *We tap the power of music to drive sales, engage customers, and increase brand awareness.*

would pay for itself because of increased sales. It was both an accurate and rational brand message, but we sought to discover why it was not driving more new business.

Brand Team and Customer Interviews

In addition to many discussions, I conducted individual interviews with Scratch team members.

I asked questions such as:

- What are the three best things that Scratch does for its customers?
- How do you want customers to feel when working with Scratch?
- What are some common misconceptions about DJs?
- What are customers most surprised by when they start working with Scratch?
- If Scratch was a superhero, what would be its superpower?

From these questions and others, I heard a lot about the attention to detail that the Scratch team brings to every customer relationship and every event. I heard about how they are motivated to make sure that their customers have great experiences. They take their responsibility of being trusted by their customers to create great experiences for their brands very seriously. Simultaneously, I heard about how they are also very serious about elevating the artistry and craft of DJing, and that they take great pride in running the Scratch DJ Academy to help aspiring DJs excel in their work.

Next, I got the perspective of DJs who are part of the Scratch DJ Network. I asked questions such as:

- As a DJ, what are the top three reasons that you work with Scratch?
- What do you think is most important to customers who hire Scratch DJs?
- How are Scratch customers different from those who use other ways to hire a DJ?
- What are the top three reasons for a corporate customer to work with Scratch?
- If Scratch was a superhero, what would be its superpower?

I felt it was super important to get the DJ perspective, since they are the people who represent Scratch at the events, and they have direct contact with Scratch customers during the event, as well as the guests those customers are hosting. It also helped me understand more about the business of being a DJ from people who work at events booked through Scratch, and those booked directly with the DJ.

As we moved into conducting customer interviews, we sought to learn more about their experience, and what they value most in their relationship with Scratch. I asked question such as:

- How does hiring a DJ fit into your overall job responsibilities?
- When hiring a DJ, what's most important to you?
- If Scratch was no longer your source for DJs, what would you miss the most?
- What are three words to describe how working with Scratch makes you feel?
- If Scratch was a superhero, what would be its superpower?

What we learned was both revealing and inspiring to the Scratch team. We learned that they hire Scratch primarily because it gives them confidence that they will have a super-energized event, and that hiring Scratch makes their life easier. Time and time again, the customers I spoke with raved about the quality of the DJs, the great experiences they have working with the Scratch team, and that overall, working with Scratch gives them one less thing to worry about when they are planning an event. They appreciate working with professionals who anticipate their needs, and they noted that not all DJs come with their level of skill or professionalism. When it came to the brand's superpower, some of what we hear included: *Mind Reader*, *Being Fast*, *Professionalism*, and *Creating Good Vibes*.

Surprisingly, the ROI of hiring a DJ, the core selling point they'd been using to date, did not come up in our customer discussions. Rob and the team were thrilled to learn that their success at providing high-quality DJs and great customer experiences was highly valued. They also recognized that their Brand Messaging focus was not as compelling as they had thought. Rob shared with me: "We felt like we understood our brand, but I'm not sure we really did understand our brand because of our own confirmation bias."

To conclude the Insights Discovery phase of work, we developed a Shared Emotional Motivation, and a new way for the Scratch team to think about what both they and their customers are striving to achieve individually and with each other:

Experiences that Keep People Coming Back for More.

This Shared Emotional Motivation has multiple meanings of equal importance. It conveys the Scratch team's motivation to consistently provide DJs for events in ways that are so easy, seamless, and high quality, that Scratch is hired again and again whenever this company has an event. It also conveys their customers' motivation to put on events that are so enjoyable for everyone that the feelings of attendees for that brand are elevated, and they want to return to that brand again and again.

This Shared Emotional Motivation became the first bookend of our brand strategy.

Connect

During the Connect phase, we worked together to hone very specific language for the other brand strategy components. But first, there was one important thing that Rob and his team wanted to address—their brand name.

Most of the time during a brand evolution, the brand name is not something you change. Occasionally, however, you recognize an opportunity to make a shift that will increase clarity. As we were on the verge of evolving the brand's expression across visual identity and messaging, it was the right time for making a brand name change, if there was going to be one.

When we started the project, the Scratch Music Group had two entities: Scratch DJ Academy and Scratch Events. It was felt by all of us that Scratch Events lacked clarity on its own. Rob had received feedback over the years that people were sometimes unsure about the scope of their capabilities when it came to producing events. The task was to make a small shift in the brand name to clarify its focus on being a source for DJs.

You may be surprised to know that this subtle but important shift in the brand name led to a lot of discussion. It was among the most important details that we needed to get right. During our exploratory we considered over a dozen variations of the name, and ultimately we landed on *Scratch Event DJs*. We liked that it carried forward the equity of the original name, while bringing the DJ focus front and center.

Core Brand Benefits

You may recall from earlier in the chapter that the "ROI of hiring a DJ" was the core brand benefit Scratch had been using. What we discovered during the Focus phase was that there are several more compelling reasons why customers choose to work with Scratch. These insights gave us an opportunity to prioritize Brand Messaging around the most compelling benefits, and ones that would also be more proprietary.

It led us to three Core Brand Benefits:

Incredible Client Service, Largest DJ Network, Amazing Event Experiences

You'll see in the Evolve section of this chapter how we brought more specificity to each of those benefits for customers, using the Brand Messaging Hierarchy.

Brand Personality Traits

You may have noticed that the Scratch team take their work very seriously. They are serious about providing great experiences and they are serious about having high-quality DJs. That came through in their Brand Expression. The Scratch team recognized that the professionalism that they bring to their work was coming through loud and clear in their brand expression, but they needed to better amplify the vibrancy and enthusiasm that they also bring to events.

It led us to the following Brand Personality Traits:

Easy, Professional and Energizing

Those three Brand Personality traits, which are already authentic to their Brand Experiences, work together to create a better balance to guide Brand Expression.

Brand Idea and Brand Positioning

As I've shared before, the process of developing a Brand Idea includes the ideation of a lot of potential territories and words. For me, it starts informally during Focus, when I'm capturing notes of insights, soundbites, and ideas that I collect throughout the process. I park those thoughts until Insights Discovery is completed, and then go into a period of ideation and refinement.

When it comes time to share Brand Ideas with my clients, I usually share a few possible territories that correspond to the Core Brand Benefits. The approach was no different for Scratch. We discussed Brand Ideas that emphasized the *Incredible Client Service* that customers get from working with Scratch. We explored ideas that emphasized the scale of the brand's

Largest DJ Network. We also explored ideas that emphasized the *Amazing Event Experiences* that Scratch makes possible.

In the end, our Brand Idea became one that brought together two of those benefits: *Incredible Client Service* and *Largest DJ Network*. We focused on those benefits because together they are competitively unmatched—what Scratch customers can't get anywhere else.

The Scratch Event DJs Brand Idea and Tagline became:

Curated DJs. Anytime. Anywhere.

Before landing on those exact words, however, we developed and considered a healthy list of options. Once we landed in that territory, we scrutinized every word. For the word *Curated* we considered alternatives like, High-Quality, Handpicked, and Vetted. For *Anytime. Anywhere* we considered alternatives like Always or Everywhere. As you can see, this process is a combination of art and science, and, once you choose the most compelling brand benefit territory, it's about getting to the words that feel right to everyone in the room.

We now had the second bookend of our brand strategy, and it was time to bring it all together with the following Brand Positioning Statement:

Scratch Event DJs is the go-to resource for DJs, anytime, anywhere, making it easy for you to consistently have energizing brand experiences that keep people coming back for more.

Evolve

Evolve, as you read in Chapter 7, is when we create Brand Expression & Experiences that address how people want to feel. Vincent and Remo from GreyBox Creative had been part of our discussions throughout brand strategy development. As we moved into Evolve, their visual identity and website design skills were central to the work ahead. Throughout this phase, and as I focused on Brand Messaging, we continued to work together to fine-tune every detail.

Visual Identity Evolution

As the GreyBox Creative team started their work, they held a kick-off discussion focused on challenges and opportunities with the current visual identity. This included discussion about what equities to consider retaining and what aspects of the current visual identity the brand team were happy to move on from. It also included several visual mood boards to elicit feedback on a range of color schemes, visual styles, and logo mark ideas to narrow the focus of which territories were most appealing.

Several inputs played an important role in guiding these discussions about visual identity evolution, including:

- The Brand Idea: *Curated DJs. Anytime. Anywhere.*
- The Brand Personality Traits: *Easy, Professional and Energizing.*
- Brand Equity: We had to consider visual identity elements that are part of the overall Scratch Music Group, such as typefaces, the use of black, and the use of a music-oriented logo mark for the Scratch DJ Academy. Its visual identity was not going to change, and we wanted to create a Scratch Event DJs logo that would demonstrate that they were part of the same family.

FIGURE 8.1 Existing Scratch DJ Academy Logo

NOTE This is the existing Scratch DJ Academy logo that we kept in mind when designing the Scratch Event DJs logo, knowing that they would be part of the same family, under the Scratch Music Group.

Remo shared a variety of approaches with the Scratch team throughout the process. His exploratory included variations on the logo typeface and a variety of logo mark ideas, such as turntable and music note images. Together with the Scratch team, we eliminated options until everyone gravitated toward the most preferred visual territory.

This territory included a logo mark of a stylized record player turntable. The way Remo designed it, you can feel the energy of a record spinning. Once this design idea was chosen, we continued to focus on the details—and every detail mattered. Remo shared several variations for how it could look until everyone on the Scratch team was happy. It was also designed to be used as a super-graphic in the visual identity system, as a holding shape for photos, or a background graphic on pages.

There was also an extensive exploration for the selection of colors and photography styles. In addition to creating the visual identity system, Remo provided layouts and templates for the website and collateral pieces, enabling the Scratch team to have everything they needed to apply the visual identity in-house.

One thing I respect most about the creative development process that Remo leads is his willingness to explore a wide range of ideas and details within those ideas. While he'd never present anything that he truly believes is a bad idea, he is meticulous about turning client feedback and preferences into great ideas, making him the kind of designer you want to work with.

The Scratch Event DJs Visual Identity is now a reflection of what the brand is all about. We created a Brand Expression that truly represents their high-quality and professional brand in a way that also expresses the energy that they bring to events for their customers.

FIGURE 8.2 Scratch Event DJs Logo Evolution

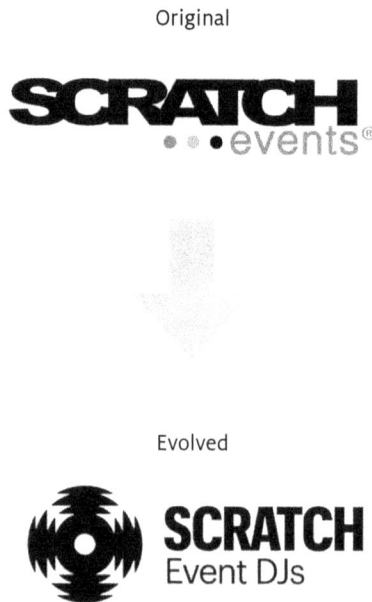

Original

Evolved

NOTE These logos represent that Scratch Event DJs brand evolution, including the name change.

Brand Messaging Evolution

While the Visual Identity work was underway, I was bringing further dimension to the Brand Messaging. Coming out of the Focus and Connect phases, we had so much insight to work with that we were eager to get started writing copy for this brand.

Before jumping into writing, however, we needed to set a few guidelines that you read about in Chapter 7: Primary Customer Personas, the Brand Messaging Hierarchy, and the Brand Messaging Style Guide. These guidelines would not only help us stay on point to address emotional insights, but they would also help any writing professionals who serve the brand to best reflect its brand strategy going forward. In this case, the Scratch team had the resources in-house to develop copy for the website and collateral pieces, and we wanted to be sure that they had documented guidelines to help them apply the evolved brand strategy and messaging.

In our guidelines, we shared a detailed summary of the primary Customer Personas. There are several distinct groups of Scratch customers, and our guidelines help the team keep what matters most to each group top of mind. (Yes, I'm being intentionally vague here due to client confidentiality.)

The next component of Brand Messaging guidelines is the Brand Messaging Hierarchy. Like you saw in Chapter 7, this is a one-page chart that highlights the Core Brand Benefits across the top, and the primary Customer Personas down the side. We fill in the grid with sub-benefits that are most meaningful for each segment. Sometimes there is a core set of sub-benefits that apply to all Customer Personas, followed by more detailed benefits that apply specifically to each persona—which is what we did with Scratch. Table 8.1 shows

TABLE 8.1 Scratch Event DJs Brand Messaging Hierarchy (abbreviated)

Scratch Event DJs
Brand Messaging Hierarchy (abbreviated)

Shared Emotional Motivation: *Experiences that Keep People Coming Back for More*
Brand Idea: *Curated DJs. Anytime. Anywhere.*

	Largest DJ Network	**Amazing Event Experiences**	**Incredible Client Service**
All Scratch Customers	• 7,600 Talented, Vetted Local Professionals	• Energized Customers & Guests	• Fast & Responsive
	• Covers All Regions, Styles, & Demographics	• Generates Buzz & Excitement	• Intuitively Understands Your Needs
	• Always A Backup Plan	• Success Made Easy for You & Your Team	• Proprietary Ops & Billing Portal
Specific Benefits for Specific Customer Personas Not Shown Here			

the top level—the benefits that apply to all personas. While you can imagine how we would get more specific below this part of the chart, I'm going to keep those details between me and Scratch.

Brand Messaging Examples

Thoughtful Brand Messaging that considers every detail of how your brand communicates with people should always be a top priority. You want people to feel like they are having a personal experience—like the brand is speaking directly to them and what they care about—so that it sparks their interest in your brand.

The Scratch team took this to heart when they brought the brand strategy into their new brand website. The combination of the new Visual Identity and Brand Messaging was a significant evolution from where they had been, rooted in a much deeper understanding of what matters to the people they serve.

The home page opens with the following message:

Curated DJs. Anytime. Anywhere.
Experiences that keep people coming back for more

Since 2002 we've been amplifying events, energizing audiences, and creating buzz for our clients. Whether one event or one thousand, our incredible client service will make you feel confident and at ease, while our highly curated DJs deliver amazing event experiences—anytime, anywhere.

We've worked with over 1,500 clients to provide talent to more than 125K events. We love what we do, and no one does it better. Come work with us and see why.

Below that, there is a section that pulls directly from the brand positioning statement. It says:

Who We Are
Scratch Event DJs is the go-to resource for DJs, anytime, anywhere, making it easy for you to consistently have energizing brand experiences that keep people coming back for more.

There's a page on the Scratch website titled *How Scratch Works*, and it opens with the following:

The Scratch Experience
How we partner with you to amplify any occasion through the power of music and DJs.

This is followed by all the details that I shared above in the Brand Messaging Hierarchy to explicitly convey the top-level Core Brand Benefits—*Incredible Client Service*, *Largest DJ Network*, *Amazing Event Experiences*—and their corresponding sub-benefits for Scratch customers.

Throughout the rest of the website there are sections that convey both the benefits and the services that are available to the industry segments they serve such as Retail and Hospitality, and the kinds of events they often support, such as Trade Shows, Conferences, and Internal Corporate Events.

It includes copy that demonstrates a unique understanding of what's important to their customers, such as:

> *We utilize our amazing talent network and operational expertise to activate environments cost effectively and hassle free. We're a one-stop-shop with flawless execution, leading to a happy team, very happy management, and extremely happy guests.*

The website also includes specific details for all their services, and customer testimonials from many recognizable brands.

Relaunching the Brand

What I remember most about this work is the conversations we had toward the end of Insights Discovery. The team was very eager to dig into the details of the customer interviews, and they were very happy, yet not surprised, to hear the highly positive customer feedback. What did prove to be very revealing were the emotional drivers behind that positive feedback—insights about customer motivations that gave them a whole new perspective on how to spark brand desire.

In speaking with Rob after our work was completed, he shared, "I would recommend that any brand take a navel-gaze, a look in the mirror, to help get out of their own heads. Now we're able to meet our clients where they are, instead of where we think they are. The outcome is a brand that's designed to better our relationships and to better our business" (Limbic Brand Evolution, 2023).

For Rob and the team, this meant that their sales and marketing materials can be less about justifying the investment of working with them, and more about the professionalism and energy that they bring to every customer interaction.

Looking Ahead

Do you have a new appreciation for the profession of DJing, or is it just me? In the next chapter, you'll read about another brand that, on the surface, does the exact same thing as its many competitors. However, you'll see how it's not the services that set this brand apart—it's the experience that they make possible for customers. If you're looking to differentiate in a crowded competitive space, you'll want to read about ServiceByte.

Brand Leadership Considerations

In your own life, are you willing to pay more for quality and convenience?

Many times, how much something costs is not the most important factor in purchase decisions. We all have an interest in spending as little as possible, or saving our organization money, but value for the money spent is usually a bigger motivator. We're often willing to pay for quality and convenience. The more something makes our life better, the less likely we are to rule it out based on cost.

In your work with brands, do you assume customers are making rational purchase decisions?

We are not rational beings. Our natural tendency is to buy on emotion and justify with logic. When a brand has a high-quality offering that's easy to access, there's a good chance that those benefits will be more emotionally motivating than saving money—even in B2B environments. When you hear directly from customers about what drives the most value for them, you'll get a good understanding of the most compelling brand benefits, and where price sensitivity fits into their decision-making.

Here are three things you can start doing today:

1 Don't assume you already know what aspects of your brand offering and experience drive the most value for customers.

2 Remember that not all buyers are price sensitive, especially when the benefits your brand makes possible are highly differentiated.

3 Be sure to identify and stand for the most compelling brand benefits, and set your pricing based on demand for your services.

References

Limbic Brand Evolution (2023) Let's Talk Limbic Sparks Podcast – episode 23, Keeping People Coming Back for More with Rob Principe, 11 March, www.limbicbrandevolution.com/podcast/rob-principe-lets-talk-limbic-sparks-23 (archived at https://perma.cc/8ENY-VCYD)

Scratch Event DJs (n.d.), Home Page, www.scratch.com (archived at https://perma.cc/53B7-X3H9)

Scratch Music Group (n.d.), Home Page, www.scratch.com/ (archived at https://perma.cc/YF3F-2KUP)

09

Differentiating on Brand Experience
ServiceByte Case Study

"We are most inspired by a love for helping people."

That's when I knew I wanted to work with Kish Melwani, who is a small business owner and founder of ServiceByte in the New York City area. Kish said this to me in our first meeting as he shared his desire to update the talking points that he uses in sales materials to better reflect his personal values and the current state of the business.

Kish comes from an IT background. Earlier in his career he was an IT technician, providing computer and software help desk support for customers of the company he was working for. He was frustrated by the norms of the industry that left a lot of people feeling annoyed when they needed tech support, rather than feeling well taken care of. It troubled Kish that people sometimes had to wait long periods of time for help, were sometimes treated with a lack of empathy for the disruption of their work, and sometimes had to transport or install their own equipment.

Kish recognized it didn't have to be this way. He decided to launch his own company knowing that he could provide a better experience for people. He envisioned more of a concierge-style approach that was more focused on customer service. Today, he and his team help many other small business owners keep their IT services and systems in good working order. They provide help desk support, installations, and security protections for computers, servers, email, and all kinds of business software. Their approach to this work is one that always prioritizes great experiences for their customers. He told me, "For us, it's all about experience. We want to improve the customer experience, from on-boarding, to support, to new initiatives, and to make it as easy as possible for them."

However, like many small business owners, while Kish had been busy running and growing his business, attention to his brand had fallen behind.

He had prioritized customer service, hiring and training his team, networking to meet new potential customers, and evolving his service offering to both eliminate some services and add new ones, based on customer feedback about what was most valuable to them.

In one of our early meetings when I was learning about the ServiceByte offerings, I asked about a service featured on his website. Kish shared, with a bit of embarrassment, that they'd stopped offering the service a while back and that the website, like most of his brand messaging, was distressingly out of date. The business had evolved but the brand had not—something he was now ready to address.

My job was to help Kish—not just to update his brand messaging, but to turn his love for helping people into a business-defining competitive advantage.

Focus

Kish and I had many conversations where I learned more and more about the heart and soul of his business, which, like this project, was very personal for him. ServiceByte is his baby—an entrepreneurial venture he had built from the ground up with his first team member and his first customers out of a tiny basement of an old office building. Despite the cramped space, he said, "We made the best of it thanks to unlimited snacks and an occasional walk to get lunch or ice cream."

He elaborated, "I firmly believe that in any service-based business, people are the driving factor for everything. If I create a fun and engaging atmosphere for them to work in, they'll be happier and my customers will feel their enthusiasm." I also learned that Kish's values set the tone for every team member and every customer interaction: *Make it easier, value people's time, help first, and encourage teamwork.*

When speaking with Kish's team members, I heard not only about the specific work they do, but also about their admiration for Kish as a leader. They talked about the customer relationship focus which they saw as unique in the IT field. They confirmed that providing great customer service is not just an aspiration, it's at the core of the ServiceByte brand.

As part of Insights Discovery, I also spoke with a handful of ServiceByte customers to understand more about the brand experience from their perspective. Here are examples of what I heard from customers in answer to four of twelve questions. You'll see I'm using the Interview Findings Summary chart that I initially shared in Chapter 3. In that chapter I shared how I include a summary insight for each question. For ServiceByte, instead, I summarized the responses with a representative quote from the interviews.

ServiceByte Customer Interview Findings

How would you describe your experience with ServiceByte?

- They take responsibility.
- Very personable.
- Really supportive.
- They take pride and it shows.
- They always put us at ease.
- I have blind trust in Kish and his team.
- Kish called me back on Christmas.

Summary customer quote:

> *"Kish sets a tone, culture and personality that comes through in the team."*

What about ServiceByte gives you the most value?

- Our network is up and running.
- Rapid response.
- Strategizing for long-term solutions.
- Communication through the process.
- Kish gets directly involved when needed.
- I'm dealing with professionals.

Summary customer quote:

> *"Strategizing to helping us think through long-term solutions is not only great, but it's added value."*

How does ServiceByte compare to other service providers in any service category?

- Top tier.
- One of the best.

- They look out for my best interests.
- They are responsive and proactive.
- Great communication.

Summary customer quote:

> *"Working with ServiceByte reminds me of how I like to do business."*

How does working with ServiceByte make you feel?

- At ease.
- Confident.
- Comfortable.
- I don't need to think about it.
- Relief.
- Secure.
- They're on it.

Summary customer quote:

> *"We can get our work done knowing the engine runs well."*

After talking with the team and hearing from customers, I knew exactly why people were feeling Limbic Sparks in their relationship with ServiceByte. Kish was clearly successful at infusing his vision and values into the customer experience.

Before turning those insights into a brand strategy, however, we needed to take a close look at the competition. When doing this work, your approach should be to develop your strategy and messaging with the insights you discover from the brand team and from customers. However, you also must ensure that you don't land in a brand positioning territory and use language that is also being used by competitors.

Since ServiceByte customers are primarily in the New York City area, we focused on local competitors—the ones that prospective customers are likely to consider. As it turns out, the landscape of managed service IT providers is a very competitive field. It consists of both small businesses like ServiceByte that are founder-led with a few technicians, and national brands with local offices and lots of technicians serving businesses of all sizes.

For me, it was also one of the most memorable competitive reviews I've conducted. One competitor's brand focused on "the fast pace of technology and threats to your business." Relying on fear tactics, they had a video that felt intense thanks to the music, the way the voice actor was speaking, and quick cuts of sports, New York City subways, traffic, people looking stressed out, fighter jets, and paratroopers. It all came together in a way that felt like the style of a movie trailer for *Top Gun*. One competitor's brand demonstrated how they are a group of good people with a video showing team members talking in their break room, by the water cooler, and at the reception desk. It was shot in the style of the show *The Office*, and was more funny than authentic. There was one competitor focused on cyber security with a photo of the founder next to a detective-like shield. Several other brands leaned into familiar language and cliché stock photography of teams working together.

Then I stumbled onto something I'd never seen before. There were three competitors—companies completely unrelated to one another—that had the same exact copy on their websites. I'm not talking about a few lines of copy. I'm talking about an entire page of bullet points with long explanation sentences for each listed under the heading "Why choose us?" that were the same, word for word, on three websites. It seemed like they'd all hired the same company to build their websites, and that company had recycled content for each client in something that I can only describe as website malpractice. While this pre-dates people using artificial intelligence for copywriting, I fear that we'll see this kind of sameness across brands when AI is used carelessly for copywriting.

Overall, the competitive set included a lot of similar messaging and imagery, uses of fear tactics, tech jargon, and a lack of authenticity. It confirmed that ServiceByte had an opportunity to be distinct by focusing on the real and relevant relationship-focused approach that their customers truly appreciate.

At the conclusion of our Insights Discovery work, we developed the first piece of their brand strategy, the Shared Emotional Motivation. It was fueled by our insights into the customer service ethic that has been part of the brand since the very beginning. It was also fueled by what we heard from customers who say that their experience is what they appreciate most about working with ServiceByte, giving them confidence that their IT systems are up and running so their business runs smoothly.

This led us to the Shared Emotional Motivation:

Always On

I love when language has multiple meanings in the same context. For ServiceByte, *Always On* means that they are constantly monitoring and proactively addressing IT issues for their customers. It also means that they, as people, are *Always On*—enthusiastic, attentive, and eager to help. For ServiceByte customers, *Always On* relates to their primary need for their business to consistently be up and running—and the need for their IT systems to be *Always On*. In so many ways, it's what both ServiceByte and its customers are most motivated to achieve individually and together.

Connect

Moving right into brand strategy development, we then identified three Core Brand Benefits:

Easy to Reach, Expert Service, Rapid Response

These three emotional benefits were the ones we discovered customers and prospects are looking for in their first moments of evaluating companies like ServiceByte, and, based on customer feedback, are benefits that ServiceByte excels at delivering.

Next, we developed a set of Brand Personality & Voice Traits to guide brand expression that reflect the values Kish has been instilling from day one. They are also what customers already feel in their experience:

- ServiceByte is *Caring*, and as a result, its brand voice should feel *Friendly*, not inauthentic.

- ServiceByte is *Expert*, and as a result, its brand voice should feel *Knowledgeable*, not full of tech jargon.

- ServiceByte is *Responsible*, and as a result, its brand voice should feel *Reassuring*, not full of hyperbole.

When it came time to write the Brand Idea, we wanted to stay very true to what matters most to customers—that ServiceByte takes care of IT issues so customers can focus on their core business. It needed to be a compelling benefit and invitation for small business owners—one that would inspire them to rely on outside experts to keep their IT services up and running. Kish also wanted what his brand stands for to be a memorable talking point in his meetings with potential customers. We agreed that it should be a phrase that Kish could say in meetings and use as a jumping-off point for other benefits when he is out meeting potential customers.

This led us to the following Brand Idea:

We Do Our Thing. So You Can Keep Doing Yours.

It's somewhat unconventional, in that it's longer than most brand taglines. However, it felt to us like a perfect fit for ServiceByte, and a refreshing departure from the competition. This brand benefit and invitation is exactly what customers care about, and unlike the competitive set, a very authentic and sincere way to ignite interest in ServiceByte.

Now, it was time to bring this to life across Brand Expression & Experiences.

Evolve

When we entered the Evolve phase, our objective was to be sure that every detail of the ServiceByte experience felt as easy and accommodating as the brand promises. Now that we had established the Brand Idea and the Brand Personality & Voice Traits, I was thrilled with the enthusiasm that Kish had to bring it to life across all brand touchpoints. I expected that we would be replacing the ServiceByte website, and that a top priority for Kish was updating his sales presentation. Kish then surprised me, wanting to go further and update the help desk ticketing system that customers use to initiate service requests, and that his techs use to communicate status updates.

Visual Identity

As this Evolve phase of work was starting, I shared with Kish that there was one common element across every touchpoint that also needed to be updated, which is the visual expression of the brand. The ServiceByte Visual Identity had been in use for a while, and it was starting to look a bit dated, which often happens with technology brands. Kish and I agreed to bring in a designer to refresh the Visual Identity.

It turned out to be a very good move. We modernized the brand logo by making some very subtle changes to lines and color. These subtle details made a big difference. We also established a palette of primary and secondary colors, selected a batch of images to establish a consistent style for stock photography, and selected a set of stock icons to represent several benefits and services. We also gave Kish a photography style guide for a photo shoot he commissioned to capture his team members—the people who he wanted customers to know by face—in a consistent way.

Overall, without a lot of time or expense, we were able to both modernize and bring vibrancy into the brand identity. We provided a set of assets for use across all brand touchpoints that was a great representation of the brand strategy. These were all important details that, if left out, would have minimized the effectiveness of the rest of our work.

Sales Presentation

The sales presentation was the top priority for Kish. In fact, updating the sale presentation was his impetus for our work together. He had not been happy with what he was using in the past—it felt too much like a sales pitch and not like a conversation. With emotional insights in mind, we understood what challenges his small business owner customers have with their technology, the stress those challenges cause, and the way ServiceByte makes customers feel.

Using those insights and the brand strategy, we were able to develop the conversation that Kish wanted to have with people, starting with the idea that ServiceByte makes IT support simple. It referenced some common IT challenges for small businesses—such as frustration, business downtime, and cyber security vulnerability—giving Kish an opportunity to reflect an understanding of those common challenges and open the conversation about other challenges the prospect might be facing.

Kish was then able to share the brand benefit and invitation—*We do our thing. So you can keep doing yours.*—and our Core Brand Benefits: *Easy to Reach, Expert Service and Rapid Response.* He introduced his team using photos and sharing their credentialed levels of IT expertise. He shared how ServiceByte is *100% Accommodating*—able to support customers remotely or on-site, and that they can schedule support at their convenience using a scheduling link. He talked about how working with ServiceByte includes *Proactive IT Strategies* such as *Protecting, Monitoring*, and *Future-Proofing* customers' IT infrastructure.

After a few weeks of road testing the new presentation, Kish was experiencing much more engagement and discussion, and several new customers. They shared that Kish and ServiceByte seemed to truly understand their challenges, with a service offering that felt like a great fit. It was music to my ears that the work was already igniting interest and creating Limbic Sparks.

Website

Our next step was to refresh the website. This work included me writing Brand Messaging, our designer laying out each page, and another collaborator I brought in, Ben Bakelaar, developing the website using WordPress.

We opened the home page with the headline, *Managed IT Services Made Simple*, and we selected a photo of a laptop on a very clean desk facing a window with a beautiful view. This photo was an important detail that we put a lot of thought into. We wanted to project a very calming environment, and knew this approach was different from so many competitive websites that feature cliché photos of people, technology, or IT security threats. Below the photo we revealed the Brand Tagline: *We do our thing. So you can keep doing yours.*

The next section of the home page included the brand benefits that were featured in the sales presentation. At the bottom of the home page, we created a rotation of customer reviews that they shared publicly on Google, or from what they shared when I interviewed them during Focus. For those, we secured two levels of permission out of respect for their confidentiality— first, I asked if they were ok with me sharing what they specifically said with Kish, and then Kish sought permission to use their words publicly.

The next page of the website is called "Why Us?" It opens with a photo of Kish and the following quote:

> *In 2010, I decided it was time for a managed service IT business that prioritizes people. We understand the stress that IT problems can cause, and our clients always know that they are in good hands. When I hear things like "Working with ServiceByte reminds me of how I like to do business," I know we're on the right track.*

And a banner that says:

> *We'll come to the rescue during an IT emergency, but our primary goal is that you won't have one.*

Like the sales presentation, it then shares our understanding of the IT challenges faced by small business owners, and what ServiceByte does to solve them. For example:

> *We understand that you don't want any IT emergencies, so we help you avoid potential problems.*

> *We understand that you are frustrated by poor performance, so we help you invest in the right tech.*

We understand that downtime can be costly, so we help you focus on what you do best.

The page also shares the brand's core values:

Our Values Set the Tone—We make it easier. We value people's time. We help first. We value teamwork.

Next there is an *Our Services* page, followed by a *Your Team* page. On the *Your Team* page, we contemplated a lot of details to bring the personality of the team to life. It includes the headline *Our People Make All the Difference* and a rotating set of photos from Kish's photo shoot of the team members in natural and fun poses. It then includes the following copy to convey more of the brand personality and approach:

Our team has deep IT expertise. We take pride in our work, have fun, and it shows. As a client you'll love how we put you first, keep you informed and take responsibility to proactively make sure that your business is always on. The less you see us the better, but when you do, know it will be a good experience.

Next came team bios that we also had fun with. Each team member bio was written from Kish's perspective sharing a heartfelt story of how they met and why he hired them. Kish's bio was also designed to convey the heart and soul of the brand, written from the perspective of team members. It says:

To call Kish caring would be an understatement. A customer refers to him as "the guy who shoveled my driveway during a winter emergency." Others talk about Kish's calming presence or his proactive recommendations. For Kish, caring for his customers and team are priority #1. Kish is the glue that makes ServiceByte different from typical MSPs. He hires the best technicians (us!) who share his core values. Kish has created a culture that inspires us all. He's also involved in the community (especially within Peekskill) where he's on the board of directors and executive committee of the Hudson Valley Chamber of Commerce. He excels at telling terrible dad jokes and playing with "his son's" Legos. Kish has many titles: boss, father, colleague, mentor, but most importantly, he's a friend. We are very proud to call Kish our friend, and as a client, you'll feel the same way.

This *Why Us?* page is deliberately designed to be non-traditional. Typically, these pages are very boring and go through the motions of sharing head-shots, titles, and bios that feel like a resume turned into a paragraph. We wanted every detail of this page to give a good feeling about the people who potential customers would have the chance to work with, and to ignite their interest. Years later, Kish let me know that people call him for the first time and they feel like they already know him—a level of familiarity that comes through thanks to this page.

After we wrote and designed the website, using a specific design guide created for development—covering font sizes, color hex codes, icon usage, and layouts for all the content—we worked with Ben to bring it into the WordPress environment. He helped with so many details such as optimizing page load time, making it both web and mobile friendly, including metadata for SEO, and bringing in WordPress widgets for certain functionality.

Ben did ask one question, a very good one, that gave me a moment to articulate one primary way that Limbic Sparks Brand Strategy is different than traditional brand strategy. Ben asked, "Why aren't the services on the home page?" sharing that most small business websites put the services front and center. Honestly, it didn't occur to me to do that, and Ben has much more experience developing websites than I do. What I shared in response was that our approach is to spark interest in the brand by highlighting benefits that matter most to people. When people go to websites for companies like ServiceByte, it's likely that they'll find that many offer the same services. Our objective on the home page is not to waste those precious few moments that they spend on it with information that they'd expect to see. Instead, it's to make them feel like we understand them and that ServiceByte was designed with them in mind.

I loved this question, because it was a reminder to me that Limbic Sparks Brand Strategy is different than what most business and brand leaders, and even brand consultants, are used to doing. It's a new approach and perspective on how brand strategy can steer Brand Expression & Experiences in the right direction. At that moment, and many others, I thought, "Maybe I should write a book about Limbic Sparks Brand Strategy," until I did.

Help Desk Ticketing System

Now that we had relaunched the brand to prospective customers, it was time to fine-tune the details of the Brand Experience for current customers. Once people become a ServiceByte customer, there's a lot of human-to-human interaction with the team. However, the backbone of tracking the status of every single issue across all customers is the help desk ticketing system.

When a customer has a need for support, they initiate the process with an email that goes to a specific address. They get an automated response confirming receipt and the tech team gets alerted. The system is used for any back-and-forth correspondence and status updates, in addition to any live conversations, until the issue is resolved and the ticket is closed. The ticketing system used is a pre-built software solution with many standard templates and features, and some room for customization. Kish, like many business owners who use this software, set it up when they first started using it and it has been running on autopilot ever since.

Kish recognized that the ticketing system was not always as friendly or simple as it could be. As a result, the brand experience did not meet his standards, and now it was not at all reflective of the evolved brand strategy. Even though customers were having an overall good experience, Kish knew it could be better.

Fortunately, Ben, we found out, had a lot of experience programming this software. He knew how it worked and where there were opportunities to customize it. So, we went to work and fine-tuned every detail. We improved the design of the support ticket emails—removing all needless information that was historically there, but not helpful. We made all the messaging more friendly and informative. We knew that customers were looking for important updates, and simultaneously we had an opportunity to help them feel reassured that their needs were being prioritized, and that everything would be resolved quickly. For example, when a client opens a support ticket there is an automated response that used to say "*Received*" but now, to make the details of that experience feel more heartfelt and reassuring, the reply says, "*We're on it*" right at the top. We also added the name of the service tech who's been assigned and a timeframe for when the challenge will be worked on. Further, we added a message at the end that says: "*Emergency? Give us a call.*" and a phone number. Now, with every interaction, customers feel taken care of, even more than before.

Re-Launching the Brand

I always tell Kish that working with him was one of my favorite brand evolution experiences. I certainly enjoy working with bigger companies that have people who are focused on brand, but it's an entirely different kind of rewarding when working with a small business owner. Kish has many roles at his company and focusing on the brand can't always be a top priority. I know that doing the work we did together was sometimes a disruption from more pressing day-to-day needs to run the business, and we had a flexible schedule to alleviate any time pressure. I also know that when we were done, Kish felt that the ServiceByte brand, his talking points in sales meetings, the website, and the day-to-day experiences that his customers have, finally felt in sync with his values. It was personally rewarding for me, knowing how personal this project was for him.

Looking Ahead

You've reached a big milestone in this book. You've read about all three Limbic Sparks Brand Strategy steps—Focus, Connect, Evolve—and corresponding cases. Next, in the final part of the book, you'll read about additional ways to bring this approach into your role as a brand leader. We'll go deeper on the difference between traditional customer research and research approaches rooted in behavioral science. You'll see how customer-centricity can fuel success for your organization and for your customers, and you'll see just how easy it is to embrace a Limbic Sparks Mindset, even if you're not kicking off a full-scale brand evolution. It's time to build on what you've already learned and to further up your game as a brand leader.

Brand Leadership Considerations

In your own life, why do you choose some providers over others when the services are the same?

We all want to feel valued and respected. When a business treats us well, it makes a difference. In fact, brand experience can be the difference that separates one business from another, when their offerings seem, on the surface, to be the same.

In your work with brands, do you have an opportunity to differentiate based on brand experience?

Competing on price is not sustainable. When your offering is the same as that of your competitors and they can always come in with a less expensive option, you must find a more sustainable way to differentiate. Competitors may be able to do what you do, but it's much less likely that they can replicate your brand experience, and that's a wonderful way to set your brand apart.

Here are three things you can start doing today:

1 Identify what makes your brand experience different than those of your competition.

2 Identify the pain points and frequent industry-wide frustrations that other brands are not addressing.

3 Become the brand known for improving the customer experience in ways and areas that other brands are ignoring.

PART FIVE

Lead

10

Revealing Emotional Insights with Research

There are times when a spark of inspiration ignites, and the status quo no longer seems right. Oliver Wendell Holmes, Sr. spoke of how a life's experience can sometimes come from just a moment of inspiration (Holmes, Sr., n.d.). It's what I love about Insights Discovery, in any form, and why this idea resonates with me so deeply.

I didn't know about the limbic system part of our brain, until I did. Then, my whole perspective about brand desire and what drives customer preference changed. It gave context to my skepticism about so many supposed best practices of traditional brand strategy. It revealed what my instincts were signaling to me, and it brought clarity to an enlightened way forward.

As you may recall from Chapter 1, after many years of being a traditional brand strategist, I became a student of a whole world of neuro-scientific understanding that had been building alongside, but rarely intersecting with, brand leadership. David Brooks, a political and cultural commentator who writes for the *New York Times*, referred to our understanding of emotion as one of the major intellectual breakthroughs since the mid-1970s (Brooks, 2024). I recognized that emotional insight is something that so many brand leaders are ignoring, misunderstanding, or under-leveraging, and that traditional brand strategy had not evolved.

My window into this field of study coincided with my introduction to behavioral science research. These approaches are newer on the scene than traditional research approaches. Learning about them furthered my understanding that emotional insight must be at the foundation of brand strategy. Knowing how to tap into emotional insight is an important step to sparking brand desire.

Why Conduct Research?

Research should always be conducted during Insights Discovery. However, not all brand evolutions require sophisticated research methodologies and big budgets to uncover insight.

Throughout this book, you've already read about some ways I conduct and use research to discover emotional insights. For example, you've seen how customer interviews led to an understanding of the true motivations of manufacturers—protecting the reputation of their own products while making them more competitive. This emotional insight helped Sundless move away from product superiority claims to emphasizing that its product is "A Material Difference" versus any other option to ignite the interest of risk-averse manufacturers. You've seen how customer interviews and an analysis of comments shared across 77 customer reviews led to an understanding that people who are responsible for inventory levels in large warehouses are in a no-win situation, expected to accurately predict the right amount of stock for each of thousands of SKUs. This emotional insight led us to expressing that with Blue Ridge they can go from doing "guesswork" to being "Supply Chain Invincible."

In each case study, you've read how we prioritized using research to discover the mindset of the customer—not just the perspective of the internal brand team—to figure out how the brand should evolve to more effectively spark desire. We dug deep, beyond surface-level assumptions, pre-conceived notions, and stated preferences.

The methods behind Limbic Sparks Brand Strategy were born out of insights I gained about how the brain works, the influence of our emotions, and the inextricable link between our emotions and our behavior. They were also born out of understanding that I learned working with my behavioral science mentors, Dr. Cyrus H. McCandless, PhD and Joe Sauer on approximately two dozen research projects. Those were not my first experiences with research, but our work gave me eye-opening recognition that traditional research techniques, like traditional brand strategy, are not always the right tools for the job. This is especially true when you want to measure how people really feel about things and what's really driving their choices.

The purpose of this chapter is to share some of my research experiences with you, so you can gain deeper insights in your work. This is not intended to be a tutorial about different research methodologies, or a fully exhaustive list of all methodologies. It's also not intended to say that some research methods are good and some are bad. Most research methods have their purpose, as well as their limitations. It's also true that some very popular methods are less reliable than others and may even lead to over-confidence in your findings. Look no further than political polling data in the United States to see how traditional polling research methods are sometimes not great at predicting election results—whether it's because the respondents were not truly representative of the whole population of voters, or people stated a preference that was not the same as how they voted.

Sometimes, as a brand leader, you'll want to conduct an incremental Customer Research Study to understand your customers and prospects better. Sometimes it's to select the best of several options, and/or validate recommendations to justify a path forward. Sometimes you'll want to use research to inspire innovation and new ways to serve customers. The trick is to know when to use each method to underpin the decisions you'll make. If I had to choose between making decisions without research and making decisions based on data from less-than-reliable methods, I'd forgo the research.

What follows are some of my experiences with lesser-known methods of behavioral science research that are becoming more and more available at cost levels that are comparable to traditional research studies. These methods are more reliable options for discovering emotional insights that correlate to actual behavior.

Choosing the Most Appropriate Research Methodology

One thing I want to be very clear about is that all research is not the same. Just because "there's research" doesn't mean that it is reliable or best suited to your needs. So many factors go into designing a research study and if they aren't carefully considered, you could be basing decisions on false assumptions. Whenever you are reviewing research that someone shares with you, or obtaining new research, be sure to look at the source and methodology before becoming too invested in what it tells you.

When considering research, there are most often two top-level options: Qualitative and quantitative.

On the Qualitative side, there are one-on-one interviews and focus groups, to name a few. These methods enable you to ask unstructured questions, ask follow-up questions, and to hear people's stated thoughts and opinions. Qualitative gives you more of an opportunity to probe why people feel and act in certain ways.

> **Qualitative Research**
>
> Research techniques that enable inquiry into how people feel and why through individualized questioning.

On the Quantitative side, there are many types of research studies that are typically survey based. They have a set of structured questions that can come in many forms, from multiple choice, to rating scale, to open ended. Thanks to a larger number of respondents, you can more reliably project the results to larger populations of the "same group" with greater confidence that the results will be consistent.

> **Quantitative Research**
>
> Research techniques that lead to statistical data showing similarities and differences between reactions to questions and stimuli across segments of people.

There are also two other ways to characterize research that many people are less familiar with: Explicit and implicit.

Research that I suspect you are most familiar with is explicit research. These are qualitative and quantitative methodologies that explore answers to research questions with people responding consciously.

> **Explicit Research**
>
> Research techniques that explore how people consciously react to questions and stimuli.

Implicit research refers to methodologies that tap into people's subconscious instincts and attitudes that they reveal without conscious awareness.

> **Implicit Research**
>
> Research techniques that explore how people react to questions and stimuli instinctively, at a subconscious level.

The majority of how we feel and behave is triggered by our instinctive emotional reactions that happen at the subconscious level. Most often we are not made consciously aware of this activity. Imagine if our brain told us about every single thing it encounters and perceives every second of the day.

You may recall from earlier chapters that we instinctively gravitate toward the things that make us feel good, and we gravitate away from the things that make us feel bad. This is why it's important, when conducting research to uncover emotional insights, that you use implicit research techniques that are designed to uncover our instinctive emotional responses.

Research Study Design Considerations

When designing a research study, there are three important considerations.

Research Study Design Considerations

1   Talking with the right people.

2   Asking the right questions.

3   Using the right methodology.

To illustrate why each of these is important, I'll share a simple example. Let's say you are the author of a nonfiction business book about brand strategy, and you want to use research to select a title for the book. You have several titles that you're considering, and your research question is: "Which of the following titles do you like the best?" On the surface, asking this question to a group of people to see which title gets the most votes seems like a good way to pick a title, but let's dig deeper.

If you were to use qualitative research methods, you may bring a few people together for a focus group or ask a handful of people what they think in one-on-one discussions. Using these approaches, you'll gather a lot of opinions and perspectives, but there won't be a statistically validated "winner." For the purposes of this example, what follows are considerations for a quantitative research approach to answer this one question.

Are You Talking With the Right People?

First, you need to be sure that your research respondents are the right people, so that you get the most projectable and reliable results. Consider the difference between 1) an open audience of people on a social media platform where anyone can respond to the survey question, or 2) a screened set of respondents who qualify to take the survey because they are "Business professionals who are involved with their company's marketing and buy three or more nonfiction business books a year." Which of these two options, do you think, will lead to more reliable data? Realize that group one most likely includes many people who have nothing to do with their company's marketing efforts and a book like that would be irrelevant to them, whereas group two are the most likely group of people who would consider buying this book.

Are You Asking the Right Questions?

Next, is "Which of the following book titles do you like the best?" the right question to ask? I'd say no. Likability, while a very popular line of questioning in research, is not always indicative of purchase intent. Just because someone says that they do or do not like the title, does not mean that they will or will not purchase the book. Further, when people are asked if they like something or not, using explicit research techniques, they don't always give the most accurate answer—often defaulting to an answer that puts them in the best light. In fact, people will sometimes avoid saying things or admitting to something controversial, or something that puts them at odds with social norms. Think about how you skew your answers to certain questions depending on who is asking.

An alternative question could be: "If you were looking to improve the results of your company's marketing and could choose a book with one of these titles to support your efforts, which book would you select?" This type of question is much more specific, and it will lead to responses that are less about likability, and more about the feeling that their selected title will help them achieve something that they would desire.

Are You Using the Right Methodology?

Taking this simple example further, it's important to be sure that you're using the right methodology for the answers that you are seeking. If you truly want to understand likability, preference, or something like the correlation between how the title makes the person feel and their intention to purchase the book, there are implicit behavioral science methodologies that I'll share later in the chapter that should be considered.

However, if we just focus for now on using research to answer the question: "If you were looking to improve the results of your company's marketing and could choose a book with one of these titles to support your efforts, which book would you select?" you may want to go further than just asking that multiple choice question.

Even if your group of respondents were the right people, and you asked the right question, just getting a data chart showing which book title "won" does not truly give you all the insight you could gather to know what to do next. Certainly, you could just go with the "winning title," but you may be missing a deeper understanding of why people made the selections that they did.

What if you were to ask respondents to rank the titles from the book that they'd most likely purchase to the one that they'd least likely purchase? With that data, you could see patterns. For example, if one title got the greatest number of high rankings, but another other option was split—half the respondents ranked it high and half ranked it low—that would be information I'd like to know. Sometimes more polarizing options are good ones because they break through the clutter and are a bigger idea worth considering. Or there is something about that title that is good but hitting some people the wrong way—something that you might be able to fix.

Going even further, I'd ask a follow-up, open-ended question: "Why?" I'd want to know why respondents chose their preferred title, and why they did not rank the other titles as high. This additional information about what drove their selections could lead to themes in the data that will help you better understand the relative strengths and weaknesses of the title options.

Getting Into People's Heads With Behavioral Science Research

Getting into people's heads is not always easy, especially when it comes to understanding the emotional drivers of their decisions. Sometimes people themselves are not consciously aware of what subconscious instincts are triggered, leading to a specific reaction or behavior. What we do know is that there is a constant interplay between our subconscious emotions and our rational thoughts, and sometimes traditional research methods will not reveal how people truly feel or how they will act.

What follows, in addition to using the carefully developed one-on-one interview questions that you read about in Chapter 3, are my experiences with some behavioral science research methodologies that will help you discover emotional insights, better than you can with traditional research methodologies.

Importantly, all the methodologies described are sophisticated research techniques that I suggest you conduct with the support of a professional research company that is a specialist in the specific data collection and analysis using the methodology you're planning to use. You may also want to approach several research companies to share your research objectives and solicit their recommendations on how best to conduct research, so you can compare their recommended approaches and methodologies.

Observational Research

Long before creating Limbic Sparks Brand Strategy, I read *Why We Buy: The science of shopping* by Paco Underhill (Underhill, 2008). He is a pioneer in shopper marketing research, known as one of our era's forefront retail anthropologists, and founder of Envirosell, a leading global shopper research company. I was fascinated by the stories he told of observing hours and hours of people shopping, and the insights that came out of that work.

The most memorable story in the book for me is about the "butt brush" effect. Underhill describes one research study about the positioning of a tie rack in a department store. They were studying the entry and exit aisles of the store, and the camera captured activity at the tie rack. They noticed that shoppers would approach the tie rack and start to shop, until they were brushed once or twice by other shoppers passing by. Then they would walk away without making a purchase. This observational research led to an insight that people are uncomfortable when other people walk by and make contact, so much so that they walk away before selecting something to purchase. After Underhill and his team reported this to the store manager, the tie rack was moved further away from the main aisle and sales of ties went up.

This is just one example of an instinctive emotional response that would most likely never have been discovered through traditional survey research. Yet in this case, and in many others that Underhill and his team have studied, insights you'd never learn from survey data are discovered. I always think of this as an early moment of recognition that traditional survey-based research is not always the best way to understand what people are thinking and feeling, or what's driving their decisions and behavior.

Observational research is not limited to shopper marketing in retail stores. You can also use it to observe website or app behavior, using tools that track how people navigate, what they click on, and where they focus most of their attention. There are many user experience research platforms available to help you conduct this research, enabling you to get real-time feedback from respondents about their experience.

Going even further into observational research, intercept interviews, such as in-home visits, in-office visits, or ride-alongs—observing and interviewing people while they shop or use a product—can shed a lot of light on whether the product is fit for purpose in its current form, whether it's helping people in ways that fuel their desire to use it more often, and what about the product experience is most and least compelling.

Implicit Association Testing

A few years later, I met my behavioral science mentors, Joe and Cyrus. They introduced me to a profound understanding of the role that emotions play in people's decisions and behaviors. They also introduced me to Implicit Association Testing.

Implicit Association Testing (Implicit) is a quantitative research online methodology that can be used to understand the strength of association between two things. It's great for evaluating "fit" between the two things being compared, measured at the subconscious level. It's important to note that implicit results are not reliable at the individual level—the study must be conducted at scale, and, when done correctly, is significantly more reliable than explicit research.

The way the methodology works is through a gamified user interface, where respondents are prompted by the two sets of variables being tested. Throughout the study, different combinations of variables are presented and based on the speed of response to a prompt (measured in milliseconds), the research can detect the subconscious strength of association or disassociation. For example, let's say you wanted to understand the subconscious strength of association between a color and a word. The respondent could be prompted with the color "red" and the word "stop," and their speed of response would be measured. In this example, as you'd expect, they would instinctively respond much faster than if they were prompted with "red" and "go," which would cause a brief hesitation in response. The research would reveal a strong association between "red" and "stop" and a weak association between "red" and "go".

Here are a few examples of how you can use this research to get reliable quantitative data on the emotional instincts of a group of people:

- How strongly are brands associated with colors, sounds, or logos? Implicit can determine the subconscious strength of relationship between a brand and brand identity elements.

- How strongly are brands associated with attributes? Implicit can determine the subconscious strength of relationship between brands and a set of attributes or benefits such as innovative, bold, friendly, convenient, luxurious, etc.

- How strongly positive or negative do people feel about a brand? Implicit can determine the subconscious strength of relationship between a brand and levels of emotional appeal from highly positive to highly negative.

Getting back to the example research question I shared earlier in the chapter—"Which of the following titles do you like the best?"—this is the methodology you'd want to use for this question. However, the question would not be asked overtly; it would be explored in the gamified Implicit user interface by including a set of possible book titles and a set of emotional responses to determine the emotional appeal rating of each title from most to least appealing. When each book title option is presented, the respondent would swipe the interface, either to indicate a positive emotional response, or in the opposite direction to indicate a negative emotional response. The speed of the response, measured in milliseconds, would provide data on the strength of the response—whether it's strongly positive or negative (if the response is fast), or closer to neutral (if the response is slow).

I've used Implicit many times to evaluate the brand fit of a variety of brand ideas, and to get on people's instinctive feelings and associations before they have a chance to consciously think about their response. It's my go-to methodology for understanding strength of association and emotional appeal—and it's much more reliable than asking people directly.

Implicit Association Testing Plus Explicit Exercises

You may recall Chapter 1 when Joe Sauer shared that "Every decision has a different blend of rational and emotional influences" (Limbic Brand Evolution, 2023). Therefore, understanding strength of association at the subconscious level is worthwhile because it reveals true instinctive responses. That said, when you combine Implicit research with what people say consciously, you can add more context, and sometimes increase your ability to predict their future behavior, adding much more confidence.

Often, when I've been part of conducting an Implicit Association Test study, we have also included conscious survey and open-ended questions to deepen our understanding and give greater context to the Implicit results. By combining the implicit responses with explicit responses, you get a more complete picture of how people feel and why.

One specific approach to improve predictability of future behaviors that I learned about from working with my behavioral science mentors is to conduct Implicit Association Testing and MaxDiff in the same research study. I'm oversimplifying here, but MaxDiff is a traditional explicit quantitative exercise where respondents choose between experimentally controlled subsets of items. They are presented with a list of items—brands, products, images, claims, etc.—and asked to indicate which of the items presented is their "most preferred" and which is their "least preferred"—or some other "most" vs. "least" question such as "most likely" and "least likely." As the full list of choices is randomly broken down into smaller groups, and respondents choose their most and least preferred, the data is being collected. Once the exercise is complete, the MaxDiff data can be analyzed to produce a ranking of most preferred to least preferred options.

Now, it's time to benefit from combining data from the Implicit and MaxDiff. When professional researchers who are practitioners of both methodologies combine the results of Implicit with MaxDiff using math that goes beyond my comprehension, they get to a degree of preference calculation that is a combination of emotion and reason. This is a blend of what people instinctively feel and what they consciously say, and leads to an even more reliable prediction of how they will behave, versus just using one of the studies independently. Based on how our brains work, combining instinctive and conscious responses to guide behavior, this combined methodology approach leads to a better indication of how people feel about and will react to the options if presented in a real-life scenario (Reid and González-Vallejo, 2009).

Joe, Cyrus and I once conducted a study like this to evaluate a variety of sounds that would occur in nature or brand experiences. We used Implicit to understand the "strength of emotional appeal" of each sound, and MaxDiff to understand the answer to "Which of the following sounds would you most and least like to experience again?" with randomized sets of pairings of all the sounds. From this study, were able to know which sounds were most to least appealing at an instinctive emotional level. We were also able to know which sounds were most to least desirable at a conscious level. We then combined the data to understand the correlation between subconscious emotional appeal and conscious desire—we confirmed an 86 percent correlation.

Therefore, one of the findings that came from this study was that if a brand's sound causes a negative emotional reaction, then there's an 86 percent chance that people will not want to have that brand experience again, and vice versa. The insight for brand experience designers, as described in an article about this study in *Wired* magazine, (Perlmutter, 2018) is that if a brand experience has poor sound design, "This adverse impression can diminish the use of a brand or device and discourage repeat purchases." Further, according to Dr. McCandless, "Sound doesn't have to be obnoxious to get someone's attention."

The more foundational insight that I took away from this and other similar studies is that our emotional instincts have a significant impact on our preferences and behaviors. This insight was a catalyst for so much of what you're reading about in this book.

Metaphor Elicitation

Henry Ford, founder of the Ford Motor Company and credited with making automobiles affordable for middle-class Americans, is also credited with saying that he would have made faster horses if he only relied on asking people what they wanted (Vlaskovits, 2011). Whether he ever really said that or not, the idea is accurate in that most people can't imagine things, let alone ask for things, that don't exist yet. Metaphor Elicitation is another example of a behavioral science research methodology, and uses metaphors to explore people's thoughts and feelings about a subject. It's great for understanding people's mindset to inform new ideas, such as ways to improve the customer experience, or gaps in the market that can lead to product or service innovation.

I had the opportunity to use this approach when exploring innovation opportunities in the customer experience of buying and selling homes. We sought to comprehensively understand the emotional context of home ownership and the emotional context of buying or selling a home—all to uncover pain points in the experience that can be solved through the elimination of bad parts of the experience and innovative new experiences. We used Metaphor Elicitation to uncover emotional insights about people's frustrations and desires that we would not have learned about asking traditional research questions. We then used these insights to develop ideas that we would not have thought of by simply brainstorming or asking people overtly what can be improved in the home buying and selling experience.

Here's how Metaphor Elicitation works:

- First, respondents are prompted with a task such as, "Please select an image that expresses your thoughts and feelings about owning a home." They select from a wide range of images such as a smiling face, a tornado, a repair truck, a rainbow, a pile of money, a family portrait, and many others.

- Next, there's a question, "Please describe the picture that you chose." If the respondent chose the tornado, they might say "It's a tornado that comes out of nowhere and causes lots of disruption and destruction."

- Next, there's a question, "Why did you choose this picture to express your feelings about owning a home?" They might say they chose the tornado because home ownership feels like it will be a lot of clean-up work, all the time.

From this series of question, using the photo as a metaphor for home ownership, you can discover a lot of emotional insights, including people's instinctive feelings about the experience—leading to a better understanding of the various mindsets that people have about the experience, and what they wish for to help them have a better experience.

This exercise can be conducted for several opening questions such as about their feeling about owning a home, about their experience buying or selling a home, about their experience moving into a new home. The methodology can be conducted qualitatively among a few people, or online quantitatively among many people. One fantastic benefit of this approach is that you get a lot of qualitative feedback from the open-ended questions that gives context to why people feel the way they do. Further, when conducted quantitatively online among many respondents, you can categorize all that qualitative detail into themes of reliable and projectable data.

Putting Research in Perspective

These are just a few of the behavioral science research approaches that you may want to consider using. From conducting a handful of one-on-one interviews to using robust implicit quantitative methods, there are many ways to collect data and discover emotional insights. The approach you choose depends on how much you're willing to spend and the level of reliability and projectability of the data that is needed.

Not every brand project needs an incremental Customer Research Study. Using the Insights Discovery steps described in Chapter 3, Limbic Sparks Brand Strategy will uncover a lot of new insight—especially if you've been using traditional brand strategy and have previously relied on only surface-level customer understanding. However, if you have a research budget and have been using traditional research methodologies, I suggest you explore behavioral science research companies for the kinds of projects discussed in this chapter.

What's most important is that you recognize the differences between traditional research and behavioral science research when it comes to measuring emotion and understanding how people truly feel about things. If you do choose to conduct a research study, you'll want to be sure it's the right one for the task at hand.

Additionally, I encourage you to recognize that research should not be just about picking a "winner." Research can be used to inform your understanding of what people think or feel, to guide your next steps in the refinement or selection of the options that you are considering, and to reveal new opportunities.

Lastly, remember that research provides data. What you discover and what ideas emerge out of that data is what's called insight.

Looking Ahead

I know. You'll never look at research the same way again. That's a good thing and maybe something you can talk about at parties. Plus, you now know that if you're not talking with your customers, then you really don't know what drives their choices, and if you're asking them in the wrong way, you may not be getting accurate answers. In the next chapter, we'll explore how customer centricity can fuel success within your organization and for your customers. You've come a long way in this book, and hopefully you're feeling energized in your desire to approach brand strategy in this new way. It's now time to inspire your team with what you've learned.

Brand Leadership Considerations

In your own life, how often do you tell people exactly what you're thinking or feeling?

If you're like most people, it's likely that you slightly or significantly adjust what you say based on who's asking. We all want to be sure that we're being perceived in the best possible light. So, our stated responses are not always what we are thinking or feeling.

In your work with brands, are you primarily relying on traditional survey-based research techniques to understand how customers and prospects feel about things?

Traditional survey-based research has limitations when it comes to reliably reporting what people are thinking and feeling. I encourage you to start using behavioral science research methodologies that are specifically designed to reveal what people are actually feeling at an instinctive, subconscious level.

Here are three things you can start doing today:

1   Continue learning about the differences between various research methodologies—quantitative and qualitative; implicit and explicit—so that you select the most reliable approach for the answers you are seeking.

2   Start investigating and using newer behavioral science research methodologies with research companies that specialize in these approaches.

3   Always keep in mind the three research study design considerations—talking with the right people, using the right methodology, and asking the right questions.

References

Brooks, D (2024) You're only as smart as your emotions, *New York Times*, 15 August, www.nytimes.com/2024/08/15/opinion/emotions-feelings-intelligence. html (archived at https://perma.cc/U3BU-SBQN)

Holmes, O W Sr. (n.d.) BrainyQuote.com, www.brainyquote.com/quotes/oliver_ wendell_holmes_sr_124488 (archived at https://perma.cc/JY5L-PQH8)

Limbic Brand Evolution (2023) Let's Talk Limbic Sparks Podcast – episode 26, Understanding Consumer Behavior with Joe Sauer, 12 June, www.limbicbrand evolution.com/podcast/joe-sauer-lets-talk-limbic-sparks-26 (archived at https:// perma.cc/U2PS-4BSD)

Perlmutter, K (2018), Beep! Bloop! Buzz! Why do UX Designers often neglect sound?, Wired, 12 November, www.wired.com/story/why-do-ux-designers-neglect-sound/ (archived at https://perma.cc/MAS6-J8FD)

Reid, A and González-Vallejo, C (2009) Emotion as a tradeable quantity, *Journal of Behavioral Decision Making*, January, www.sentientdecisionscience.com/wp-content/uploads/publications/emotion-as-a-tradeable-quantity.pdf (archived at https://perma.cc/5KKK-HCZE)

Underhill, P (2008) *Why We Buy: The science of shopping—updated and revised for the internet, the global consumer, and beyond*, Simon & Schuster, US

Vlaskovits, P (2011), Henry Ford, innovation, and that "faster horse" quote, *Harvard Business Review*, 29 August, hbr.org/2011/08/henry-ford-never-said-the-fast (archived at https://perma.cc/AQW2-4TX6)

11

Championing Customer Centricity

Adam Grant talks about the idea of deriving success through helping other people succeed (Grant, 2014). This sentiment is at the heart of what it takes to create Limbic Sparks, and the emotionally intelligent approach to brand strategy that you've been reading about.

My core belief is that brands should exist to make people's lives better, and when they do so in a way that's highly relevant and emotionally appealing, they simultaneously fuel their own business success. Brands that make life more complicated and frustrating end up turning away customers–detracting from both customer and business success.

When you, in your role as brand leader, champion customer centricity, you help people succeed—inside and outside of your organization. By prioritizing customer insight, you can guide your organization to serve your customers as best as possible.

FIGURE 11.1 Fueling Success with Customer Centricity

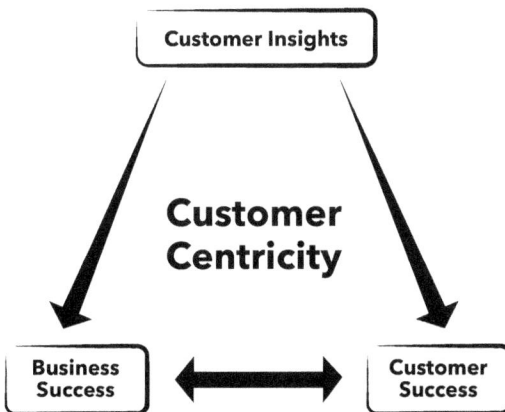

```
         ┌──────────────────┐
         │ Customer Insights │
         └──────────────────┘

              Customer
              Centricity

┌──────────┐              ┌──────────┐
│ Business │ ◄──────────► │ Customer │
│ Success  │              │ Success  │
└──────────┘              └──────────┘
```

NOTE By championing customer centricity and using emotion-centric customer insights, you'll fuel both business success and customer success. Even better, they fuel each other.

That said, I do completely understand that the realities of brand leadership are complex, and that the role is not so easy. In fact, brand leadership is becoming more and more challenging to navigate every day. While this chapter is about simplifying complexity and fueling success with customer centricity, I do want to acknowledge an understanding of the challenges you face in your role.

Confronting The Complexities of Brand Leadership

I work with and speak with a lot of brand leaders. They confide in me with their ambitions and their challenges. Together, we not only discuss how to evolve their brand to improve business results, but we also talk about how to do so in ways that are right for their organization. The larger the organization, the more stakeholder alignment is key to successfully implementing any initiative.

If your situation is like that of many brand leaders, it's likely that you, too, are under the pressure of an ever-expanding, rarely consistent set of responsibilities, along with new skill sets to learn, technologies to navigate, and media channels to consider. The number of ways to reach people and serve them continues to grow and become more fragmented. There are always escalating demands on brand and marketing performance concurrent with the expectation of continuously reduced costs. You're increasingly expected to drive toward greater efficiency through automation and artificial intelligence, while improving the customer experience. Simultaneously, there's a growing customer expectation of seamless and personalized experiences wherever customers interact with your brand.

I've seen some brand leaders struggle to get initiatives off the ground because of the pressure that they're under to drive short-term sales. They get sucked into the day-to-day of putting out fires, which diverts their attention away from longer-term efforts that can help the brand evolve and drive more sustainable growth. They find themselves feverishly moving forward without robust customer insights guiding the way. As a result, they fight uphill battles internally to secure the resources needed for product, service, or customer experience innovation, or to conduct valuable customer research that can unearth new opportunities for stronger connections and growth. All because short-term performance expectations are prioritized over longer-term brand-building investments.

Externally, brand leaders that I know have historically found themselves pushing their advertising and digital marketing agencies to do highly effective work, yet they are unable to equip them with insights that would make the work as engaging and effective as possible. Creative briefs are heavy on the brand's "why," loaded with details about the company and its products, including proof points and reasons to believe that internal teams want to talk about. These creative briefs are, on the other hand, very thin on the brand's "who" and reasons to care, leaving their agencies with the task of igniting customer connections without meaningful emotional insights.

If any of this feels familiar to you, I want to assure you that there is a way forward that can help you simplify the complexity of many disparate aspects of your brand leader role and align your team around beneficial paths forward. By championing customer centricity, you can use insights about what matters most to the people your brand serves as a point of orientation for stakeholder alignment. I've seen firsthand how customer insight puts brand leaders on the front foot, better positioned to guide their teams forward to simultaneously solve business, brand, and customer challenges.

Fueling Success With Customer Insight

Business leadership is about driving company growth and profitability. Brand leadership is about being a catalyst for that growth. Limbic Sparks Brand Strategy is all about sparking brand desire by discovering and standing for the benefits that matter most to people and then helping them feel how they want to feel through Brand Expression & Experiences. When people feel good about your brand, they gravitate toward it and want to experience it again and again. These Limbic Sparks have the potential to drive business growth through customer retention and acquisition.

Emotional insights give you a deeper understanding of people's mindsets and the drivers of their behavior. Those insights are incredibly valuable. When it comes to cross-functional collaboration within an organization, you as the brand leader can use your deep customer understanding to guide companywide efforts—including strategic planning, capability building, and innovation—to better serve customers and drive business growth.

Despite all the growing complexities and challenges of brand leadership, you are the voice of the customer within your company. You are also the customer advocate as they strive for whatever kind of success they are seeking with or without your brand. Based on what your brand does for customers, and more importantly, how your brand makes them feel, they instinctively determine the strength of their relationship with your brand—if it's one they want to avoid, one they are indifferent about, or one they prefer not to live without.

Recognizing the Illusion of Brand Loyalty

At the crux of a Limbic Sparks Brand Strategy is customer centricity. It's about ensuring that whenever people interact with your brand, it's a good and satisfying experience at minimum, and igniting Limbic Sparks as often as possible. You've read before about how important it is that Brand Expression & Experiences feel like they were designed with the customer in mind—which you can make possible with an understanding of what matters most and great attention to detail.

Customer Centricity

Making customer understanding and positive customer experiences a business priority.

It's simultaneously important to keep up with evolving customer needs and periodically refresh your set of customer insights. Many brands have a large customer base and sometimes get too comfortable in the feeling that they understand their customers. Sometimes, organizations get overconfident in the predictability of future revenue from existing customers. Meanwhile, customers have an ever-expanding set of choices combined with a low tolerance for unfulfilling brand experiences. The challenge with this is that everything is evolving—customers are evolving, the competitive landscape is evolving, the world around us is evolving—and customers will only keep coming back to your brand if it is fulfilling their evolving needs.

This is why it's important to recognize that customer loyalty is sometimes an illusion. The fact is that loyalty can be fleeting if the brand and the customer become out of sync. Scientifically, there's a behavioral distinction between loyalty and habits. Loyalty, by definition, is a conscious choice based on perceived value or desire for association and allegiance—it's when people actively choose and desire your brand. Habits, on the other hand, are more instinctive. While they resemble loyalty, they are more passive in nature. Habits, by definition, are repeated behaviors that often go unnoticed because there is no need to engage in self-analysis when undertaking routine tasks.

Dr. McCandless says, "Don't mistake habit for loyalty; many brand relationships are actually quite fragile. In most cases, we instinctively follow the path of least resistance. Repeat purchases are often just the result of our brain's effort to simplify decision-making versus evaluating choices available in the moment" (Perlmutter, 2020). Brand leader Megan Baker puts it this way: "Sometimes it may seem like loyalty, but really many people are loyal to the easiest way to keep moving forward on their own terms" (Perlmutter, 2020).

On this topic of brand loyalty, the 25th Annual Brand Keys Customer Loyalty Engagement Index shared that while brand loyalty is growing, the factors that lead to them are becoming more complex and more challenging to sustain. The study acknowledged that much brand behavior today is driven by emotionally based attitudes and drivers, and that customers instinctively evaluate whether a brand is meeting their expectations or not (Customerland Editor, 2020). Brand leader Beth Knight suggests that thoughts around brand loyalty should be reframed, saying "It ultimately comes down to need fulfillment. If a brand can continue to serve the needs customers have, and adapt fast enough as needs change, people will keep coming back" (Perlmutter, 2020).

The implication is that it's important for you to help your team not only to avoid risks of complacency, but to proactively address unmet customer needs. Sometimes you'll need to advocate and fight for what's best for customers with your organization, knowing that it's ultimately what's best for everyone. Brand leader Samantha Liss shares, "Often, you need to make decisions that lean toward the customer versus what someone else in the organization thinks" (Limbic Brand Evolution, 2022a).

Three Ways to Ensure Customer Centricity

Three Ways to Ensure Customer Centricity

1 Turn your Brand Idea into the beacon.

2 Make it easy for your customers.

3 Beware of artificial intelligence and automation shortcuts.

Turn Your Brand Idea Into the Beacon

Sometimes brand evolution work is seen as separate from the work done by people in other parts of the organization. However, you are the bridge between business strategy and brand strategy. Therefore, you are also the bridge between internal organizational activities and customer-facing Brand Expression & Experiences. To create that bridge you can use emotional insights about what matters most to your customers, and what your brand stands for and delivers. The stronger the bridge, the better position you are in to help everyone succeed—your customers and your internal team members.

I once heard a CEO refer to the work of the brand leader as "arts and crafts," revealing a sad lack of respect for their brand leader and a primitive understanding of the role brand can play in fueling business objectives. This is a tough mindset to break through in some organizations, but it's a reminder of the important role you play in bridging business objectives and brand desire. Brand leader Michelle Holmes, whom you read about in Chapter 2 about the AT&T Performing Arts Center, described it this way: "It's important to ensure that your brand and business strategy are really in lockstep and that it's not a superficial engagement" (Limbic Brand Evolution, 2021a).

One of the most powerful things you can do as a brand leader is leverage your Brand Idea—your compelling brand benefit and invitation—to be the guiding light for your internal team. Gregg Heard once shared with me, "Brand serves as a beacon of inspiration for where the company can go. It creates belief of a future and creates a gravitational pull toward a future state" (Limbic Brand Evolution, 2021b).

So often when I work with brand leaders, the Limbic Sparks Brand Strategy process, and the results of it, bring people together internally. The self-reflective work of clarifying brand motivations gets people out of the day-to-day and back to the purposeful ambitions that their work is all about. The outside-in work of discovering deeper customer insights and emotional motivations brings a renewed perspective, breaks down pre-conceived notions, and reinvigorates commitments to serving customers well.

The resulting Shared Emotional Motivation and Brand Idea set the foundation for a refreshed way forward to help customers feel like your brand was designed with them in mind, rooted in things you discovered were important to them. Your Brand Idea can also be an inspirational tool to help you champion customer centricity within your organization. It can help you ensure continual improvement in how customers and potential customers feel with every brand interaction. It can even inspire new ways to deliver on the brand benefits that customers crave. Brand leader Jess Kessler talks about customer centricity this way: "The brands that do it the best are always one step ahead of the game. They're always delivering something that a customer maybe didn't know they needed, or maybe that they didn't ask for yet" (Limbic Brand Evolution, 2024).

Think about the Brand Ideas throughout this book—"Yours to Discover" for the AT&T Performing Arts Center, "Be Supply Chain Invincible" for Blue Ridge, "We do our thing. So you can keep doing yours." for ServiceByte, and others. Not only are these the primary brand benefits and invitations to spark customer interest, but these ideas also play an important role in bringing people together within the organization around the brand benefits that matter most. Internally, they keep everyone focused on product and service offering evolution, brand messaging, and brand experience creation that increasingly delivers on those benefits. It trains their attention not on what they do, but on the impact that they have on the people they serve, and how they can further that positive impact with their ongoing work.

One crucial way to turn your Brand Idea into a beacon internally is to be sure that everyone feels connected to it. In addition to all the activities that I described in Evolve for applying the brand strategy to how the brand comes to life externally, you want to be sure that you also prioritize bringing the brand to life internally. For example, I shared that for Blue Ridge, there was a companywide townhall meeting where all employees learned about the "Be Supply Chain Invincible" brand evolution. During that presentation we described the steps we took to gather customer insights, and what we learned were the most compelling brand benefits and emotional drivers that cause customers to continue to work with Blue Ridge. We shared how we turned that insight into the Brand Idea and Core Brand Benefits. We then shared how we brought it all to life through Brand Expression & Experiences, and energized employees around the new brand positioning. Additionally, we had already evolved the presentation that the sales team uses when meeting with potential customers, bringing the Brand Idea and Core Brand Benefits to the top of the conversation. Through these and other activities, helping customers *Be Supply Chain Invincible* became a customer-centric beacon internally to guide how the offering will continue to evolve and deliver on the promise to customers.

You'll recall as well that for the AT&T Performing Arts Center, we flipped the brand idea from "Staging the Amazing" to "Yours to Discover." In doing so, we further instilled a customer-focused orientation point rooted in helping people discover all there is to experience at the Center. Igniting discovery became an internal priority in the development of new programming and marketing.

As you'll read about in the next chapter, social services nonprofit Rise has "Together, We Rise." as a Brand Idea. It serves as motivation internally for stepping up in a crisis, as well as for the ongoing efforts to increase capacity in areas of need for better serving the community. It's gotten to the point where Rise is a first point of contact for community leaders when support is needed in a crisis—whether that's a pandemic or a fire that destroys an apartment complex. Naturally, the Rise team accepts that responsibility with open arms and steps up every time.

Brand leader Ruth Gaviria says, "Brands are built from the inside out" (Limbic Brand Evolution, 2021). Ensuring that everyone internally is clear on the Shared Emotional Motivation that the organization has with customers, and the Brand Idea that invites them to feel successful, you can turn your Brand Idea into a beacon of inspiration for keeping customer centricity on track.

Make It Easy for Customers

The fact that our brains are wired to choose the path of least resistance is something that more brand leaders would benefit from understanding and addressing in their work. How many times have you walked away from something because it was too complicated, too frustrating, or just not worth your effort?

You may recall in Chapter 1 when I shared that Forrester ranks brands based on their customer experience and how that correlates to brand loyalty. Their ranking is based on three primary customer experience factors – Effectiveness (value of the experience), Ease (level of ease or difficulty to get the value), and Emotion (how customers feel about the experience). Throughout this book, we've been talking about Emotion – the factor that has the most impact (Parrish, 2019).

It's important to recognize that Ease is also a primary factor, and it contributes to overall emotion. In Forrester's 2021 US Customer Experience Index report, they revealed the most influential positive emotions that lead to loyalty. While some would guess that delighted, happy, and surprised would rank at the top – many brands focus on "surprising and delighting" their customers – there are three other feelings that people want to have that rank higher. Forrester has reported that customers want to feel valued, appreciated, and respected. Those three feelings come from brand experiences that demonstrate a recognition that customers have many things going on in their lives that have nothing to do with the brand. As such people appreciate when a brand respects their time, avoids making them jump through hoops to accomplish a task, provides relevant and timely feedback, and rewards customer loyalty (Yaiser, 2021).

It's why a big priority should be to root out all the sources of friction in your brand experience. This starts with making it easy for potential customers to immediately understand the benefits that they get from becoming a customer of your brand – something you will accomplish with Limbic Sparks Brand Strategy.

Further, you'll want to be sure that the presentation of your benefit, product, and service offering is easy to navigate, so people can find what they are looking for. You may recall that for ServiceByte, we prioritized putting the Core Brand Benefits front and center on the website home page – *Easy to Reach, Expert Service and Rapid Response*. These benefits are not only what customers said are the reasons why they choose to work with ServiceByte, they also reflect the fact that ServiceByte helps customers feel valued, appreciated, and respected. We also make it easy to find the service offering details on another page as opposed to jamming too much information on the home page. It's important to not overwhelm people with information, because we naturally avoid complexity and are sometimes overcome with decision paralysis – which happens when we're unable to make decisions because we are overwhelmed by choices.

Making it easy for people to shop and purchase should be another area of focus. One famous example of this is 1-Click, one of Amazon's earliest innovations. It's a technology that they patented and trademarked, as well as licensed to other brands, such as Apple. In 1999, Amazon recognized that most e-commerce checkouts were time consuming and included lot of steps. They sought to make it easier and created a one-step checkout experience that set a new high bar for e-commerce.

Beyond making it easy for customers to understand your offering and buy from you, you must also consider the customer service processes you have in place and strive to make that as easy as possible for customers to get support or make returns. Many companies see support and returns as a cost to minimize. However, it can become even more of a cost if it's not handled well. When people decide to buy a product or service, and companies then make them jump through hoops to get relief when something doesn't go as planned, it's the opposite of customer centricity.

The fact is, nobody makes a purchase hoping to contact customer support, so when they do, it's already a negative experience. Customers are inclined to anticipate that resolving the problem will be the beginning of a frustrating process. We can all point to bad customer service experiences that stick in our mind and cause us to question buying from that brand again. However, when the support experience goes very well, it's an opportunity to turn a potentially negative experience into a highly positive one. As Ruth Gaviria shared on my podcast, "When the brand goes the extra mile to support the customer when things are not going well, and they're able to show up and help solve that problem, that's how you build a business" (Limbic Brand Evolution, 2021c).

One example of a great experience I had was with a company called Orbit that sells the B-Hyve Sprinkler Control System for programming automatic sprinklers. My controller had suddenly stopped working. I was concerned because it was out of warranty and I expected an unsympathetic response from the company. On their website, I found the number for customer support, and to my surprise, I had a fantastic experience. Instead of me waiting on hold, they offered a callback option—something all customer support call centers should offer—and I was talking with a live person less than 10 minutes later. They quickly walked through a few troubleshooting steps that were unsuccessful. Without me saying a word, the support representative offered to replace my product for free, giving me a code to order a new one on their website. Within a total timeframe of under 15 minutes, they made it so easy for me to solve the problem. In that short interaction they hit on all three emotions that Forrester referenced—helping me feel valued, appreciated, and respected—and they created Limbic Sparks which will ensure that I buy from them again whenever I'm looking for a product they sell.

It's up to you to advocate for making the support experiences as easy as possible for your customers. Brand leader Karen Moffitt suggests, "It's about how you can solve for them and how you can help them" (Limbic Brand Evolution, 2022b). This includes making it easy for them to achieve whatever kind of success they are hoping for with your offering, at any point in their experience with your brand.

Beware of Artificial Intelligence and Automation Shortcuts

A friend who runs a marketing services company shared a story with me that I hope represents an unusual perspective. A potential client pushed back on a project proposal because it included a copywriter, suggesting that a copywriter is not needed because of AI. I suspect that if you made it this far into this book, you feel as appalled as I do by the suggestion that AI can fully replace a human for a task such as copywriting.

There's no doubt that AI is here to stay. It will improve over time and create vast amounts of efficiency across many industries. However, in most cases it is only a tool to aid, not to replace, human activity. A *Harvard Business Review* titled "How AI Can Power Brand Management" outlined ways in which AI can support brand managers, such as automating creative tasks that are complex and expensive, but it also made clear that AI's ability to replace the more delicate work of a brand manager—such as developing the brand story, ensuring that the brand fully reflects its competitive positioning, and earning loyalty through the management of customer relationships—are things that a brand manager won't be able to exclusively rely on AI for anytime soon. Nonetheless, AI is becoming an integral part of brand management and understanding its limitations is key (De Freitas and Ofek, 2024).

Recognizing the long-term potential of AI and automation, we should be open to experimenting and supplementing human activity. However, as the bridge between your organization and customers, it's important that you resist the calls for greater efficiency through AI and automation when it is likely that they will degrade the humanity of Brand Expression & Experiences. In addition to the challenges with over-using AI to create things within your organization, I'd like to share the results of several research studies that have been conducted to gauge how customers respond to AI and automation in brand experiences. Understandably, people will get more comfortable with AI over time, but as a brand leader, you should understand how they feel about it before assuming it will get a positive response.

In a study published in the *Journal of Hospitality Marketing & Management*, AI has been found to be a deterrent in product descriptions. It found that including "AI" in product descriptions makes the product less appealing to people – citing that when customers see the words "artificial intelligence" their purchase intentions go down because it lowers emotional trust (Cicek, Dogan, and Lu, 2024).

Another study that explored how people would feel if companies used AI for customer service was conducted by Gartner. It found that 64 percent would prefer that they did not, and 53 percent would consider switching to a competitor if they knew AI was in use for servicing customers (Gartner, 2024).

Another study, published by Steve Keller and SiriusXM Media's Studio Resonate in the 2024 Neuromarketing World Forum Yearbook, was about brands using AI-generated voices in brand experiences. This study evaluated both emotional appeal and trust-related reactions to AI voice versus human voice in three ways. First, respondents were asked if the voice they heard was AI or human, and their results indicated that they were correct as much as they were incorrect—that the difference was undetectable at a conscious level. The second experiment was conducted using Implicit testing to evaluate the strength of each option for overall appeal and trust. It found that at a subconscious level, the real human voice was 25 percent more positive and 23 percent more trustworthy than the AI voice—indicating that our brains can detect the subtle differences that inform our instinctive perceptions. In the third experiment, both human and AI voices were tested again Implicitly for overall appeal and trust, but this time they were told that all the voices were created using AI. As a result of this information, there was a drop in instinctive associations for the real human voices, with positivity falling by 8 percent and trust associations falling significantly, down 24 percent (Keller, 2024).

When it comes to the automation of customer service, one big area of growth is in the use of kiosks that are replacing live people for placing orders or paying for purchases. In fast food, we're seeing more and more ordering kiosks, which are touted for saving on labor costs and being good for suggesting up-sells with orders. A study from Temple University researchers found that, when a line forms behind customers using kiosks, customers experience more stress when placing their orders and purchase less food. It also found that some customers take longer to order when attempting to navigate the kiosk versus placing the order with a person. The study suggested that customers will be happier with the kiosk when it is perceived to add value to the experience, rather than being seen just as an attempt to save on labor costs, creating more customer inconvenience and stress than benefit (Lu and Lee, 2024).

Personally, I recall stopping into a local café for coffee. I stepped up to the counter where there was no line, and the barista would not take my order. Instead, I was asked to walk back to the entrance of the store where there was an order-placing kiosk. Suddenly, the feel of this local café turned very cold. I walked back toward the kiosk and right out the door.

It's also important to recognize that AI and automation can be used for good, when prioritizing the humanity of the experience. One great example is the brand Lemonade—an online seller of insurance. Their automated, AI-driven brand experience feels wonderfully human because every detail is so well considered—the product offering, the user experience, the design, the copywriting, and the overall tone/personality.

I first experienced Lemonade when my daughter was getting insurance for her cat, Poutine. It started with asking her cat's name. Then, referring to him by name throughout, it asked questions in a very conversational style. After the automated forms collected everything that they needed to know about Poutine, it was time for Lemonade to present the cost of annual pet insurance. It started with a screen that indicated it was working on the quote, with a blinking cursor. Even though we know that it could have shared the quote instantaneously, the experience was designed to feel more human. Suddenly, a bunch of random characters replaced the blinking cursor, then they were backspaced away, followed by the following text: "Sorry, my cat just ran across the keyboard." This experience, moments before they presented their quote, was so emotionally endearing—creating such Limbic Sparks—that we were smiling and predisposed to accept their insurance quote. From the moment you're introduced to the Lemonade brand, you're made to feel that it's a brand that you want in your life, because it's an experience that feels so human even though it's fully automated. Who says that about an insurance company?

Technology analyst Jeremy Goldman says, "When it comes to AI and automation, it's all about balance. These technologies have incredible potential to enhance customer experiences, but they shouldn't make things harder or more impersonal" (Perlmutter, 2024).

As the allure of and pressure to use AI and automation technology grows, it's so important for you to recognize not just the upside, but also the watchouts. There is no doubt that customer apprehension of AI will lessen over time. No matter where customers are on the apprehension-adoption continuum, your job as a brand leader remains the same. It will always be critical that you view the technology from the customer perspective, and that you prevent it from degrading the humanity of Brand Expression & Experiences. If the technology can successfully improve how people feel about your brand, for sure, use it to your advantage. On the other hand, if the technology will cause people to feel worse about their experience with your brand, then it's your responsibility to prevent its negative impact.

Turning Customer Centricity Into Your Mission

Limbic Sparks Brand Strategy is specifically designed to get to the heart of what matters most to people, so that customers feel like you "get" them. It gives you the insight to serve customers in ways that feel relevant and desirable. By taking responsibility for championing customer centricity internally, you'll be working to ensure that your brand is easy to navigate and that it's easy to get support, so that customers feel like every detail of your Brand Expression & Experience is thoughtfully designed with them in mind.

Brand leader Dominik Prinz-Barley puts this responsibility as follows: "You need to get a really in-depth understanding of what drives people— what it is they want and need. Then design your products, services, and experiences with exactly that in mind. No compromise." He goes on to say, "If you really want people to fall in love with your brand, you must first fall in love with the people who you serve" (Limbic Brand Evolution, 2022c).

With customer centricity as your mission, you can fuel success inside and outside of your organization.

Looking Ahead

Brand evolution is not an overnight project. It's a long game, where you are the leader, orchestrator, and catalyst for change, using customer insights and customer centricity to guide the way. The next chapter shares a case study that demonstrates how you and your Brand Idea can guide ongoing brand evolution in your organization, using all that you've learned to date, even when a full-scale brand evolution is not underway. It's also about a brand that is near and dear to my heart, that I'm proud to share with you.

Brand Leadership Considerations

In your own life, are you more open to other people's ideas when they help you solve a pressing challenge?

If you said yes, you're not alone. It's our human nature to prioritize our own needs over the needs of other people. One of my earliest lessons as an account manager in advertising was to share insights with my creative teams that would help them come up with better creative ideas. When they saw me as a threat to their creativity, they ignored me. But when I shared insights that inspired their work, I was invited into their process.

In your work with brands, do you wish that there was more coordination and collaboration between departments within your organization?

Organizations are run by people who each have their own priorities. Their work is being judged and they are on the hook to deliver results. Customer insights and centricity can be a galvanizing orientation point that you can use to help cross-functional teams move in the same direction. You have an opportunity to bring people together around the mutual goal of driving business success, by helping them understand what will be most appealing to customers and prospects.

Here are three things you can start doing today:

1 Support your cross-functional teams by uncovering and revealing customer insights that will help them be more successful in their individual roles.

2 Turn your Brand Idea into the beacon of inspiration for customer centricity that everyone internally feels connected to and is inspired to deliver for customers.

3 Prioritize efforts to make customer experiences as easy as possible and reject the temptation and pressure to do so with AI and automation technology when it will degrade, rather than enhance, how customers feel about your brand.

References

Cicek, M, Dogan, G and Lu, L (2024) Adverse impacts of revealing the presence of "artificial intelligence (AI)" technology in product and service descriptions on purchase intentions: The mediating role of emotional trust and the moderating role of perceived risk, *Journal of Hospitality Marketing & Management*, 19 June, www.doi.org/10.1080/19368623.2024.2368040 (archived at https://perma.cc/9XTN-5FN3)

Customerland Editor (2020) Brand loyalty drivers are growing, more complex, Customerland, 29 January, customerland.net/brand-loyalty-drivers-growing-more-complex/ (archived at https://perma.cc/9TD8-3YCZ)

De Freitas, J and Ofek, E (2024) How AI can power brand management, *Harvard Business Review*, September-October, hbr.org/2024/09/how-ai-can-power-brand-management (archived at https://perma.cc/H484-6DWH)

Gartner (2024) Gartner survey finds 64% of customers would prefer that companies didn't use AI for customer service, Gartner, 9 July, www.gartner.com/en/newsroom/press-releases/2024-07-09-gartner-survey-finds-64-percent-of-customers-would-prefer-that-companies-didnt-use-ai-for-customer-service, (archived at https://perma.cc/HPV6-HAMB)

Grant, A (2014) *Give and Take: Why helping others drives our success*, Penguin Books, US

Keller, S (2024) Reality Bytes: The power of human voice in an age of AI, *Neuromarketing Yearbook*, March, www.researchgate.net/publication/381313207_Reality_Bytes_The_Power_of_Human_Voice_in_An_Age_of_AI_Neuromarketing_Yearbook_2024_Neuromarketing_World_Forum_Pages_88-89 (archived at https://perma.cc/VKN9-BSUL)

Limbic Brand Evolution (2021a) Let's Talk Limbic Sparks Podcast – episode 2, Fueling Brand Evolution with Emotional Insight with Michelle Holmes, 11 April, www.limbicbrandevolution.com/podcast/michelle-holmes-att-pac-lets-talk-limbic-sparks-2 (archived at https://perma.cc/W8JB-9HUQ)

Limbic Brand Evolution (2021b) Let's Talk Limbic Sparks Podcast – episode 7, Creating Brand Desire Through Design with Gregg Heard, 7 October, www.limbicbrandevolution.com/podcast/gregg-heard-sage-lets-talk-limbic-sparks-7 (archived at https://perma.cc/HB7K-KY3F)

Limbic Brand Evolution (2021c) Let's Talk Limbic Sparks Podcast – episode 5, Using Empathy to Strengthen Brand Relationships with Ruth Gaviria, 9 August, www.limbicbrandevolution.com/podcast/ruth-gaviria-elevate-prize-lets-talk-limbic-sparks-5 (archived at https://perma.cc/95PD-8FP3)

Limbic Brand Evolution (2022a) Let's Talk Limbic Sparks Podcast – episode 13, Demystifying Consumer Insights for Service Brands with Samantha Liss, 9 May, www.limbicbrandevolution.com/podcast/samantha-liss-lets-talk-limbic-sparks-13 (archived at https://perma.cc/KZE6-YYXR)

Limbic Brand Evolution (2022b) Let's Talk Limbic Sparks Podcast – episode 19, Baking Kindness into Every Brand Experience with Karen Moffitt, 14 November, www.limbicbrandevolution.com/podcast/karen-moffitt-lets-talk-limbic-sparks-19 (archived at https://perma.cc/59SZ-HWVA)

Limbic Brand Evolution (2022c) Let's Talk Limbic Sparks Podcast – episode 10, Prioritizing Brand Purpose and People's Emotions with Dominik Prinz-Barley, 8 February, www.limbicbrandevolution.com/podcast/dominik-prinz-barley-lets-talk-limbic-sparks-10 (archived at https://perma.cc/G2L3-W8SQ)

Limbic Brand Evolution (2024) Let's Talk Limbic Sparks Podcast – episode 32, Staying One Step Ahead to Create Brand Value with Jess Kessler, 15 January, www.limbicbrandevolution.com/podcast/jess-kessler-lets-talk-limbic-sparks-32 (archived at https://perma.cc/4LZZ-LTYX)

Lu, L and Lee, W (2024) Feeling rushed at the food ordering kiosk? You're not alone, Temple University [blog] 12, April, https://news.temple.edu/news/2024-04-12/feeling-rushed-food-ordering-kiosk-you-re-not-alone (archived at https://perma.cc/M9X3-SN3Z)

Parrish, R (2019) The US Customer Experience Index, 2019: some small gains, widespread stagnation, no real leaders [blog] Forrester, 11 June, www.forrester.com/blogs/cx-index-2019-results/ (archived at https://perma.cc/S4T9-S85M)

Perlmutter, K (2020) How brand leaders overcome the illusion of customer loyalty, *Brandingmag*, 13 November, www.brandingmag.com/2020/11/13/how-brand-leaders-overcome-the-illusion-of-customer-loyalty/ (archived at https://perma.cc/2TWL-XEQ5)

Perlmutter, K (2024) Humanity in Branding: Is AI Driving or Hindering Your Customers' Trust?, *Brandingmag*, 17 December, www.brandingmag.com/kevin-perlmutter/humanity-in-branding-is-ai-driving-or-hindering-your-customers-trust/ (archived at https://perma.cc/2QKR-ZRJ7)

Yaiser, M (2021) To win customer loyalty, make customers feel valued, appreciated, and respected [blog] Forrester, 3 November, www.forrester.com/blogs/to-win-customer-loyalty-make-customers-feel-valued-appreciated-and-respected/ (archived at https://perma.cc/2Q5R-QD3B)

12

Sustaining Ongoing Brand Evolution

Rise Case Study

"When our community is challenged, we Rise."

These were some of the first words I heard after being introduced to Rise, the central New Jersey social services nonprofit where I ultimately became a board member. Those words inspired me to want to learn more, to understand the challenges Rise helps people work through, and ultimately to decide to devote a significant amount of my time to helping Rise serve our community in the years that followed. Right away, Rise captured my attention.

For a long time, I had a personal interest in getting involved with a nonprofit. However, for much of that time I had young children, long work hours, and a long commute to and from New York City. As soon as I started my own business and took control of my time, I prioritized starting my nonprofit work. In early 2020, I started seeking a nonprofit to devote some of my time to, and I had a conversation with Keith Timko, Executive Director onprofit capacity-building organization, Support Center for Nonprofits. He was helping me make connections to local organizations that he knew were seeking potential board members.

Before making any suggestions or referrals, he asked me what type of nonprofit I was looking for. I thought a lot about how to respond, as there are so many types of nonprofits in my area, all with meaningful causes. A few things initially came to mind such as distance from my house, levels of time and financial commitment, and the type of services they offer. However, what I realized was more important than any other consideration was that I wanted to support an organization that "felt" like one I really wanted to be a part of. I knew the answer wasn't too helpful for Keith, but for me it meant I was seeking an organization doing work that I felt passionate about, with a group of people who I'd enjoy working side-by-side with, in support of a mission that solves pressing community needs. Those criteria rose above all others.

After Keith introduced me to Rise, I had initial conversations with Leslie Koppel, its Executive Director, and Nancy Walker-Laudenberger, President of its board of directors. I started attending board meetings as a guest and meeting other board members. Leslie also invited me to volunteer at a food drive-thru event. This event was taking place within the first year of the Covid-19 pandemic. While many people were staying home, the Rise team was busier than ever helping people in need.

To my surprise, on that October morning in 2020, over 1,000 cars lined up to have their trunks filled with food and household goods. Cars weaved their way through the streets in a line until they got to the distribution area. As they drove through, volunteers at each station added food or household goods to their trunks. Inside the cars I saw families who were so happy for the support they were getting. They waited in line for hours, but their smiles conveyed so much gratitude. Outside the cars, a massive operation was underway, led by Leslie, with the support of members of the Rise staff, members of the Rise board of directors, and an army of volunteers. There were also representatives of the Trenton Area Soup Kitchen who collaborated with Rise on this event. All around, I saw signage that said, "When our community is challenged, we Rise."

It happened on that day. The Limbic Sparks ignited, and I knew I had found the organization I had been looking for. As my commitment grew deeper, I attended more volunteer events and I spoke with Leslie about all that Rise does—social services for community members, distributions at the Rise Food Pantry several days a week, subsidizing goods for families at the Rise Thrift Store, earning revenue from the sale of donated items to support the work Rise does, and more. Soon thereafter, I was invited to join the board of directors—an offer I was eager to accept.

Knowing my background as a brand strategist, Leslie was curious about my perspective on the Rise brand. She acknowledged that it didn't fully represent the heart and soul of the organization. She also shared details about how the need for the services that Rise offers was increasing and putting a strain on the organization's resources. It meant that to meet the expanding need for services, the organization needed to increase funding from grants, sponsors, and individual donations to support operations, as well as enlisting more volunteers, and continuing to improve collaboration between Rise and the local community leaders. As these conversations continued, I started seeing more and more opportunities where Rise had potential to create stronger connections within its community through its brand.

Before long, I was bringing the fundamentals of Limbic Sparks Brand Strategy into Rise and helping the team apply it every day. On the board of directors, I assumed a newly created role as the head of the Strategic Planning & Brand Development committee. It meant that I was not only volunteering at events to support the Rise community, but I was also leveraging my professional skills to help the Rise brand evolve. Talk about Limbic Sparks! I couldn't be happier.

A Solid Strategic Foundation

My work with Rise does not follow the linear Limbic Sparks Brand Strategy approach that you've been reading about. We didn't kick off a big brand strategy initiative, or a full-on Insights Discovery phase of work followed by Brand Idea development. As I've shared before, I'm a big fan of carrying forward brand equity that's working and building on it, and Limbic Sparks is a mindset that can be applied to any brand, at any time—something you'll read more about in the next chapter. For Rise, I knew we had an opportunity to fine-tune the details of Brand Expression, with a relatively solid base to work from.

Under Leslie's leadership, the foundational elements of the Rise brand strategy were strong. Insights Discovery is built into the day-to-day operations, as the Rise team are talking with the people they serve every day—in the office, at the Rise Food Pantry, at the Rise Thrift Store. The Rise team are embedded in the community and listening closely for how they can best support individuals and families in need. They then act on those insights to help people. Being responsive to community members is what the Rise team are so incredibly good at.

Further, long before my introduction to Rise, a strategic plan had been developed with the support of an outside nonprofit management consultant, Allison Trimarco, who is founder of Creative Capacity. This strategic plan established the Rise Mission:

> *Through community partnerships and direct services, we assist local families and individuals in recovering from setbacks and achieving their full potential.*

The plan also has details about key areas of operational focus—each with strategic objectives and tactics to deliver on the Mission. Overall, this plan serves to inspirationally guide the organization, as well as prioritize initiatives and resources. A draft was first created in 2014, and the strategic objectives are updated every few years to stay ahead of how the community and the organization are evolving.

Growing Pains and Growth Opportunities

In my early conversations with Leslie, I asked a lot of questions. I wanted to understand as much as I could about the organization, the people it serves, and how I should prioritize my time helping her and the board of directors. The more we spoke, and through my own observations, I recognized that there was a missed opportunity for the role that brand could play. The core elements were there—the Mission, the Brand Idea, and so many fulfilling Brand Experiences. However, when it came to Brand Expression, there seemed to be a lack of cohesiveness and energy.

Further, Leslie shared that for as much as Rise does in the community, the organization was not as well understood as it could be. Rise quietly went about its work, providing life-enhancing miracles for people on a daily basis. However, until you are part of a Rise experience, or have a discussion with a Rise staff member, the brand and all its breadth, and all the good that it makes possible, was not completely clear.

Solving these challenges was important for a variety of reasons. One is the reality that people may benefit from some of what Rise is doing, but they may also be unaware of other ways Rise can support their needs. For example, people who only know Rise for the Thrift Store may be unaware of the benefits they can receive from the Rise Food Pantry, and people who show up to an occasional Rise drive-thru distribution for food and household goods may be unaware of the services that Rise Case Managers can help them with throughout the year.

Another challenge has to do with raising donations, attracting sponsors, and enlisting volunteers—Rise relies on all of these, in addition to grants and Rise Thrift Store sales, to fund daily operations. Thanks to the Covid-19 pandemic, and ever since, the need for Rise services has been steadily increasing, as has the cost to keep up with demand.

As Leslie shared with me, these challenges were not just items on her to do list, they were mission critical. We agreed that the more people understand about Rise, and the more they feel Rise in their hearts, the more likely they will be to contribute their money or time.

Evolving the Rise Brand

As I'm writing this, I'm over four years into my board membership and work with Rise. It's important to also note that there are so many people—board members, staff members, consultants, volunteers—who are responsible for the many things that get accomplished, and my role is that of an advisor.

Once asked what I do for Rise, I answered, "I make observations and recommendations." Leslie gives me more credit than that, saying that I introduced a way of thinking about brand that prioritizes focus on how we make people feel, and using that insight to bring greater relevance, cohesion, and inspiration to all our efforts. It's fair to say that Leslie has embraced a Limbic Sparks Mindset. She champions ongoing brand evolution efforts so that the Rise brand increasingly becomes a factor in inspiring people to do what they can in support of the Rise mission. Further, our slightly evolved Brand Idea, "Together, We Rise." is the compelling benefit and invitation that inspires us to all to keep evolving, so we can get better and better at serving our community.

FIGURE 12.1 Rise Logo and Brand Idea

Together, *We Rise*.   **rise**
njrise.org

NOTE This is the inspirational Rise Tagline that motivates and inspires us all to serve our community as best as we can every day.

Our work evolving the Rise brand has fallen into three primary areas: Community Relations, Brand Expression, and Mission Fulfillment.

Community Relations

I joined Rise at the height of the Covid-19 pandemic, which, as mentioned earlier, created a skyrocketing demand for social services and help with basic needs. Local families were struggling with unemployment and all the challenges that come with it. Rise stepped up to serve a 300 percent increase in the number of families seeking assistance. Many of those people did not know about Rise before but were suddenly seeking services. The Rise Food Pantry, only one aspect of how Rise was helping people, ramped up to distribute food to 300 families a week, all outdoors, with lines wrapped around neighborhood streets several times a week. Additionally, in 2020, 7,121 families benefited from 10 drive-thru Food Pantry events, each with cars lining up hours in advance and creating traffic jams for everyone in the area.

While Rise was doing all it could to help people, the increased activity was creating some frustrations around town. At board meetings we discussed the challenges. Neighbors of the Rise Food Pantry were frustrated by people lining up on their street, overflowing dumpsters with corrugated cardboard or spoiled produce, and delivery trucks coming and going. Additionally, local police suddenly found themselves directing traffic jams with a lot of frustrated drivers on typically quiet downtown streets.

At first, the board and staff were disturbed that our relief efforts were upsetting people in town—the opposite reaction to what we had expected. Then, we took a moment to think about things from their perspectives. To help mitigate the challenge, I introduced the idea of the Shared Emotional Motivation—what both Rise and the local community are most motivated to achieve individually and with each other. We created an initiative to open conversations with people in local government, the local police, and neighbors, to hear their concerns, understand their motivations, and develop ways of working for Rise that were better for everyone. Built into our solution, we took the opportunity to share more about what Rise does and the impact we're having, as we worked to mend fences.

To better manage and avoid traffic jams, we took steps to coordinate our events with the local police. Our discussions led to a deeper appreciation for their concerns, and we sought locations for our events that would be less disruptive. This more open dialogue helped us earn their greater support and forgiveness when needed.

For neighbors of the Rise Food Pantry, we held an open house event and personally invited neighbors to stop by. Our objective was to ensure that each neighbor felt heard and respected, despite all the activity on their street. One neighbor came up to me and Leslie, asked who was in charge, and shared her frustration about the garbage cans overflowing. Leslie brilliantly defused the situation by saying that she was in charge. She listened to the concerns, thanked the neighbor for sharing, promised that it would be addressed, and let the person know that she could call Leslie directly if anything needed to be addressed in the future. This kind of conversation happened several times that day.

This open discussion with local officials and with neighbors at the open house were important steps we took to listen to people, recognize their concerns, share details about our work that they weren't aware of, and, overall, give everyone a stronger appreciation for each other. It's something that is now part of how Rise approaches things, leading to a community that feels more connection to the Rise brand.

Brand Expression

When I first became aware of Rise, I did what most people would do—I looked at their website. It was comprehensive, but I have to say, it didn't leave much of an impression. It had more text than images, lots of information and announcements, and it felt a bit dated. That incredible Brand Idea that drew me in—"When our community is challenged, we Rise."—was nowhere to be found. Overall, it was uninspiring.

When I asked Leslie about the website, choosing the words of my question carefully, she immediately knew what I was getting at, and she let me know she was eager to update it. This was music to my ears. Leslie had just opened the door to our gradual work to fine-tune the details of Brand Expression.

Between 2021 and 2024, working with Leslie's outside creative consultants, we updated the Rise website twice to progressively improve the visual presentation and the messaging. We also optimized the website based on traffic patterns and to make it easier for people to navigate so they can easily find the most relevant content.

Coinciding with the website evolutions, we took important steps to improve the brand's Visual Identity elements and Brand Messaging. The primary shift that we made was to focus more on Brand Expression that is designed to be intrinsically motivating. In behavioral science, the spectrum of motivation runs from extrinsic to intrinsic. When people are motivated extrinsically, it means that they are motivated by incentive—for example, if you achieve this goal, you'll get this reward. Intrinsic motivation, at the other end of the spectrum, happens when people are inspired to do things because of how it makes them feel—for example, you choose to support a cause because it makes you feel good.

The intrinsic motivation approach introduced a change in perspective for all forms of Brand Expression, and a whole new way of inspiring people to get more involved with Rise.

It was still important to ask people for their support, and to display impressive statistics, such as those from 2023: 189,117 bags of food distributed, 827 families helped each month at the Rise Food Pantry, 26,940 volunteer hours worked across all Rise programs and events, and so much more. However, we focused more on sharing the impact that our efforts have on the people served by Rise.

To bring our more intrinsically motivating approach to life, we utilized photographs taken at Rise events, showing the real people who benefit from Rise, and those who work for and volunteer with Rise. It's these wonderful photos of people in action, and the stories behind them, that convey contagious enthusiasm and inspire people to get involved.

When it comes to Brand Messaging, we combine details about our services and programs with positive outcomes. All details are purposeful to share what each part of Rise is all about, while simultaneously, sometimes subtly, encouraging people to get involved. Our copywriting style conveys the positive impact that you, the reader, can have on members of your own community when you get involved.

Here are some examples:

At the top of the home page, there's a photo of the Rise staff and our Brand Idea (shortened since the end of the Covid-19 pandemic):

Together, We Rise.

Also, on the home page we share details about the four areas of Rise that all our services emanate out of:

Rise Home Office: *Providing a range of complimentary services from assistance with official documents, school supplies, or any other type of support.*

Rise Thrift Store: *Where it's easy and affordable to find great things, and previously loved items get a new loving home.*

Rise Food Pantry: *Nourishing every family member. From wholesome foods to personal care, baby essentials, and even pet food, we're here to support our community.*

uRise: Discover. Connect. Enjoy.—*uRise is your center to learn, connect and grow, offering enriching programs to help you discover your unique talents.*

We also share details throughout the website to inspire people to get involved:

When you support Rise, you support your community.
You can help people in our community overcome challenges and rise to a better future. A donation of any kind will do a lot for our neighbors in need. When you give to Rise, you're helping us provide direct support—food, clothes, household goods, school supplies—and peace of mind that things can and will get better.

Make a charitable donation
Your donation will do a lot for our neighbors in need. Thanks to you, we'll be here when people need us the most.

When you volunteer at Rise, you change lives!
If you'd like to share a few hours of your time, or bring a whole group, we'll welcome you with open arms.

Shop for the greater good.
Every dollar spent at Rise Thrift Store is reinvested back into our community.

Join the Rise Good Neighbor Program
Your monthly donation will make a difference in your local community all year round.

Beyond the website, this style of Brand Expression made its way into all forms of how the Rise brand comes to life, including the communications style of the monthly newsletter that is sent to hundreds of subscribers, and social media posts to promote and share highlights of Rise events. The intrinsic motivation approach also evolved to how we inspire potential corporate sponsors, those who offer grants, and individual donors about the benefits of their involvement—shifting from getting increased brand recognition to having a meaningful impact on members of their own community by funding our ability to deliver on our mission.

Throughout all forms of Brand Expression, we prioritize emotional benefits with the specific intent of igniting people's emotional connection to Rise and interest in getting involved—whether through donating, sponsoring, shopping, or volunteering.

Delivering on Our Mission

The third area of our ongoing brand evolution at Rise ties directly to the second half of our Mission. Our mission has two parts: *assist local families and individuals in "recovering from setbacks"* and *"achieving their full potential."* Much of what you have read thus far focuses on the first part— the day-to-day work of helping people who are in need.

During the Covid-19 pandemic, while many nonprofits were struggling to keep up with the demand for their services, we leaned into the *"achieving their full potential"* part of the Mission. Our Limbic Sparks Mindset helped us stay close to community members. Through ongoing conversations, we understood that coping with the pandemic was challenging. We heard their desire to get beyond their current situation. We then started exploring ways to help.

It was at that same time that PenFed, the wonderfully generous Federal Credit Union, shared with us that they were also interested in providing meaningful support to uplift and strengthen communities. Thanks to Leslie and her team's deep understanding of community needs and proactive thinking, she was prepared to propose a substantial initiative to PenFed and enable Rise to better deliver on the second half of the Mission.

PenFed funded our ability to create and launch uRise as an online hub for community members to reframe their Covid-related anxiety, loss of purpose, and hopelessness into personal growth, strength, and optimism (PenFed Credit Union, 2021). Rise enlisted the support of local creators who were inspired to share their passions and skills with others through live online classes and pre-recorded on-demand videos. Topics included wellness, English as a second language, professional development, arts, and more. Not long after launch, uRise had hundreds of registered members, dozens of volunteer content creators, and thousands of website visitors. It gave people a way to connect with community, manage their well-being and mindfulness, and acquire new skills and knowledge.

As the pandemic subsided, we kept listening to feedback on all that uRise was offering. Based on community interest, we transitioned uRise to include more live classes, as people were eager to get together in person. The most popular class by far—one that started online and transitioned to live—has been English Language Learners, where hundreds of community members have learned English as a second language thanks to volunteer instructors. There have also been very popular art classes, dance classes for students, nutrition classes, and more.

At Rise, our Mission is not just a set of words—it's the foundation of our ongoing organizational and brand evolution. Combining that with a Limbic Sparks Mindset, we are constantly listening to our community to help us understand and address the most critical needs. This now includes thinking long-term about how to increase our capacity in areas of importance.

In 2024, we took another big step by starting to think more proactively about how we will deliver on our Mission over the next 10 years. It was clear that the need for our services continues to increase, and that there are unmet community needs that we would like to start addressing. Up to this point, our strategic plan was only written to guide short-term strategic objectives that could be funded by the annual operating budget.

With the help of our management consultant Allison, we've amended the Rise strategic plan. Now we have a new goal that is all about what more we can do in the future, with a long-term time horizon and through incremental funding sources. The plan begins with formal efforts to better understand the evolving needs of our community, then exploring how best to enhance capabilities.

One area of focus is strengthening our ability to do what we already do. For example, in 2025 we transformed the experience of our Rise Food Pantry into a choice pantry with an upgraded indoor space. Another area of focus is building new capabilities to serve the needs of our community member needs that we are not yet serving. For example, some of the people who Rise supports are living in precarious housing situations, and it's our ambition to help them get into more stable and secure housing.

Around the same time that we evolved our strategic plan, we were approached by a local foundation that was preparing to sunset, and to grant large sums of money to a few local organizations to help them exponentially expand their capabilities. They have supported Rise over the years, and they included us in a round of meetings they were having with candidate organizations. They were looking to understand how we would use a large sum of money, should they grant it to us, and making their selection based on those that they felt were not only in need, but ready for a large infusion of funds.

Not only were we prepared for their question, but they were super-impressed with our track record of evolution, our ambition for the future, and the specificity of our forward planning. After meeting all the other organizations in a months-long evaluation process, we received our largest one-time grant ever—over $1 million. This incredibly generous transformational grant will accelerate our ability to deepen our capabilities and build out our expansion efforts, enabling us to have an exponentially greater impact on our community.

Ongoing Brand Evolution

Applying the Limbic Sparks approach at Rise is an example of how any organization can progressively evolve by putting the needs of its community and/or customers front and center. In 2023, while discussing the evolution of the Rise brand with Leslie on my podcast, she shared: "The way I think about the brand is simplicity. Before we had to explain why this is valuable, but now we don't need to do this. Now, we focus more on how it's going to make people feel. What we've been able to create for our Rise brand is something that is intrinsically good. It sparks joy—an emotional response to the connection that people feel when they're helping other people and showing kindness" (Limbic Brand Evolution, 2023).

It's hard for me to express just how grateful I am to have the opportunity to support such an incredible organization. My time with board members, with Leslie and her staff members, and working alongside volunteers at events, is always time that I look forward to. What continues to be so fulfill-ing to me is how I'm able to blend my time directly supporting community members, with time leveraging my professional skills to help Rise be an organization that people are increasingly motivated to support.

Looking Ahead

If you'd like to learn more about Rise or if you're inspired to support our community, please check out NJRise.org. In the next and final chapter, we'll review how your Limbic Sparks Mindset can help you lead your brand by putting emotional insights at the center of how your brand sparks desire—whether you're embarking on a big brand evolution or managing the ebb and flow of everyday activities. You'll also hear from other brand leaders about how they create Limbic Sparks for their customers. Then, you'll be well on your way to creating Limbic Sparks.

Brand Leadership Considerations

In your own life, do you have a set of personal values that you work hard to live up to?

Sometimes we talk about this as being our "best self"—an aspirational version of who we want to be when we're living our best life. The thing is, our natural tendency is to want more and to keep improving. No matter how much progress we make, there's always something that we're still trying to achieve.

In your work with brands, do you foster and encourage progressive improvement?

In brand leadership, if you're standing still, you're probably falling behind. Setting high standards and always striving to achieve them is a good thing. I'm not talking about stretch goals that seem to be too far away to ever achieve. I'm talking about progressively improving what benefits people get from your brand and how it makes them feel to increasingly deliver on your Brand Idea.

Here are three things you can start doing today:

1 Think of brand development as a marathon, not a sprint, knowing there are always ways to get better at serving the people your brand is for.

2   In addition to delivering on your brand promise today, use it as inspiration for ways you can increasingly deliver on it over time.

3   Put in place a mindset of progressive evolution, fueled by the ongoing collection of customer insights, and don't be afraid to evolve further as needed.

References

Limbic Brand Evolution (2023) Let's Talk Limbic Sparks Podcast – episode 25, 8 May, https://www.limbicbrandevolution.com/podcast/leslie-koppel-lets-talk-limbic-sparks-25 (archived at https://perma.cc/WH3S-FUKP)

PenFed Credit Union (2021) PenFed Credit Union and Rise partner to launch "uRise", a local resource for learning, community and care, PR Newswire, 25 May, https://www.prnewswire.com/news-releases/penfed-credit-union-and-rise-partner-to-launch-urise-a-local-resource-for-learning-community-and-care-301299054.html (archived at https://perma.cc/VK3L-Z54Y)

13

Embracing Your Limbic
Sparks Mindset

When I become aware of new insights or a better way forward, I'm energized to move down that path. I enjoy shaking up the status quo and applying what I've learned. Mark Twain was an advocate for getting started without delay, and I'm a subscriber to his belief that striving for incremental progress is better than waiting for the right time to achieve perfection (Twain, n.d.). My suspicion is, since you've made it this far into this book, that you're feeling like you want to start applying what you've learned.

Perhaps you and your organization are ready to kick off a robust brand evolution, following the playbook of Focus, Connect, and Evolve. Perhaps it's not the right time, but you still want to bring your new perspective into your day-to-day. Regardless, now is time for you to get started putting Limbic Sparks Brand Strategy into practice.

This last chapter is about embracing and cultivating your Limbic Sparks Mindset, no matter where you are in your brand evolution journey. It will help you put emotional insight at the center of how you lead your organization to spark brand desire every day—not just when a big brand evolution is underway. Most importantly, it will help you keep that one fundamental question, from the opening words of Chapter 1—"How do people want to feel?"—in the forefront of your mind as a guidepost for thought and action.

> **Limbic Sparks Mindset**
>
> An approach to brand leadership that uses emotional insight to address how people want to feel, so your brand ignites interest and sparks desire.

A New Mindset for Brand Leadership

Limbic Sparks is more than an approach to brand strategy to call upon when you need a full-scale brand evolution. It's also more than the outcome of a successful brand interaction. Limbic Sparks is a mindset for brand leadership and an approach that you can use every day—one you can get better and better at over time.

Before I created Limbic Sparks Brand Strategy, I was a traditional brand strategist. Once I started developing and fine-tuning all the details that you've read about here, I became more and more fluent in this approach. Now, my perspective is such that it's not even possible for me to consider developing brand strategy, brand expression, or brand experiences without an understanding of what matters most to customers. I promise, you'll never find me basing strategy only on what company insiders tell me, or expressing a brand's "Why" as a brand idea. Always remember, "Why" in the absence of "Who" is a half-baked strategy.

As you embrace your Limbic Sparks Mindset, you'll train yourself to think from your customer's perspective; you'll know how to always ask the right questions and use emotional insights to guide your work forward. Over time, this approach will become second nature. You'll break free from the limitations of traditional brand strategy. You'll become more in tune with your customers. You'll become more capable of effectively guiding your internal team and your external agencies. Your brand will become more relevant and compelling, and more likely to ignite Limbic Sparks among the people who it's intended to serve.

When you embrace your Limbic Sparks Mindset:

- You'll use your curiosity to investigate beyond the internal echo chamber of customer understanding or preconceived notions about how to position your brand's offering.

- You'll be inclined to push back on the gut instincts of agencies, consultants, and team members who have more answers than questions, and you'll ask for insights to back up their recommendations.

- You'll think more about the methodologies of the research you rely on to make important decisions, knowing that traditional Explicit Research is not the best approach to reliably measure subconscious human instincts.

- You'll ensure that it's easy for people to navigate your brand's offering, easy for them to make purchases, and easy for them to get customer service issues resolved, because you know that how those experiences make them feel has the most significant impact on their desire to do future business with your brand.

- You'll ensure that when people interact with your brand, they are made to feel valued, appreciated, and respected, so that they always want to come back for more.

The Essentials of a Limbic Sparks Mindset

Starting today, you can embrace your Limbic Sparks Mindset by answering three questions, in any situation:

1 What are people's frustrations, unmet needs, and motivations?

2 How do people want to feel?

3 What should your brand say and do to make people's lives better?

You can bring these three essential questions into conversations about any brand activation. You can use them to reframe discussions with your leadership team, and with your outside agencies. Anytime you're making decisions about your brand, these questions can help you keep your Limbic Sparks Mindset on track. Answering these questions, however formally or informally, will help your brand be more successful at addressing how your customers want to feel, so when they interact with your brand, they feel like you truly care about them, and they feel the Limbic Sparks.

FIGURE 13.1 Embracing Your Limbic Sparks Mindset

NOTE By prioritizing these three questions and using the answers to guide your actions as a brand leader, you'll be embracing your Limbic Sparks Mindset.

What Are People's Frustrations, Unmet Needs, and Motivations?

This question is about ensuring that emotional insights play an increasingly valuable role in guiding decisions within your organization.

Customers don't care about your business objectives. They want to solve their own challenges. They want to be happier and more successful. When it comes to your brand, they want to know what's in it for them. Brand leader Eric Fernandez once said to me, "Revenue is the result, not the objective" (Perlmutter, 2023). While so many people in organizations are rightly focused on revenue, you're the one who advocates for what's best for customers, leading your entire organization to solutions that achieve business objectives by solving customer objectives.

I was once told of a conversation between a brand leader and their CEO. The brand leader was advocating for a bold initiative to solve significant systemic frustrations that people have with the typical customer journey—not just for their brand, but for their entire industry. The brand leader saw an opportunity to reimagine the entire customer journey and give the brand an unmatched competitive advantage. It was then that this CEO expressed that these challenges had been part of the industry for a very long time, and said, "who are we to think we can solve them?" This CEO ultimately guided the team to focus on making the status quo as good as it could be, rather than meaningfully improving the customer journey.

This example is the opposite of one that embraces a Limbic Sparks Mindset. In stark contrast to this scenario, brand leader Dominik Prinz-Barley once said to me, "Great brands solve problems that matter" (Limbic Brand Evolution, 2022a). One of the most powerful change agents you have in overcoming traditional approaches is when your company leaders hear the voice of their customers. It reveals what customers care about, why they really choose the brand, and where there are opportunities for improvement. This emotional intelligence can lead to new ways for your team to not just understand, but solve customer frustrations, unmet needs, and motivations, leading to strengthened connections with your brand.

Your Limbic Sparks Mindset will help you bring emotional insight to the forefront of conversations, so that everyone in your organization is directing their efforts toward improving the lives of customers.

How Do People Want to Feel?

This question is the game changer. It puts your work directly in the path of making people's lives better. It also flips traditional perspectives on emotion—from "about the brand" to "for the customer."

Historically, emotion has been thought of in terms of how the brand presents itself, not what motivations it addresses for customers. In advertising, emotion is often about using humor, nostalgia, fear, or sentimentality—which is not always a bad thing, but also not what Limbic Sparks Brand Strategy is all about. In B2B, emotion has sometimes been avoided by business leaders with excuses like, "I don't want our brand to be emotional. We want to be taken seriously," even though we know that our instinctive emotional responses plays an outsized role in how people make decisions, whether it's for a home or work purchase.

By now, you see how that way of thinking is misguided and backward. You now know that the role of emotion is not about the brand expressing emotion, it's about brand leaders understanding and addressing the emotions of their customers and other people they'd like to serve.

This question—How do people want to feel?—is the bridge between the emotional insights that you discover, and the initiatives that you prioritize for your brand. It's where you see the opportunity to make people's lives better and turn insight into action. The answer to this one question sets the brief to guide decisions within your organization that will benefit customers and stimulate their greater interest in your brand.

Your Limbic Sparks Mindset will help you guide the entirety of your organization with an understanding of how people want to feel, so that what your brand puts into the world is relevant and desirable to the people your brand is intended to serve.

What Should Your Brand Say and Do to Make People's Lives Better?

This question is about ensuring that when people interact with your brand, they feel like it was designed with them in mind.

Marketing should not feel like persuasion and customer experiences should not feel purely transactional. Regardless of how many people your brand serves, no one wants to feel like they are just a number, or that they're being pushed through a production line, or that their business is not appreciated. Brand interactions that feel good—from everything went smoothly to life-enhancing—are the ones that people want to re-live again and again.

Brand leader Joe McCambley says, "Brands that help, sell. Brands that sell, don't" (Limbic Brand Evolution, 2021a). It's so true. Every interaction is felt personally and has an impact on how much or how little people care about your brand. Prospects who encounter your marketing will ignore it when it is not personally relevant. Customers who are expecting a positive outcome of any kind from your brand want to feel like their needs were addressed, that their time and money were not wasted, and that you value their business.

Brand leader Joanna Hutchins once said to me, "There's no amount of media spend that can compensate for a poor execution that doesn't emotionally connect" (Limbic Brand Evolution, 2024a). Marketing is no longer about reach and frequency. It's about relevant and desirable interactions. The better people feel when they interact with your brand, the more likely it is that Limbic Sparks will keep them coming back for more.

Your Limbic Sparks mindset will help you fine-tune the details of how your brand comes to life at all touchpoints, informing what your brand says and does, so that anytime people interact with your brand, it feels like it was designed with them in mind.

The Best Ways to Create Limbic Sparks

I've found so much inspiration talking with brand leaders who navigate the challenges of brand leadership every day, and who also have an appreciation for using emotional insights in their work. They are people who embrace the Limbic Sparks Mindset, even if they've never officially gone through a Limbic Sparks Brand Strategy project.

When I talk with them on my podcast, I always ask, "What do you believe are the best ways to create Limbic Sparks—those moments when emotional motivation meets brand desire?" Each brand leader brings their own experience and perspective, but I've noticed that most responses fall into two categories—customer understanding or brand experience. Here's what I hear most often.

On Customer Understanding

Brian Reed says: "If you want to help someone, you need to first connect with them on a human level. You need to understand where they're coming from" (Limbic Brand Evolution, 2024b).

Esther-Mireya Tejeda says: "Everyone has a deep ocean of feelings, somewhere deep in their soul, that is making them like the things they like and see the world the way they see it. If we do the hard and important work, of understanding that layer of truth for our customers, and really understand the diversity of those emotional profiles, then and only then can we create those Limbic Sparks" (Limbic Brand Evolution, 2023a).

Lisa Richner says: "Empathy is at the heart of it all. It's not just about them in the moment with your brand, but it's everything outside and around it" (Limbic Brand Evolution, 2023b).

Rhys Powell says: "If you want to create a brand that people emotionally connect to, you've got to tap into some part of their being. Figure out what story to tap into—the very basic human part of life that our limbic system controls. Then latch on to that and make sure you're speaking to that part of the brain" (Limbic Brand Evolution, 2021b).

Joanna Hutchins says: "You really need to deeply understand your consumer, and that doesn't happen by reading reports or staring at spreadsheets. There's no substitute for getting close to human beings and understanding how they think, behave, and what matters to them" (Limbic Brand Evolution, 2024a).

On Brand Experience

Kim Christfort says: "Your brand is only as good as the experiences you put behind it" (Limbic Brand Evolution, 2022b).

Abby West says: "A brand needs to make sure that their consumer, their audience, feel like they are more than just a transactional interaction" (Limbic Brand Evolution, 2023c).

Karen Moffitt says: "Simply put, it's to genuinely care about your customer and their needs" (Limbic Brand Evolution, 2022c).

Samantha Liss says: "Listen to customers and make sure that they're having the best experience possible" (Limbic Brand Evolution, 2022d).

Stephan Gans says: "The intersection of relevance and authenticity. If you hit that sweet spot, then you can have all the sparks you want" (Limbic Brand Evolution, 2021c).

Ignite Your Brand Evolution

Brand evolution is a marathon, not a sprint. As a long-distance runner, I've come to realize that the things I love about long-distance running are also the things I love about brand evolution. Both involve a lot of strategy, and both benefit from a mindset of progressive improvement. If you want to be successful in the long run, you must have stamina to keep moving forward and to keep getting better:

- You can always learn more insights about the landscape.
- You can always build more effective techniques into your approach.
- You can always find ways to evolve strategy and tactics, to prioritize those that will have the most impact.

Once you embrace your Limbic Sparks Mindset and cultivate it among your team, your collective values revolve around ensuring that your brand—inside and out, and across every detail of Brand Expression & Experience—is all about making people's lives better through an understanding of what matters most. When you're making people's lives better and helping them feel the way they want to feel, you'll ignite their interest and spark ongoing desire for your brand.

Looking Ahead

You're ready! It's time to start applying your Limbic Sparks Mindset. You can keep this book by your side and use it as a reference guide for how to Focus, Connect, and Evolve. You can go to LimbicBrandEvolution.com for additional information, supporting materials, and ways to learn more from me. No matter how you choose to get started, it's time to bring your Limbic Sparks Mindset into your day-to-day work.

Most importantly, always ask: *How do people want to feel?*

Then, let the answer be your guide.

Brand Leadership Considerations

In your own life, are you good at new things right away, or does it take practice?

Very few people take on a new hobby or attempt a new skill and are at expert level right away. Anything worth doing well takes practice and ongoing effort. As a woodworker, I have a ritual of bringing a new tool and new skill into every project. Over many years and many projects, I have a lot of tools and lots of skills. The more we stretch ourselves to be better at something, the more natural it becomes, and the easier it gets.

In your work with brands, what are the best ways for you to create Limbic Sparks?

Every brand leader I've asked this question to comes at the answer from their own experience and perspective. While it's true that most of their responses involve either a focus on customer insights and/or brand experience, every situation is different. You now have the insight and the tools to bring a Limbic Sparks Mindset into your work. With practice, you'll get better and better at this over time. It will become your instinctive approach to brand leadership, so that your brand is more emotionally intelligent and better able to spark desire.

Here are three things you can start doing today:

1 Embrace your Limbic Sparks Mindset and start practicing every day by keeping those three questions top of mind.

2 Prioritize bringing customer insights into any discussion about how your brand comes to life so that every interaction at every touchpoint is designed to address how people want to feel.

3 Enjoy learning about your customers and take pride in making their lives better.

References

Limbic Brand Evolution (2021a) Let's Talk Limbic Sparks Podcast – episode 6, Breaking Through in a Competitive Category with Joe McCambley, 13 September, https://www.limbicbrandevolution.com/podcast/joe-mccambley-saatva-lets-talk-limbic-sparks-6 (archived at https://perma.cc/5XPL-BCF8)

Limbic Brand Evolution (2021b) Let's Talk Limbic Sparks Podcast – episode 4, Spreading Joy with Culturally Relevant School Food with Rhys Powell, 14 June, www.limbicbrandevolution.com/podcast/rhys-powell-red-rabbit-lets-talk-limbic-sparks-4 (archived at https://perma.cc/7AFU-77MM)

Limbic Brand Evolution (2021c) Let's Talk Limbic Sparks Podcast – episode 17, Evolving Global Consumer Insights with Stephan Gans, 17 March, www.limbicbrandevolution.com/podcast/stephan-gans-pepsico-lets-talk-limbic-sparks-1 (archived at https://perma.cc/55DJ-CHWV)

Limbic Brand Evolution (2022a) Let's Talk Limbic Sparks Podcast – episode 10, Prioritizing Brand Purpose and People's Emotions with Dominik Prinz-Barley, 8 February, www.limbicbrandevolution.com/podcast/dominik-prinz-barley-lets-talk-limbic-sparks-10 (archived at https://perma.cc/FYW4-GEVV)

Limbic Brand Evolution (2022b) Let's Talk Limbic Sparks Podcast – episode 11, Challenging Brands to Go Beyond Status Quo with Kim Christfort, 14 March, www.limbicbrandevolution.com/podcast/kim-christfort-lets-talk-limbic-sparks-11 (archived at https://perma.cc/FU5N-QFVL)

Limbic Brand Evolution (2022c) Let's Talk Limbic Sparks Podcast – episode 19, Baking Kindness into Every Brand Experience with Karen Moffitt, 14 November, www.limbicbrandevolution.com/podcast/karen-moffitt-lets-talk-limbic-sparks-19 (archived at https://perma.cc/B573-FF7Y)

Limbic Brand Evolution (2022d) Let's Talk Limbic Sparks Podcast – episode 13, Demystifying Consumer Insights for Service Brands with Samantha Liss, 9 May, www.limbicbrandevolution.com/podcast/samantha-liss-lets-talk-limbic-sparks-13 (archived at https://perma.cc/8ASD-X3DQ)

Limbic Brand Evolution (2023a) Let's Talk Limbic Sparks Podcast – episode 30, Marketing with Precise Emotional Drivers Insight with Esther-Mireya Tejeda, 16 October, www.limbicbrandevolution.com/podcast/esther-mireya-tejeda-lets-talk-limbic-sparks-30 (archived at https://perma.cc/MG52-4TNR)

Limbic Brand Evolution (2023b) Let's Talk Limbic Sparks Podcast – episode 29, Talking with Users to Improve Digital Products with Lisa Richner, 18 September, https://www.limbicbrandevolution.com/podcast/lisa-richner-lets-talk-limbic-sparks-29 (archived at https://perma.cc/5CQ9-VXNQ)

Limbic Brand Evolution (2023c) Let's Talk Limbic Sparks Podcast – episode 21, Respecting Cultural Nuances to Connect Authentically with Abby West, 14 January, www.limbicbrandevolution.com/podcast/abby-west-lets-talk-limbic-sparks-21 (archived at https://perma.cc/S3ZF-NSU7)

Limbic Brand Evolution (2024a) Let's Talk Limbic Sparks Podcast – episode 37, Ensuring Your Brand is Culturally Relevant with Joanna Hutchins, 9 September, www.limbicbrandevolution.com/podcast/joanna-hutchins-lets-talk-limbic-sparks-37 (archived at https://perma.cc/69UK-MT9L)

Limbic Brand Evolution (2024b) Let's Talk Limbic Sparks Podcast – episode 34, Shifting from Tech-Speak to People-Centric with Brian Reed, 11 March, www.limbicbrandevolution.com/podcast/brian-reed-lets-talk-limbic-sparks-34 (archived at https://perma.cc/2447-8YT4)

Perlmutter, K (2023) Consumer insight makes for a uniquely influential CMO, Brandingmag, 28 September, https://www.brandingmag.com/kevin-perlmutter/consumer-insight-makes-for-a-uniquely-influential-cmo/ (archived at https://perma.cc/T3BY-EHUZ)

Twain, M (n.d.) AZ Quotes, www.azquotes.com/quote/615556 (archived at https://perma.cc/6NAF-MQXY)

LIMBIC SPARKS
BRAND STRATEGY GLOSSARY

Limbic Sparks Brand Strategy is a remedy for traditional brand strategy that often sends brand leaders down the wrong path. Part of the challenge is outdated terminology rooted in the persuasion era, or broad definitions that don't lean toward a customer-centric approach. It's time to eliminate terms like unique selling proposition, proof points and reasons to believe—which all put your focus on selling versus solving.

This glossary replaces old terms, updates definitions, and introduces new terms that put you in the mindset of understanding and addressing the emotional motivations of the people who your brand is for. Words matter, and these will help ensure you and your team prioritize a customer-centric approach that puts emotional motivations at the center of consideration.

Brand: A unique combination of elements representing an organization, product, or service that evoke an overall impression people have based on all their associations and experiences.

Brand Descriptor: Succinct statement to bring clarity to what the brand does, sometimes paired with a non-descriptive brand name.

Brand Dynamics Review: Absorbing existing information about the brand's current business objectives, strategy, messaging, marketing, products, services, customer experiences, long-term ambition, and customer metrics.

Brand Expression & Experiences: How your brand comes to life through visuals, sounds, words, and all forms of interaction at every touchpoint, leading to an overall brand impression.

Brand Idea: The Limbic Sparks Brand Idea is the overarching compelling brand benefit and invitation. It can also serve as the customer-facing brand tagline.

Brand Leader: Anyone who is responsible for attracting and retaining customers to what a brand has to offer.

Brand Messaging: The words and language style your brand uses when communicating with people.

Brand Messaging Hierarchy: The overarching Core Brand Benefits and sub-benefits that are most emotionally motivating for each Customer Persona segment.

Brand Messaging Style Guide: The dos and don'ts that guide your brand messaging.

Brand Personality & Voice Traits: The humanistic traits that guide the feel of Brand Expression & Experiences.

Brand Positioning Statement: The statement of distinct customer promise, identifying the brand, who it's for, and what it does to make their life better.

Brand Strategy Success Criteria: Internal alignment on the magnitude and specific objectives of the brand evolution, determined after insights discovery and before brand strategy development.

Brand Team & Customer Interviews: Discussions with people at all levels of the brand's organization who represent a variety of functions, and hearing directly from customers about their experiences with the brand, their brand perceptions, their emotional motivations, and what it is about the brand that drives the most value.

Category Dynamics Review: Understanding how customers navigate the category, any category-specific peculiarities, and comparing the nuances of product and services offerings across primary competitors.

Competitive Audit: Investigating details about primary competitors to see how they differentiate themselves, the language they are using, and what makes them uniquely compelling.

Confirmation Bias: A behavioral tendency that humans have to interpret new information in ways that confirm existing beliefs.

Connect: Strengthening connections with customers by standing for the emotional benefits they care about the most.

Core Brand Benefits: The most emotionally desirable and sought-after benefits across all customer segments. They answer the questions "What's in it for me?" and "Why should people care?"

Customer Centricity: Making customer understanding and positive customer experiences a business priority.

Customer Personas: Insightful descriptions of like-minded customer segments that highlight the emotional motivations of each in the context of your offering.

Customer Research Study: Fielding an incremental investigation of customers and prospects, often using an outside research company, to glean more precise details and new insights about people's lives in the context of your offering, their motivations, and the emotional drivers in your category.

Emotional Insights: A deep understanding of the underlying emotions that drive our decisions and behavior.

Emotional Motivations: The driving forces behind our decisions and behaviors.

Evolve: Creating evolved Brand Expression & Experiences to address how people want to feel.

Explicit Research: Research techniques that explore how people consciously react to questions and stimuli.

Focus: Discovering the Shared Emotional Motivation that your brand has in common with the people it's for.

Implicit Research: Research techniques that explore how people react to questions and stimuli instinctively, at a subconscious level.

Insights Discovery: A concerted effort to gain a deep understanding of the brand, its context, and the emotional motivations that drive customer behavior, as critical inputs to developing brand strategy, marketing, and customer experiences.

Limbic Sparks: What you feel when your emotional motivation meets brand desire.

Limbic Sparks Brand Strategy: The non-traditional brand strategy approach that puts emotional insight at the center of how brands attract and retain customers.

Limbic Sparks Mindset: An approach to brand leadership that uses emotional insight to address how people want to feel, so your brand ignites interest and sparks desire.

Qualitative Research: Research techniques that enable inquiry into how people feel and why through individualized questioning.

Quantitative Research: Research techniques that lead to statistical data showing similarities and differences between reactions to questions and stimuli across segments of people.

Reasons To Care: Meaningful emotional benefits that are intended to ignite customer desire.

Shared Emotional Motivation: The core Limbic Sparks insight identifying what both the brand and customer are most motivated to achieve individually and with each other.

Social Conformity Bias: A behavioral tendency that humans have to adapt what we say and how we behave based on how we want to be perceived.

Sonic Identity: The guidelines and assets for how your brand sounds.

Strategy: A plan of action designed to achieve an objective, or setting the foundation for a future that has yet to unfold.

Traditional Brand Strategy: Familiar approaches to brand strategy that are lacking meaningful emotional insights about what matters most to customers.

Visual Identity: The guidelines and assets for how your brand looks.

INDEX

NB: page numbers in *italic* indicate figures or tables.

Looking for another book?

Explore our award-winning
books from global business
experts in Marketing and Sales

Scan the code to browse

www.koganpage.com/marketing

More from Kogan Page

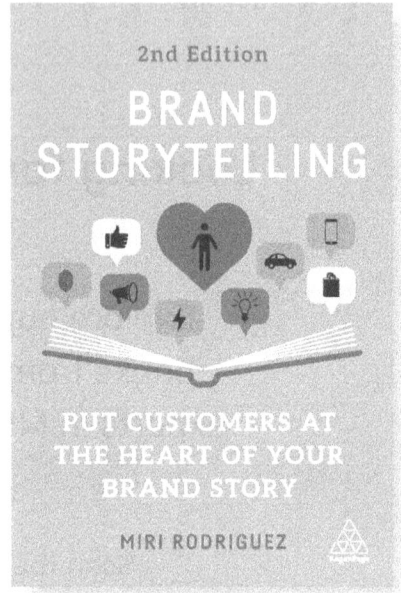

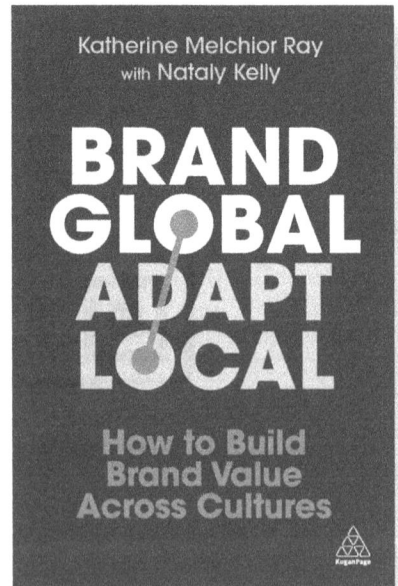

www.koganpage.com

From 4 December 2025 the EU Responsible Person (GPSR) is:
eucomply oÜ, Pärnu mnt. 139b – 14, 11317 Tallinn, Estonia
www.eucompliancepartner.com